CANADA IN AFGHANISTAN

CANADA IN AFGHANISTAN
the war so far

PETER PIGOTT

DUNDURN PRESS
TORONTO

Editor: Michael Carroll
Design: Alison Carr
Printer: Tri-Graphic Printing Ltd.

Library and Archives Canada Cataloguing in Publication

Pigott, Peter

      Canada in Afghanistan : the war so far / Peter Pigott.

Includes bibliographical references and index.
ISBN 978-1-55002-674-0

      1. Afghan War, 2001- --Participation, Canadian.
2. Canada--Armed Forces--Afghanistan. 3. Afghanistan.
4. Canada--Military policy. 5. Postwar reconstruction--
Afghanistan. I. Title.

DS371.412.P45 2007   958.104'7   C2007-900858-5

1   2   3   4   5   11   10   09   08   07

Conseil des Arts du Canada / Canada Council for the Arts

Canada

ONTARIO ARTS COUNCIL
CONSEIL DES ARTS DE L'ONTARIO

We acknowledge the support of the Canada Council for the Arts and the Ontario Arts Council for our publishing program. We also acknowledge the financial support of the Government of Canada through the Book Publishing Industry Development Program and The Association for the Export of Canadian Books, and the Government of Ontario through the Ontario Book Publishers Tax Credit program, and the Ontario Media Development Corporation.

Care has been taken to trace the ownership of copyright material used in this book. The author and the publisher welcome any information enabling them to rectify any references or credits in subsequent editions.

J. Kirk Howard, President

Printed and bound in Canada.
Printed on recycled paper.

www.dundurn.com

Dundurn Press	Gazelle Book Services Limited	Dundurn Press
3 Church Street, Suite 500	White Cross Mills	2250 Military Road
Toronto, Ontario, Canada	High Town, Lancaster, England	Tonawanda, NY
M5E 1M2	LA1 4XS	U.S.A. 14150

This book is dedicated to those Canadians who have given their lives in the service of peace while serving in Afghanistan

Contents

Preface

In his book *Marching as to War*, Pierre Berton writes about the Boer War:

> The Boers, too, were baffled, as George Shepherd of Paris, Ontario, discovered later that year when he encountered an imprisoned Boer general in a military hospital. "Would you kindly tell me why it is that you have left a civil peaceful life to come here to fight a selfish war and endure all the hardships of the field?" the general asked him. "I am not surprised by the action of the English or Cape volunteers, but it puzzles me why you identify yourself with the quarrel. I don't suppose it was the mere love of fighting that brought you here."
>
> To which Private Shepherd replied, "It was not so much to actually assist England as to show the world the unity of the Empire, and to show that if one part of the Empire is touched, all are hurt."
>
> "He did not say anything for a while," Shepherd wrote home, "but stroked his beard and appeared lost in thought."

One can imagine Taliban leader Mullah Mohammed Omar (if he's ever caught) asking the same question.

The South African War, in which 7,000 Canadians volunteered and 277 died, was overshadowed by the carnage that followed when more than 60,000 Canadians were killed in World War I and 42,000 died in World War II. And even after 1945, Canadians answered the call to arms — no longer for the British Empire but for the United Nations and the North Atlantic Treaty Organisation (NATO). In Korea in the early 1950s, 500 Canadians lost their lives.

However, what occurred on September 11, 2001, changed everything. If the tragic drama of that day didn't herald a new era in world history (more significant, for example, was the dissolution of the Soviet Union in 1991, leaving the United States as a single superpower) or precipitate the "clash of civilizations," it did introduce Afghanistan to Canadians. Since the Suez Crisis of 1956, Canadian soldiers had served in Cyprus, the Golan Heights, Somalia, and Kosovo. But these were regional conflicts where the threats were self-contained and Canada itself was in no danger. Not so with Al Qaeda (The Base) and its Afghan sanctuary.

"The image was of the twin towers coming down on September 11," reflected Member of Parliament John McCallum (later minister of national defence), "with a mental footnote to the effect that this could also happen in Canada." Lieutenant-Colonel Pat Stogran, commanding officer of the Princess Patricia's Battle Group, recalled upon returning to Edmonton after service in Afghanistan: "We had a tremendous welcome home from Canadians. I think the reason is that on September 11 our lives changed. It was a real and profound challenge to our way of living … and we were the spearhead for Team Canada." When asked why Canada was in Afghanistan, Brigadier-General David Fraser replied frankly: "This is the home of the Taliban, the Taliban are a threat to nations around the world, including our own. It's naive of us to think that Canada is not a pathway to get to America and that Canada would not be the next objective." As Private Shepherd explained to the Boer general, "If one part of the Empire is touched, all are hurt."

That Canada was risking its national security unless its soldiers fought in Afghanistan became the cornerstone for involvement in that country. When irrefutable evidence confirmed that the Taliban was based in Pakistan, when the labelling of any anti-Coalition insurgent as "Taliban" proved too simplistic, and when in June 2006 the Royal Canadian Mounted Police (RCMP) could find no connection between 17 Canadian citizens arrested in Toronto as terror suspects and the Taliban or even Afghanistan, the mantra did not falter. The Taliban might only know the Hindu Kush mountain range and the deserts of Rigestan, but it supported jihad and home-grown jihadists such as those who bombed London in July 2005. The defining case is that if Afghanistan fails again as a state and becomes a platform for jihadists, all NATO countries will be threatened. What occurred on September 11, 2001, was not a war-game scenario, the cancer of extremism has since bloomed, the war in Afghanistan has become firmly linked with that of global terrorism, and if Canada hadn't confronted terrorism at its source, it would have come to Canadian shores. Abandoning Afghanistan was never an option.

I first came to know Afghanistan through the works of Rudyard Kipling. An Anglo-Indian author like myself, Kipling has always been a favourite writer of mine. In fact, I can still recite his poem "If." Family history has it that one of my ancestors, as editor of the *Allahabad Pioneer* newspaper, gave the young Kipling his first job as a journalist. Whether that tale is true or not, it was Kipling's novel *Kim* that introduced me to the Great Game that the British Raj and the Russian tsar played out in Afghanistan. However, what really brought the country home to me was the British writer's short story "The Man Who Would Be King." In it two British ex-soldiers, Peachey and Danny, hatch a plan to be crowned kings of the Afghan province of Kafirstan with the help of the latest weaponry — in this case Martini-Henry rifles. Everything ends badly when, led by the local mullahs, the Afghans exact a terrible revenge on the pair. Kipling based the story on the life of American adventurer Josiah Harlan (1799–1871) who, in a similar fashion, had himself made Prince of Ghor, the province north of Kandahar. The moral of the story was a metaphor for colonialism and a lesson that no foreign power, even with a technological advantage, should impose itself on what it considers to be a backward people.

While I was doing the research for *Canada in Afghanistan: The War So Far*, Eric Newby, author of some of the best travel literature books, died. His *A Short Walk in the Hindu Kush* (1958) is quintessentially

English, though the "short walk" is actually an arduous journey through the more remote parts of Afghanistan, with elements of comedy that describe both the Afghans and the author — never more so than when tribesmen test the waterproof nature of Newby's watch by immersing it in goat stew. Newby met the legendary British explorer Wilfred Thesiger on the banks of the Upper Panjshir in Afghanistan. (He had hoped that the significance of the event would rival that of Stanley meeting Livingstone, but the great man looked with disgust at Newby's blow-up mattress and called him "a bloody pansy.")

It has been said that Canada is a country with too much geography and too little history and that with Belgium (and Britain) it is the opposite. While the comparisons are wildly inaccurate, Afghanistan is overburdened with too much of both — and in its case, neither the history nor geography are particularly appealing. Indeed, both have been described as mainly "Dust and Blood." Perhaps because of this, Afghanistan has captivated authors as diverse as Herodotus, Ibn Battuta, Marco Polo, Winston Churchill, James Michener, Ken Follett — and myself.

Even if you don't believe that Kabul was founded by the biblical Cain, son of Adam, the city was still said to be as exotic as Casablanca, as lawless as the Shanghai of the 1930s, and as far off the tourist trail as Lhasa before the package tours. I knew that the legendary Silk Road passed through Afghanistan, and so did the Koh-i-Noor diamond. That the traditional Afghan sport remains *buzkashi* (a type of polo) where only recently the carcass of a goat has been substituted for that of an enemy. That the Greek/Buddhist/Indian cultures co-existed peacefully at Bamiyan, once famous for the serenely beautiful giant Buddhas. Today, where no corner of the planet has escaped the proliferation of Coca-Cola and McDonald's, Afghanistan outside its cities remains in another era where fable and fact abound, populated by mysterious burka-clad women and shaggy, bearded frontiersmen shouldering bolt-action Lee-Enfields. There are said to be no people more handsome, more devious, more hospitable, more cruel, and more fascinating.

But all of that was the Afghanistan of the past — before the Soviet invasion of 1979. According to the United Nations Office on Drugs and Crime (UNODC), Afghanistan's harvest of opium in 2006 was 6,100 tonnes, a staggering 92 percent of the total world supply, exceeding global consumption by 30 percent. An estimated 35 percent of Afghanistan's gross domestic product, or around US$2.7 billion, is earned through illicit poppy cultivation. Despite massive injections of foreign aid, the majority of the Afghan population continues to suffer from insufficient food, clothing, housing, and medical care, with three out of ten children dying before the age of five, and half of those who survive being severely malnourished. The United Nations estimates that 35,000 Afghan children died in 2006 alone from measles, simply because they weren't vaccinated. The United Nations de-mining office has stated that at current clearance rates it will take 500 years to clear the mines from Afghanistan completely. And if Kandahar is the birthplace of the beautiful Mughal princess Nur Jehan called "Light of the World" and the home of the Shrine of the Prophet Muhammad's Cloak, it is also where the terrible events of 9/11 were first planned.

In writing a book about a war that is currently underway, the author risks rebuttal and embarrassment. By the time this book is published, events could take an unforeseen turn. Pakistan might implode in its own civil war like Iraq. Depending on the results of an imminent federal election, Canada might pull its troops out earlier than the intended 2009. *Canada in Afghanistan* was written to give perspective to what Canadians see nightly on their televisions and read in their newspapers or on the Internet. The canvas is unashamedly ambitious, incorporating the 3Ds — Defence, Diplomacy, and Development — between two covers. Even the book's subtitle, "The War So Far," is contentious. For years the Canadian government, Liberal and Conservative, refused to call this conflict a war. The Boer War was so identified as was the Korean War, but five years and 45 Canadian deaths later, the deployment in Afghanistan is still called "stabilization" to prevent another terrorist atrocity like that of 9/11. Before that date Afghanistan rarely figured in our consciousness and an "afghan" was a shawl one's mother knitted. Few Canadians could find the ancient city of Kandahar on a map then, let alone the mud-walled villages of Pashmul, Panjwai, and Zhari. Few had heard of Operations Athena, Mountain Thrust, and Medusa, or knew what ramp ceremonies, IEDS, G-Wagons, and PRTs were, or could discuss shuras, Pashtuns, and Loya Jirgas. All these names and terms are now commonplace in Canada's vocabulary, and it is a rare television newscast that doesn't feature RPGS, LAV IIIs, or the Taliban.

At this moment those world leaders who were there when Operation Enduring Freedom began — George W. Bush, Tony Blair, Pervez Musharraf, and Hamid Karzai — are still in power. For Prime Ministers Jean Chrétien and Paul Martin, Afghanistan never figured highly on the agenda. Afghanistan is Stephen Harper's war, a commitment, one suspects, that suits him just fine. Written while Harper was facing increasing pressure to define Canada's role and ambitions in Afghanistan, there are three themes in this book. The first sets the stage on which the drama is being played out — Afghanistan. The second is why and how Canada got to Afghanistan and attempts to find a coherent pattern to the events, political and military, that have shaped Canadian involvement since Operation Enduring Freedom began. The third focuses on the good things Canada is doing in Afghanistan, and for that I was fortunate to be able to make the journey to the heart of such benefits, the Provincial Reconstruction Team (PRT).

"One of the things that I found when I was commander of international operations," said Chief of Defence Staff General Rick Hillier, "was that the most dangerous thing of all was the individual who visited the theatre for 48 hours and then left an instant expert with the solution to everything, which was invariably wrong." (Fortunately, General Hillier was talking about the conclusions of the Paris-based Senlis Council, not mine.) The trail over which my research took me was difficult and dangerous, beginning with the flight into Afghanistan. As an aviation author, I knew well the checkered history of the Ariana Afghan Airlines Boeing 727-200 that brought me to Kabul. Thirty years before, when it was owned by Faucett Peruvian Airlines, I had watched its wings buckle as it corkscrewed into the airfield at Cuzco. That flight was an experience I will never forget, as hard as I try.

Having never been in the military, I owe a particular debt of gratitude to many who are and who were generous with their time in helping me write this book. Captain Doug MacNair, Canadian Expeditionary Force Command (CEFCOM), arranged for me to be embedded with the Canadian Forces (CF) at Kandahar Airfield in the summer of 2006. Others in the CF who gave of their expertise were: Captain Richard Perreault, public affairs officer, CEFCOM, who told me of the airdrops; Master Corporal (now Sergeant) Chris Stringer, FCS

Tech/NSE/Maint. Coy, Camp Julien; Captain Richard Little of Surveillance and Target Acquisition; Lieutenant-Colonel J.D. (John) Conrad, commanding officer of the National Support Element, Task Force Afghanistan; and Master Seaman (now Sergeant) Bill Pritchett. At the PRT it was my pleasure and privilege to interview three extraordinary Canadians whose experiences appear in this book: Captain Tony Petrilli, the Civil Military Cooperation (CIMIC) Projects officer; Major E.A. Leibert, the deputy commander of the PRT; and RCMP Superintendent Wayne E. Martin, police adviser.

An unexpected source of research was the Air Cadet 632 Phoenix-Telesat Squadron in Orleans, Ontario. Not only is the squadron fortunate to have within its ranks my two daughters, Sergeant Holly Pigott and Corporal Jade Pigott, but the parents of the cadets put me in touch with two of the main sources for this book. Colonel J. Grondin, CD.MHE.CHE, found me Major J.A. Bradley, the deputy commanding officer at the Multinational Medical Unit, Kandahar Airfield; and Colonel Ralph Schildknecht put me in touch with Lieutenant-Commander Rob Ferguson of the Canadian Strategic Advisory Team. In the words of the squadron's motto, the contributions of both men were *Nulli Secondus*.

For the diplomatic side, I was yet again fortunate to have Réjean Tremblay at the Lester B. Pearson Library track down the inter-library loans. Program Manager Peter Marshall is a member of the unsung band of administration officers who open our embassies around the world. His account of creating the Kabul Chancery should be recorded in a departmental history on embassy buildings, if one is ever written. By an amazing coincidence, I already knew Bruce Gillies, who 20 years earlier had been a key person in the operation to bring the Russian defectors out of Afghanistan. In his book *Out of Afghanistan*, David Prosser described Bruce in 1987 as slightly reserved and immaculately dressed and sporting a goatee. I can safely report that he hasn't changed at all. I owe much to him and his charming wife, Christina. I would also like to thank the photographers of Combat Camera and Rosie DiManno of the *Toronto Star*.

In the years to come, more books about the war in Afghanistan will be written by others. The military analysts will move the chess pieces about and the generals, both armchair and in the field, will reminisce about the dust, the Boardwalk, and the IEDs. The government will commission an official history of Canada's involvement in that far-off country. Monuments will be erected to the fallen in parks and city squares, schoolchildren will recite poems about Panjwai and Spin Boldak, and on November 11 the veterans of the Afghan war will polish their medals. Until all of that happens, there is on a footbridge that crosses the North Saskatchewan River near downtown Edmonton a plaque with a name. It is called the Ainsworth Dyer Bridge.

Peter Pigott
December 31, 2006
Ottawa

1

"The Petri Dish of Afghanistan"[1]

Fortress of Islam, heart of Asia,
Forever free, soil of the Aryans,
Birthplace of great heroes.
— Afghan National Anthem

To the sophisticated Persians, the land of rocks and desert at the edge of their empire was Yaghestan. Filled with savages who would never accept the rule of law, it was simply where civilization ended. There is some evidence that the country's most ancient name was Avagana, a Sanskrit term, but another school of thought believes the land was originally called Ab-bar-Gan, or "High Country," which derives from the Sumerian language and dates back as far as 3000 BC. In religious terms, the Afghan or Pashtun origin is said to stem from the Old Testament's Abraham. Afghana, Saul's grandson, was raised by David and was made chief of the army. His family became so powerful that in the sixth century BC, Nebuchadnezzar, king of Babylon, exiled them to Khor, the site of modern Afghanistan. Greater Khorasan is a historical region that includes territories in today's Iran, Pakistan, Tajikistan, Turkmenistan, Uzbekistan, and Afghanistan. Persian travellers referred to the many tribes in its mountainous area as Pashtun from the language spoken there, and it was only in the 18th century that Europeans called the area Afghanistan, after the Afghans, the ruling tribe then.

The Afghans themselves have an explanation for the physical features of their country. After creating the countries of the world, God had some rubbish left over. This he moulded together and dropped on an area of the planet that no one wanted, creating Afghanistan. Trapped historically between Persia, Russia, India, and China, the country has been cursed throughout history. From ancient times this collision of mountain ranges, tribes, and empires has had a strategic importance, even more so today since its modern neighbours are Pakistan, China, Iran, Tajikistan, Uzbekistan, and Turkmenistan, the first two being nuclear powers and the third suspected of trying to join that club. The British historian Arnold Toynbee thought Afghanistan was "the roundabout of the world" ("traffic circle," in Canadian terms). For Lord Curzon, British viceroy of India at the beginning of the 20th century, it was the cockpit of the world.[2] After the disastrous British and Soviet invasions, Afghanistan earned the title of Graveyard of Empires. A geographical expression in search of a state, Afghanistan is more commonly called the Corridor of Asia. Whatever the name, to the great powers of any day, Afghanistan has always been a vacuum that has to be filled.

Located in Central Asia on the geologic Iranian Plateau, Afghanistan is 647,500 square kilometres, an area similar in size to Manitoba and slightly smaller than Texas. Like Switzerland and Austria, it is landlocked, mountainous, and heir to a few languages and religions. Its present-day boundaries are artificial, having been drawn up early in the 20th century in London and Moscow. Because of its past, Afghanistan was known for the ferocity of its warriors. In fact, so impressed was Lord Kitchener with an Afghan tribe called the Hazaras that in preparation for a Third Afghan War (1919) he raised a battalion of Hazara Pioneers. When London wisely cut its losses and refused to get involved with pacifying Afghanistan, the Hazara battalion accompanied Kitchener home and during World War I went to France, Kurdistan, and Baghdad, fighting for the British with distinction.

The Hindu Kush slices through the country, beginning in the high northeast where the former Soviet Union, China, and Pakistan meet, then continuing to the barren lowlands of the Iranian border. Because of these mountains, Afghanistan is chopped into the Central Highlands, the Northern Plains, and the Southwestern Plateau. Deep, narrow valleys, the storied Khyber and Bolan passes, the Suleiman Mountains that march across the border with Pakistan, and the Central Highlands form the popular notion of Afghanistan.

Rarely reported in the media is that better distribution of water is critical if Afghanistan is ever to become a stable nation. Although the country has experienced several years of drought, it still possesses tremendous water resources. Drought, ineffective management, and lack of available infrastructure have created conditions for massive internal displacement of the population. The dearth of water has caused opium cultivation to increase, inflamed local conflicts over access rights to water, and raised health concerns. The recent proliferation of thousands of tube wells has also led to a decrease in the water table, further disrupting the local community as control over wells becomes an issue. Despite all this, there is no shortage of available water in Afghanistan.[3] The problem is one of management. There are three types of irrigation systems in the country: surface, *karez*, and formal. Fifty-five percent of irrigation is by traditional methods such as diverting surface river water. *Karez* systems use the groundwater by digging tunnels that channel the liquid from underground to the surface where it can be redirected to crops. With streams and seasonal springs, *karez* systems comprise 30 percent of the nation's irrigation, with the remaining 15 percent consisting of formal systems such as large-scale government projects.

The United Nations' Food and Agriculture Organization (FAO) estimates that only 1.4 million hectares of land out of a potential 5 million hectares is currently available for extended seasons. The average production of wheat is 1.3 metric tonnes per hectare, but with improved water management this figure could potentially triple. The application of surface systems is often based on traditional use, and local management of these includes the distribution of water as well as responsibilities for maintenance. Samandar, a 40-year-old peasant from Andarab, a district in the northern province of Baghlan, told the United Nations' Integrated Regional International Network that he had lost a son and a brother to a water dispute in his village. "They were killed by farmers of a nearby village," he said. He believed that more than 70 percent of the tensions and anxieties affecting his village arose from disputes over the distribution of irrigation water.

Vineyards have flourished for centuries along the Arghandab River valley in Kandahar Province, and before the Soviet war, Afghanistan was the source of 60 percent of the world's raisins, exporting them largely to Iran and Pakistan. Only known as a battleground to Canadians, this lush farmland is divided into rectangular sections called *jeribs*, roughly equal to 2,000 square metres. Farmers usually surround their *jeribs* with thick mud walls and work the land using the methods employed for centuries. They create row upon row of parallel chest-deep ditches, either by building upwards with mud or digging down into the beige earth. These troughs serve as trellises for green grapes, which tend to be smaller than the grapes found in Canadian supermarkets but which have a more intense flavour. Other crops include wheat, pomegranates,[4] watermelons, squashes, marijuana,[5] and poppies. The last is harvested for opium and also the tasty seeds. Almonds (especially a thin-shelled variety known as *khargazi*) and pomegranates from Kandahar Province were once famous throughout the Indian subcontinent. The country's agricultural base suffered severe damage during the frequent wars, and the recent drought further jeopardized the industry.

The country's future hopes and wealth lie in the untapped mineral deposits and natural gas in the foothills of the Northern Plains where the Amu River, historically known as the Oxus, flows. The u.s. Geological Survey and the Afghanistan Ministry of Mines and Industry Joint Oil and Gas Resource Assessment Team estimate that there are huge deposits of crude oil, natural gas, and natural gas liquids in northern Afghanistan. In 2003 the Ministry of Mines, in partnership with various donors, made great strides in identifying priority projects and ensuring the regulation of the sector. The Minerals Law was passed in July 2005, and the Hydrocarbons Laws were approved by the Afghan government in December 2005. The World Bank estimated that Afghanistan's existing mining operations were worth about us$60 million annually, and on June 30, 2006, the Bank announced that it had approved a us$30 million grant to assist the government to "effectively regulate the country's mineral and hydrocarbon resources and foster private-sector development in a transparent manner." By March 20, 2007, the Afghan government hopes that an enabling regulatory environment for commercial extraction of the country's mineral wealth and other natural resources will be in place, not only for the oil but for more mundane resources such as the crushed rock, sand, and gravel necessary to build schools, houses, and hospitals. But without more stability and security, Mining Watch Canada has warned, private investors won't feel safe, and as long as the Taliban remains in the country, any mining development will become the focus for insurgents, either as political targets or as a source of "revolutionary taxes."

With no particular home are nomadic tribes like the Kochi, who despite decades of war continue to herd goats and the fat-tailed Afghan sheep. Many herdsmen have taken to long-distance truck driving, which because there is no railway system is the country's only means of internal and international trade — and smuggling. Within the Hindu Kush live the Persian-speaking Hazaras, distinctive with their Mongol features and Shia religion, two reasons they have endured centuries of persecution by the Pashtun majority, who consider them *munafaqeen* ("hypocrites" or "false believers"). South of the Hindu Kush are the historic cities of Kabul, Kandahar, and Ghazni, home of the Pashtuns. In the north are the smaller, less-populous cities of Faizabad and Mazar-i-Sharif, where the Turkic ethnic groups live. Rising out of the western desert, or Registan, is the cultural jewel of Herat. An ancient oasis on the Silk Road, it has benefited from its distance from Kabul and proximity to the Persian (and now Iranian) trade routes. The civility and culture of the Persian Heratis so impressed (or duped) the Russians that they allowed their officers stationed there to bring their families with them. When on March 15, 1979, the city's inhabitants rose up and massacred those families, the enraged Soviets bombed the ancient city into rubble, so much so that a British journalist likened what remained to the ruins of Hiroshima. But, as the Soviets discovered, this did little to stop the insurrection.

In the first days of the current war, on October 7, 2001, when the u.s. military claimed it had "taken out" the Taliban's "command and control" bases in Kabul and Kandahar, nothing was really affected.[6] Cities in Afghanistan aren't cities in the usual sense, i.e., sources of industry, religion, learning, or government. Afghans depend on the countryside for all of that. Occupying or laying waste to the nation's cities has little effect on an overall military campaign against the Afghans. Rather, Afghan cities are liabilities, sucking in troops for garrison duties and food aid to feed starving refugees. Parasites, cities are also infested with media, both national and foreign, who are quick to report on human-rights abuses. Their historical/spiritual antecedents notwithstanding, the strategic worth of cities like Kabul and Kandahar is not in their industrial or intellectual wealth — for there is none — but in their *airports*.

The capture of the former Russian air base at Bagram outside Kabul was essential to both the Taliban and its enemies. The great Afghan military tactician Ahmed Shah Massoud knew that whoever occupied Bagram's runways had a portal to the outside world, allowing allies to funnel in supplies by air. The airport at Kandahar, essential to the International Security Assistance Force (ISAF), and now sporting an inukshuk erected by the first Canadian Forces to arrive, deserves a book of its own. Originally built by the Americans in the 1960s, expanded by the Russians to take heavy bombers, the airport at Kandahar, its terminal architecture reminiscent of airfields in the former Yugoslavia, takes its place in the ranks of historic airports such as those in Berlin, Hong Kong, and Saigon.[7] It was in a hardened compound at Kandahar Airfield that Osama bin Laden first lived in suburban bliss with his wives and children, his private jet parked outside the terminal like the family station wagon.

When the Americans arrived at Kandahar Airfield and set up base in November 2001, the sprawling complex became a cash cow for the local warlord, Gul Agha Shirzai. Allotted to him by President Hamid Karzai for his help in forcing the surrender of the Taliban, the airport allowed the governor to consolidate his power and wealth. When the United States wanted to pump money into the local economy and not use its own construction battalions or fly in foreign workers, all necessities to rebuild the base, including supplying interpreters, gravel, cell phones, and Toyota pickups, as well as all contracts to provide local labourers and essential fuel supplies, went through Gul Agha Shirzai. Kickbacks to Pakistani middlemen, nepotism for Shirzai's own tribesmen, and a protection racket to ensure no one else could bid on contracts soon flourished. And with the governor's militia wearing U.S.

Army fatigues and guarding the base's outermost ring, no one else, from Western media to rival contractors, could get access without Shirzai's permission. It was no wonder that by 2003 the Afghans equated Shirzai's thugs with the foreigners who had arrived to help them. Worse was the common perception that the warlord's atrocities were being ignored and/or condoned by President Karzai.

The dominant ethnic group in Afghanistan is the Pashto-speaking Pashtuns, accounting for about 42 percent of the population. Persian (Dari) and Pashto are official languages of the country. Dari is spoken by more than half of the populace as a first language and serves as a lingua franca for most Afghans. Simply put, Pashto is spoken in the south, while Uzbek and Turkmen are spoken in the north. Smaller groups throughout the country also speak more than 70 other languages and numerous dialects. The Tajik (27 percent), Hazara (9 percent), Uzbek (9 percent), Aimaq (4 percent), Turkmen (3 percent), Baluch (2 percent), and other small groups (4 percent) make up the remaining number.

The Pashtuns are the largest segmentary lineage tribe in the world. There are an estimated 12 million in Afghanistan and more than twice that number in Pakistan, with communities in the United Arab Emirates, the Netherlands, Germany, and Britain. A warrior tribe renowned since they fought Alexander the Great, the Pashtuns through the centuries have successfully defeated more numerous and better equipped invaders that have included the Macedonians, the Mauryans, the British, and the Soviets. Sometimes called Pathans, they are usually tall with light skin and green eyes and have captured the imagination (and photo lenses) of the Western world. They are Sunni Muslims and consider themselves a Semitic race, tracing their origins to Qais, a friend of the Prophet Muhammad. Two tribes, the Ghilzai and the Abdal, dominate the Pashtuns, each claiming descent from Qais's sons. The Pashtun religious code, Pashtunwali, is rooted in Mosaic Law and has core tenets that include self-respect, independence, justice, hospitality, love, forgiveness, and tolerance for all (especially to strangers or guests). It is a decentralized religion and government — no single person can rule and/or interpret the Word.

Thus, throughout history would-be conquerors didn't have a single king or chief to subvert, since Pashtun government is based on the collective wisdom of the people in the *jirga*, an assembly of tribal elders called to wage war or broker peace, tribal or intertribal. It has always been this way, a truth that continues to elude foreign governments. No matter who has occupied the throne or Presidential Palace in Kabul, monarch or Marxist, he has never exercised control over the tribes in the countryside. They have always managed their own affairs and have never called any man their master. The drawback to this tradition is that foreigners from the Macedonians to the Pakistanis have preyed upon the various Pashtun factions for their own purposes, creating a disjointed front.

If there is a centralized authority in the typical mud-walled village, it is the *minbar* in the mosque. Here is the pulpit from which the mullah delivers his Friday sermon. And if the mosque is adjoined by a religious school, or madrassa, so much the better. Here the *taliban* ("seekers of truth" or "students") learned by heart from a mullah not much better educated than themselves the Koran, the tenets of Islamic law, and the life and sayings of the Prophet Muhammad.

The rural people have never wanted anything from Kabul except to be left alone. As with the Vikings, Afghans have long practised trading and looting as essential elements of their customs and economy, a way of life highly idealized in Edwardian literature, as noted by Philip Mason in *A Matter of Honour*: "The harsh soil of the rocky valleys and windswept tops gave only the barest of necessities of life — for anything else — a wife, a horse, a rifle — a man must either go down into Hindustan with a caravan and hope to come back with a full purse or he must raid across the border for camels or cattle or ransom."[8] Robert Byron in *The Road to Oxiana* summed up this romanticized Afghan tribesman with: "Here at last was Asia without an inferiority complex."

Today Western society views the same Afghan warrior as damnably misogynistic. The plight of women in Pashtun society has received global media attention, and arguably there isn't a more disadvantaged group in the world. As late as September 2006, the Afghan human-rights commission reported that women were still being persecuted by a legal system that should have been protecting them and that the number of "honour killings" was rising — 185 Afghan women had been killed by their own families so far that year, although the number was thought to be much higher because many more cases were unreported.[9]

Besides the cultural inhibitions that the Pashtun and Taliban cultures have traditionally imposed on women in Afghanistan, hundreds remain widowed due to the incessant wars in their lifetimes. Left without incomes, these women try to support families, even though they possess no skills or education and lack the ability to travel freely. This situation has occurred in an economy that offers little opportunity for meaningful employment, whatever the sex. Usually, extended families will help women who need to support their own families, but a woman who is raped or even approached by another man brings shame to the extended family and is banished from the only institution in the country that has held together.

"Some of these women we found in prison where they live with their kids," says Captain Tony Petrilli, a Canadian Forces Civil Military Cooperation (CIMIC) officer with the Provincial Reconstruction Team. "Such is the shame in this that when we visited the prison we could not get a straight answer when we asked why these women were in jail." To be a woman in Afghanistan, comments Petrilli, takes great courage, and to have a public role is almost a death warrant. Petrilli goes on to say: "My colleague Lieutenant Gwen Bourque had many discussions with the director of women's affairs, Aman Jana Sapia, regarding gender issues. During a meeting in Washington with President Karzai, President George W. Bush praised her courage. Sadly and in typical Taliban cowardice, Aman Jana Sapia was killed on September 25, 2006. The Taliban was quick to take credit for the assassination. She clearly had an impact that threatened the Taliban's backward way of thinking. We had at the PRT an Afghan doctor who was our medical liaison with the Directorate of Public Health. Dr. Wali came in one morning tired after his night shift as a surgeon at Mirwais Hospital. He remarked that Afghans needed more time off like Westerners. We offered to make him famous by starting "Walidays," to which he countered that famous Afghans were soon dead. Sadly, this remark by Dr. Wali was shown to be the case with Aman Jana Sapia."

Afghanistan has one of the highest mortality rates for children and mothers dying during childbirth, and this unfortunate statistic is exacerbated by the inability of male doctors to examine and treat women. Given the shortage of female doctors everywhere in the country and their non-existence in rural areas, untrained midwives are employed, causing more harm than good with their brand of folk medicine.

Other nations with similar topographical, religious, ethnic, and language mixes — Spain, for instance — have overcome their bloody past to prosper as modern states. What impedes Afghanistan is a xenophobia and fanaticism that have no equals on the planet. There are few braver, more honourable people — or more bigoted, cruel, and untrustworthy. And the barbarity stretches back through Afghanistan's history century after century. In 1150 the warlord Alaudin Jahansoz, who called himself "The World Burner," compelled his captives to carry a heavy pack of soil to his mountain capital of Firoz-Koh. There he butchered them, mixed their blood with the soil, and built victory towers from the mortar. When Genghis Khan crossed the Oxus River in 1221, he spared only 40 of the inhabitants of Herat, a city of 160,000. Genghis's biographer noted that "with one stroke a world which billowed with fertility was laid desolate, and the regions thereof became desert ..."

In 1747 Nadir Shah punished a rebellious tribe with cruelties that were even by the standards of a cruel age exceptional. A French priest who accompanied Shah records that "wherever he halted, he had many people tortured and put to death, and had towers of their heads erected." Fast-forward to 1933 when Abdul Khaliq, a Hazara student avenging the persecution of his people, assassinated the Pashtun king Mohammed Nadir Shah. Nadir's son and successor, Mohammed Zahir Shah, had Khaliq tortured by first cutting off his fingers, pulling out his tongue and eyeballs, and then slicing off his ears and nose. After that the assassin was slowly executed. Four decades later little had changed. In June 1979, President Hafizullah Amin had 200 of his countrymen bound up in their own *pugris* ("turbans"), soaked them in petrol, and burned them to death, starting with their heads. A year later the *Daily Telegraph* revealed that the president's wife, his nephew, his seven children, and his 20 aides were shot when he was killed.

The campaign of wanton cruelty makes for sad, repetitive reading in the reports of Amnesty International: "While the soldiers started pulling down and burning the houses, 13 children were rounded up and stood in a line in front of their parents. The soldiers then poked out the children's eyes with steel rods. The mutilated children were then slowly strangled to death. Next it was the parents' turn." The fate of invading forces was equally gruesome. During the Soviet occupation captured Russian soldiers could expect no mercy from the mujahideen. "One group," John Fullerton recounts in *The Soviet Occupation of Afghanistan*, "was killed, skinned, and hung up in a butcher's shop."[10] Another captured Russian, Fullerton writes, "found himself the centre of attraction in the game of *buzkashi*." Instead of the headless goat usually used as a ball, the Russian served the purpose while still alive. Proving that nothing has changed even in the 21st century, an email from a British soldier describes a failed rescue of Afghan troops and French Special Forces: "The scene was like a human abattoir. We fought off the Taliban, but were too late to save the French guys. All of us were shaking when we were flown back to base. One of the Afghan survivors said the French had been tied up, then gutted alive by the Taliban. It was one of the most shocking things I had ever heard."[11]

In 2006 it was a rare newscast, magazine article, or newspaper editorial in Canada that didn't mention Kandahar, an Afghan city unknown to most Canadians four years earlier. Kandahar is one of the 34 *wilayats* ("provinces") in Afghanistan, each further divided into *uluswali* ("districts") and *alaqdari* ("subdistricts"). Only Kabul is large enough to be divided into *karts* and then subdivided into *nahias*. Kandahar Province's capital city of the same name is very ancient and is mentioned in the *Mahabharata*, the Hindu epic. Built on the Bronze Age city of Mundigak, Kandahar is thought to derive its name from a localized transliteration of Alexandria, one of the many cities Alexander the Great created or renamed. Descendants of the Macedonian rulers traded the city to the Indian Mauryans for 500 elephants.

Because Kandahar sits astride the main (and only) road between the Indian subcontinent and Central Asia and Europe, its citizens have always been horse traders or caravanners, though today they are more likely to be truck drivers, auto mechanics, innkeepers, and tollbooth attendants — or highwaymen when the situation demands. (In Rudyard Kipling's *Kim*, the title character's mentor, Mahbub Ali, is a Pashtun horse trader and spy.) And because of its strategic location, Kandahar has changed hands more times than Poland or the French provinces of Alsace and Lorraine. Among other Afghans, Kandahar is envied, but it is also regarded with loathing, since it seems to be the origin of everything adverse. Like an Italian city-state during the Renaissance, the Pashtun city contains great vision, wealth, and savagery.

Kandahar was originally settled by Iranian tribes, the most prominent being the Pashtuns. Once an outpost of the Indian Mauryan Empire, Kandahar had a pillar with an inscription in Greek and Aramaic erected by the Indian emperor Ashoka. The Greek/Buddhist/Hindu melding of societies continued here until 654 AD when the Arabs began invading and converting the population to Islam. Like the cathedral cities of medieval Europe, Kandahar has always had great religious significance. At the north entrance to the old city and adjacent to the Governor's Palace are the Mausoleum of Ahmad Shah Durrani (the Father of Afghanistan) and the nearby Shrine of the Prophet Muhammad's Cloak. This is where Mullah Mohammed Omar appeared in 1996 on a balcony overlooking an assembly of thousands of Taliban. A poor farmer from the lesser Ghilzai clan, Mullah Omar needed the approval of the mainly Durrani Taliban, and by waving the holy relic the village mullah was able to elevate himself to "commander of the faithful," thus legitimizing his rule. Among the devout, this declaration effectively made him second only to the Prophet Muhammad.

The Mirwais Nika Shrine is west of the city on the road to Herat, nearly 2.5 kilometres beyond the Panjwai turnoff. The bright blue dome in a park-like setting is the Mausoleum of Mirwais Khan Hotak, the Ghilzai chieftain who declared Kandahar's independence from the Persians in 1709. The more recent Eid Gah Mosque, next to Kandahar University, was built for Mullah Omar by Osama bin Laden. The mosque was intended to be Mullah Omar's pulpit, and its large blue dome dominates the Kandahar skyline. Today the mosque remains unfinished and is used twice a year to celebrate the two Eid festivals. (The Eid al Fitr marks the end of the Ramadan fast; the Eid al Adha commemorates the Prophet Abraham's willingness to sacrifice his son.)

Finally, as befitting an ancient "cathedral city," there is Kandahar University. Located in the northwest suburb of Kandahar on a site previously used as a madrassa by Mullah Omar, it is the only Pashto-speaking university in the world and attracts many students from Pakistan.

Important to Canadians at the PRT, the university has Faculties of Agriculture, Medicine, and Engineering. A Faculty of Education was added in 2002. In 2006 there were approximately 1,100 students attending the university, 32 of whom were female. The Government of Afghanistan (GOA) has contributed the land and buildings to the campus and pays some of the instructors. Significantly, one of the biggest contributions was the GOA's removal of the Taliban from the area and ongoing security, though more security is needed to allow female students to stay on campus in the dormitories. India's government supplied a computer lab and also provided some professors.

The present campus consists of 11 main structures with nearly identical floor plans, plus a larger building for meals and prayers. One building is used for administration, one for storage, five for men's hostels, one for each of the faculties, and one for the library, information technology centre, and English-language training centre. There is also a women's hostel, with a second recently completed detached from the main complex of buildings. There are currently no laboratories or other facilities for conducting practical training, and the university lacks a gymnasium, other recreation facilities, and a student clinic. Kandahar University's Faculty of Medicine is Mirwais Hospital, the main medical facility for Kandahar City, Province, and much of the country's south. It is a 200-bed surgical hospital. Built by the Chinese, it is referred to by locals as the Chinese Hospital.

The city also has a technical college begun in 1957. Providing technical education in Pashto, it has six departments: Electrical, Small Engine Repair, Automotive Engine Repair, Welding, Plumbing, and Carpentry. Originally, there were 900 students, but in 2006 attendance dwindled to 60, largely because more money can be made working for the vast foreign-aid industry than fixing local plumbing. As the Canadians at the nearby PRT are aware, the importance of a technical college in the country's future can't be overlooked. Such an institution has the potential to provide Pashto speakers in southern Afghanistan with highly marketable technical skills that the region requires.

The symbolic significance of Kandahar is so strong that even when the Taliban captured Kabul in September 1996, Mullah Omar and his hardcore supporters decided against relocating to the Afghan capital.

Throughout the reign of the Taliban (1996–2001) and beyond, the local population has remained loyal to this movement. Kandaharis see the Taliban as a symbol of the revival of old Pashtun glory, and it is this Pashtunwali nationalism that is the driving force of the current insurgency. The historical antecedents to the present rebellion in Kandahar Province can be traced back to the fact that Kandahar City was the birthplace of great political and military leaders from Ahmad Shah Durrani to Sardar Mohammed Daoud Khan to Hamid Karzai. No matter what the world thinks, to Pashtuns, Kandahar is the centre of Afghanistan. The Pashtun nation includes three tribes that dominate the south from their ancestral city: the Achakzai, who traditionally run the cross-border trade; the Barakzai, who control the city's government; and the Alokozai, who have the finances and President Hamid Karzai's Popalzai, the nobility. Below these are the tribes of lesser importance: the Kakars, the Sakzai, the Tareen, and the Noorzai.

Babur, founder of the Mughal (the Persian word for Mongol) Empire, annexed Kandahar in the 16th century, but his son, Humayun, lost it to the Shah of Persia. Kabul was Babur's beloved city where he wandered the hillsides above it, recording 33 varieties of wild tulip, observing the migratory patterns of birds, and commissioning wells, reservoirs, and watercourses for its inhabitants. The city was lost to him through treachery. After a near-fatal poisoning attempt, Babur had his food taster cut to pieces, his cook skinned alive, and the female accomplices thrown under elephants. His grandson, Akbar, regained both Kandahar and Kabul, but subsequent Mughal emperors lost the territory of Afghanistan forever.

When the Shah of Persia attempted to convert the Sunni Pashtuns of Kandahar into Shias in 1709, they rose up under the Ghilzai warrior Mirwais Khan Hotak and drove the Persians out. Mirwais's descendants followed them across the border into Persia, occupying that country until 1729. The tensions between the Sunni Arabs and the Shia Persians for the prize of Afghanistan continued into the 21st century and accounts for Iranian and Pakistani meddling in the country's internal affairs today.

The Pashtun Abdali tribe invited all the clans in 1747 to a Loya Jirga (council of community elders) where Ahmad Shah Abdali was elected their king.[12] Considered to be the Father of Afghanistan, Ahmad Shah

Abdali changed the name of his tribe and his own last name to Durrani. Kandahar became the capital of his Pashtun kingdom. The Father of Afghanistan laid out the present city, and his very ornate mausoleum remains there as a place of worship. Ahmad Shah Durrani soon invaded India, where the tottering Mughal Empire was already under siege from the Mahrattas and the British. By 1761 the Afghan king was ruling Delhi, and with the expansion to the east the family seat at Kandahar was considered too isolated. So in 1772 Ahmad Shah Durrani's son, Timur Shah Durrani, moved the capital to Kabul, where it has remained.

By 1857 the Pashtun kings ruled a country that stretched from the Oxus River in the north to Delhi in the east and Herat in the west. A modern nation-state of Afghanistan might have occurred by then, but even as early as Timur Shah's death in 1793 a familiar Afghan sickness had asserted itself and the Durrani dynasty tore itself apart in bitter fratricidal wars and was replaced by a dynasty of kings from the Barakzai, another leading Pashtun tribe. This tribe retained the Afghan throne until 1973, "reigning but not ruling," as an astute British historian once put it.

Too preoccupied with internal dissension to hold off the Russians in the north and the British in the east, the Pashtun kings gradually lost their territories outside Afghanistan's present-day borders. Fearing that Afghanistan would be assimilated into an expanding Russian Empire and thus provide the tsars with a launching pad for an invasion of India, the British attempted three times to conquer the country. In each instance they were defeated by Afghan guerrillas, the intense heat, scarcity of water, and the difficult terrain, all factors familiar to other foreign armies, namely, the Soviets, the Americans, and Coalition forces today. In retrospect the campaigns by the British were entirely unnecessary since the Russians wisely stayed out of Afghanistan — at least for another century.

Afghanistan really entered European consciousness in 1838 as an outcome of the Great Game when the British colonial government in India heard from its spies that the current king of Afghanistan, Dost Mohammad Khan, was about to allow Russian troops to enter his country due to the Russian siege of Herat. If Kabul, too, fell, reasoned Lord Auckland, the governor general of India, it would only be a matter of time before the Russians controlled ports on the Arabian Sea. As it turned out, the intelligence was incorrect — the Russians *were* expanding their empire, but east into China. War, as historians have noted, has its own momentum.

Auckland insisted on raising the siege at Herat and replacing Dost Mohammad with his government's own choice of ruler, in this case a previous and unpopular king of Afghanistan, Shuja Shah Durrani, who had been in exile for the past 30 years in India. In 1839 the great Army of the Indus set out for Afghanistan. With 9,000 troops under British command and 6,000 sepoys under Shuja Shah's, it was (as the supply line between Afghanistan and Calcutta was a long one) followed by a caravan of some 30,000 camels and 38,000 non-combatants — wives, families, servants, and other camp followers. All arrived triumphantly in Kabul that summer when on August 6, 1839, Shuja Shah, astride a white horse and protected by British bayonets, was restored to his throne.

In the next two years the British discovered what other armies later would: Afghanistan was difficult to invade but impossible to occupy. Far from the nearest British outpost, they were immersed in an ocean of hostile natives. Even hunting parties venturing outside the walls of Kabul were caught and hideously tortured. The British government in London had never seen this venture as a long-term one and began recalling home sections of the army for duty elsewhere. When the second winter began, what was left of the Army of the Indus lost heart and panic set in. Now the soldiers wanted out of Afghanistan at any price.

Shuja Shah was conveniently murdered, Dost Mohammad was put back on the throne in return for the guarantee of safe passage for the British troops back to India, and in January 1842 the dispirited, homesick, disorganized procession set out on the nine-day journey to Jalalabad on the Indian frontier. Struggling through the mountain passes, fighting the winter cold and snow, they were cut to pieces by Afghan snipers and sword-wielding cavalry. All were inevitably massacred, and the British families were sold into slavery. Only one Englishman, Dr. William Brydon, survived to tell the tale, his famous escape the subject of many Victorian illustrations. To the Afghans, and all Asians and Africans, it was a salutary lesson: the British, indeed the white man, was not invincible. It was a lesson not wasted during the Indian Mutiny 15 years later.

Forty years after the First Afghan War (1839–42), with the British and Russian empires at their height, history repeated itself almost exactly. In the Second Afghan War (1878–80), Prime Minister Benjamin Disraeli was so convinced of a Russian threat to the Northwest Provinces of British India that he and Lord Lytton (then the Indian viceroy) resolved to station a Permanent Resident in Kabul before the Russians did. To the Afghans this action was the first step towards annexation. Sher Ali Khan, the current Afghan king, steered a neutral course between the two powers, but his son, Mohammad Yaqub Khan (who had already been imprisoned for rebelling against his father), welcomed the British. He signed the Treaty of Gandamak on May 26, 1879, giving the British the cities of Quetta and Peshawar and ceding control of Afghanistan's foreign affairs to the British viceroy in Delhi. Most dangerous of all, he guaranteed the safety of a permanent British Resident in Kabul.

The complicity of the Afghan royal family in what happened next was never proven, but Afghan soldiers (who hadn't been paid for months) were told they could loot the British Resident's home in lieu of pay. Under attack the British Resident appealed to the king, claiming he was under royal and legal protection. If there was a reply, it came too late. Joined by mobs from the streets of Kabul, the Afghan soldiers hacked to pieces everyone inside the Residence, allowing once again a single survivor to escape to India. Forgotten by the West, the memory of the Second Afghan War that followed was kept alive by the Afghans who, admiring bravery above all, continue to this day (as the author Jan Morris discovered) to speak in admiration of British heroism.

The war achieved nothing beyond adding to Afghan xenophobia. After 1880, with British military equipment and an annual subsidy of 1.85 million rupees (as Winston Churchill wrote, silver is a good substitute for steel), Emir Abdur Rahman Khan ruled Afghanistan without upsetting London, or any foreign power, and the country returned to its prewar role as a neutral buffer state between India and Russia. Abdur Rahman tried to keep the expansionist British at bay — they wanted to annex Kandahar permanently — by allowing Sir Mortimer Durand and his commission to negotiate the border between India and Afghanistan in 1893. As was the fashion of the day, local sensibilities were ignored by the colonial power, and the artificial border, dubbed the Durand Line, was drawn through neighbourhoods and ethnic homelands with clinical indifference. As a reward for settling the Afghan issue, Durand was made ambassador to the United States where, because Canada had no treaty-making power then, he oversaw negotiations concerning the u.s.-Canada border on the Pacific coast. The legitimacy of the Durand Line in Afghanistan was to extend for a century, ending in 1993, and today no Afghan (and few Pakistanis) recognizes its validity. It didn't take London long to realize that with cash subsidies and arms the Afghans could be kept occupied fighting one another and both the British and the Russians could stay out of the country and engage in what Rudyard Kipling immortalized as the Great Game of spying, bribing, and playing members of the Afghan royal family off against each other.

Abdur Rahman Khan, Afghanistan's "Iron Emir," was the autocratic ruler who unified the country by crushing everyone who opposed him without exception, from his own Pashtun tribe to the minority Hazaras and Uzbeks. He accomplished this feat by starting the forerunner to Khidamate Aetilaati Daulati (KHAD), literally the state information services or Afghan secret police force. Like his Russian neighbours, Abdur Rahman had whole communities transported from their homelands and settled in the midst of other ethnic populations, relocations that continue to create tensions in the 21st century. Since the Pashtuns were Sunni, Abdur Rahman's wrath was especially reserved for the Hazaras, Shias who had always been semi-independent. In 1893 his government forced Hazara girls into marriage with Sunnis, confiscated all cattle from Hazara families, and had 350 men and women of the Jaghori district sold at the Kabul markets as slaves. Like the Taliban, the Iron Emir relied on fundamentalist Pashtun mullahs to insulate Afghanistan from outside (and therefore liberal) influences. Even as railways and telegraph wires spread across the world during the Victorian Era, Afghanistan retained its mule and dirt tracks. For, as Abdur Rahman reasoned, "As long as Afghanistan does not have enough weapons to ward off acts of aggression by the big powers [the British Empire and the tsar], it would be crazy to allow the construction of a railway track leading into my country."

Abdur Rahman's sons were a lot more accommodating, especially Amanullah, who introduced Western-style schools, the emancipation of women, and a constitution. Encouraged by these measures, the British gave Afghanistan its independence in 1919 (since Russia was no longer a threat) and stopped the annual subsidy. Signs of progress continued as the sales of enslaved Hazara men, women, and children ended when the institution of slavery was abolished in 1923, the year Afghanistan entered the Railway Age. Three steam engines manufactured by Henschel, a German enterprise, travelled on a test track from Kabul southwest to Darulaman Palace, seven kilometres from the city. Whether there were plans to extend the railway farther isn't known, since the project was short-lived and ended in 1929 when the parent German company went bankrupt. Even today Afghanistan remains one of the few countries in the world without a railway system.[13] Because of this situation, its long-distance truck drivers wield power out of all proportion, not only in the transport of people, goods, and information, but also in the opium trade, which is exported in their vehicles. Every Afghan politician understands full well that the truck-driver mafia has to be courted if his government is to remain in power long.

Without roads or railways, Afghanistan was ideally set up for the 20th century's greatest invention — aircraft. Unfortunately, the Air Age came to the country in the form of history's first mass evacuation by air. In the winter of 1928–29, to prevent another massacre of foreigners, the Royal Air Force sent several Victoria IIIs (a variant of Vickers's Virginia bomber) to evacuate British staff and other Europeans (for a total of 582 passengers) from the Residence.

Mohammed Zahir Shah inherited the throne in 1933 after his father's assassination and became adept at accepting aid and advisers from the democracies and Nazis equally. The British supplied 19 Hawker Hind fighter aircraft to the Royal Afghan Air Force in 1938 (the last of which is improbably in the Canada Aviation Museum in Ottawa) and trained its first pilots.[14] Joseph Stalin's mass murders of Muslims within the Soviet Central Asian republics — the little-known Basmachi Revolt — made Kabul wary of Moscow and no doubt played some part in its international politics. Afghanistan joined the League of Nations, the German airline Lufthansa was granted permission to fly into the country, and the first American ambassador to Kabul was accepted. (He wasn't the first to fly the Stars and Stripes in Afghanistan; that honour belonged to

American adventurer Josiah Harlan [1799–1871], who had done so in 1823.) Aware that continuing to court the Nazis during World War II would invite, as in Iran, a British/Soviet military occupation, Zahir Shah managed to keep Afghanistan neutral.

Afghanistan's problems with neighbouring Pakistan — historic Pashtun territory — began in 1947 when that country became independent. In September 1953, Prime Minister Sardar Mohammed Daoud Khan began agitating for the reunification of all Pashtun people, especially those on the other side of the Durand Line. To discourage his reunification efforts, Pakistan closed its borders with Afghanistan in 1961, causing a tribal and economic crisis. When the United States, a staunch ally of Pakistan, refused Daoud Khan military weapons and loans, he turned to the Soviet Union for aid, especially for the completion of the Helmand Valley project, which radically improved living conditions in southwestern Afghanistan.[15] The present-day formal irrigation systems in Afghanistan were built between 1950 and 1970 with the aid of both the United States and the Soviet Union and gave the country a nearly self-sufficient agricultural economy.

Tensions between itself and China and U.S. support of Pakistan prompted the Soviet Union to believe that control of Afghanistan was essential. What was later dubbed the Brezhnev Doctrine was simply another manifestation of traditional historic Russian insecurity over its borders, and between 1954 and 1970 some 7,000 Afghan army officers were trained in the Soviet Union, a farsighted move that paid dividends after the Soviet invasion in 1979.

Prime Minister Daoud Khan resigned in March 1963, and the Pakistani border was reopened. King Mohammed Zahir Shah introduced a constitution in 1964, excluding for the first time all members of the royal family from the council of ministers. When Moscow reasserted its sphere of influence four years later by using tanks to crush the revolt in Prague, the West "rediscovered" Afghanistan on the Soviet Union's "soft under belly" southern border and aid poured in. By 1970, with more than half of Afghanistan's expenditures dependent on foreign aid, the country was in reality under foreign control. The United States managed the country's agriculture, the Germans oversaw the police force, the French supervised the hospitals, and the Soviet Union held sway over the army. Without a railway system, both the Russians and the Americans built asphalt roads; the Russian roads all ran north to south, while the American ones stretched east to west.

When Zahir Shah flew to Rome for medical treatment, Prime Minister Daoud Khan seized power on July 17, 1973, keeping the king in exile there. The move wasn't unexpected or unacceptable. Daoud Khan was a cousin of the king and a prince in the royal family. He declared Afghanistan a republic with himself as president and packed the Loya Jirga with his supporters. A growing Islamic fundamentalist movement was persecuted, and its young leaders, Gulbuddin Hekmatyar, Burhanuddin Rabbani, and Ahmed Shah Massoud, all future mujahideen, fled to Pakistan, where Prime Minister Zulfikar Ali Bhutto welcomed them.

Daoud Khan began the Marxist-style People's Democratic Party of Afghanistan (PDPA), which unfortunately for him splintered into two Communist groups, the Parcham (Flag) and the Khalq (Masses). Neo-socialists who held that a true proletarian revolution could never occur in Afghanistan, the Parchamis were controlled by Soviet intelligence, the GRU. Aligned with the KGB, the radical Khalq faction was old-style Bolshevik, agitating for an immediate, violent overthrow of the government. It suited the Kremlin to keep both groups at each other's throat. Led by their mullahs, the rural people wanted nothing to do with either faction and declared a jihad or holy war against all Communists, who were seen as infidels or non-believers. Using the army and KHAD, Daoud Khan repressed all opponents equally — Parcham, Khalq, and Islamic religious extremists. To reduce dependence on the Soviets, he courted India, Saudi Arabia, and Iran, whose Shah, flush with petrodollars (and advice from Henry Kissinger), was only too willing to help. The Shah advised Daoud Khan to drop the Pashtun reunification issue and pursue friendlier relations with the other American ally in the region, namely, Pakistan.

Afghan turmoil gave the Shah an opportunity to replace the Soviet Union in Afghanistan and re-establish the ancient Persian hegemony in the country. Beginning in 1974, Tehran put millions of dollars in aid into its neighbour and sent in SAVAK, the Shah's secret police, to help destabilize the Afghan Communist parties. On a state visit to Moscow on April

12, 1977, Daoud Khan begged Leonid Brezhnev to rein in Parcham and Khalq. But it was when he dropped the Pashtun reunification cause, on the advice of the United States, and visited Pakistan's General Muhammad Zia-ul-Haq in March 1978, that the radical Afghan elements on both the left and right made common cause to overthrow him.

At the funeral of Mir Akbar Khyber, a murdered Parchami leader, on April 19, 1978, the Afghan Communists rallied against Daoud Khan. Their leaders, Nur Muhammad Taraki, Hafizullah Amin, and Babrak Karmal, were ordered to be arrested, but Taraki went into hiding, Karmal escaped to the Soviet Union, and Amin was only put under house arrest. That was Daoud Khan's last mistake, for on April 27 a *coup d'état* took place at Kabul International Airport, and the next day, as the new government led by Taraki declared that President Daoud Khan had "resigned for health reasons," the overthrown president and his family were shot in the Presidential Palace.

President Taraki renamed the country the Democratic Republic of Afghanistan (DRA) on May 1 and welcomed Soviet military advisers. On their advice, positions in his Marxist government were divided between Khalq and Parcham leaders. Taraki and Deputy Prime Minister Hafizullah Amin were from the Khalq faction, while Babrak Karmal and Mohammad Najibullah were Parcham leaders. Taraki sent both Parcham leaders out of the country as ambassadors and then began a purge of all Parcham party members. On December 5, 1978, he signed a treaty of friendship and cooperation with Moscow that permitted the deployment of Soviet troops in Afghanistan if requested. This treaty would later be used as a pretext for the Soviet invasion.

As with all Afghan reformers, Taraki meant well. He passed laws to change the country's medieval marriage customs and redistribute land equitably, but both measures were contrary to Afghan traditions. He was soon preoccupied suppressing a rebellion in Herat led by Ismail Khan, a former Afghan army officer who was influenced by Ayatollah Khomeini's teachings. In February 1979, the American ambassador, Adolph Dubs, was kidnapped and held hostage by a Tajik group demanding the release of their colleagues who had been jailed by Taraki. The Afghan police bungled Dubs's rescue and he was killed in the shootout, tilting the White House towards the freedom fighters.

On his way home after attending a conference of the non-aligned nations in Havana, Cuba, on March 20, 1979, Taraki visited Moscow and begged Brezhnev for Soviet ground troops. The Politburo, especially Premier Alexei Kosygin, were wary of getting involved and grudgingly gave him helicopter gunships with Russian pilots, maintenance crews, and 700 paratroopers to defend Kabul Airport. Brezhnev advised Taraki to gain popular support by ending the drastic social reforms. He also warned that Hafizullah Amin was preparing to eliminate him, but it was too late. On March 28, 1979, Amin was made prime minister and Taraki was sidelined as president. Then, on October 10, 1979, Amin ordered the commander of the palace guard to execute Taraki. He was reportedly suffocated with a pillow.

With increased Soviet aid pouring into Afghanistan, President Jimmy Carter authorized the CIA to begin conducting covert propaganda operations against the Amin government. Carter's national security adviser, Zbigniew Brzezinski, with his eye on the Soviets' clampdown in his native Poland, saw that Afghanistan could well become the Soviet Union's Vietnam and urged the White House to do whatever it could to make that a reality.[16]

The Russians, too, had their misgivings about Amin, even as in July they deployed the first motorized rifle divisions, an airborne division, and an assault brigade into the country. The KGB chairman, Yuri Andropov, and Dmitry Ustinov, the minister of defence, reported to the Politburo that Amin was eliminating everyone who opposed him, including Soviet sympathizers, while at the same time furthering diplomatic relations with Pakistan. When the KGB suspected that Amin had been subverted by the CIA, the decision was taken to invade Afghanistan on Christmas Day 1979. As the British had done in 1838, Moscow was intervening to replace one Afghan ruler with another who would be more subservient to its agenda. Even the propaganda put out was eerily similar: the Soviets insisted they were entering Afghanistan because the Afghan government had requested them to do so, and as soon as their mission was accomplished, they would send their army home.

The Kremlin had an operational contingency plan to invade Afghanistan as early as March 1979, but the U.S. hostage crisis in Iran on November 4 provided the perfect cover, keeping the United States preoccupied. Moscow sent up a smoke screen by offering Ayatollah Khomeini support as Soviet forces mobilized on the Afghan border. When his airborne special forces landed at Kabul Airport on December 22, Brezhnev told his concerned ambassador in Washington that the conflict would be finished in three weeks. On December 27, Soviet tanks entered Afghanistan from the north, parachute divisions landed at the strategic Bagram Airfield, and KGB special forces in Afghan uniforms took over all government, military, and media buildings in Kabul. The Tajbeg Presidential Palace where Amin was hiding was stormed and he was executed. Radio Kabul (actually a Soviet military radio station in Uzbekistan) announced that the Soviet Union was only complying with the 1978 Treaty that former President Taraki had signed. The Parcham faction was put into power and its Afghan Revolutionary Central Committee elected Deputy Prime Minister Babrak Karmal as head of government.

Initially, the Soviet military intended only to occupy Kabul, Kandahar, and the large cities. The rural areas had never been under government control, and the Russians were unable to establish any sort of authority outside the urban limits. Since 1945 the Red Army had trained to fight on the plains of Europe with armour and supporting air and artillery bombardment, its tanks sweeping over all opposition according to a well-rehearsed plan. In wild and mountainous Afghanistan, without roads, communications, or a centralized authority, the Soviet army found itself ill prepared. If most of the army officers were Russian, the rank and file were not. More than 50 percent of the Red Army forces in the Southern Command were conscripts from the Asian and Muslim regions of the Soviet Union, their political and military unreliability making them poor fighters against the mujahideen.

The set-piece plan to invade another country wasn't adapted to the situation. The anti-aircraft ZSU-23 mobile batteries trucked in were useless (the guerrillas had no aircraft). The famed Soviet tanks that had crushed revolts in Hungarian and Czech cities proved ineffective and vulnerable in the Afghan environment. In total the Soviets lost 147 tanks and 1,314 armoured personnel carriers, even as the deadly, highly accurate, shoulder-launched Stinger surface-to-air missiles supplied to the mujahideen by the CIA increased the aircraft losses of the Soviet air force.[17]

To the Russians the Afghans were amazingly resilient and were called *dukhi* ("ghosts") because they blended with the locals so well. Of the rings of land mines sown around the garrisoned cities, the most numerous were the ashtray-size PMN especially designed to maim and not kill. The idea was that while the dead were buried and forgotten, the sight of a legless man or child had a more demoralizing effect. Other mines were air-dropped such as the "butterfly" type designed for mountainous paths — no wonder Afghanistan has been described as one vast minefield. The spraying of toxic chemicals in scorched-earth campaigns that destroyed whole regions were also employed, but the international condemnation that arose from their use, in particular from the non-aligned nations and the Muslim world, negated their effects. It was only when Russian tactics were changed to close support of ground troops with effective use of SU-25 Frogfoot aircraft (the equivalent of the American A-10 Warthog) and the humped-back Hind Mi-24 gunships and Mi-8 Hip troop transports that some measure of success was achieved.

"The Soviets," writes Sarah Chayes in *The Punishment of Virtue*, "shot at from a village, would come back with their invincible helicopter gunships and raze the village, bring down the mud-brick houses on their occupants, splinter the bones of the elders, eviscerate the women never once seen by a stranger's eyes, sow mines among the almonds and apricots so those who longed to tend the trees would be blown up trying. A million Afghans would be killed in that decade of war, most of them civilians."[18] But even with an estimated 300,000 men at their disposal and a complete disregard for human rights, the Soviets were unable to pacify Afghanistan. To paraphrase what a character in *Lie Down with Lions*, Ken Follett's novel about the conflict, says: the only way that they were going to do so was to turn the whole country into a radioactive desert.

To the historically xenophobic Afghans, the Soviet invasion was yet another attempt by foreigners to replace their religion and traditional way of life. So, as their ancestors had with the Persians and the British, they fought a jihad against this new enemy.[19] Officially, between 1979 and 1989, 15,000 Soviet troops were killed (though veterans of the war claim the tally was two to three times that) in addition to many hundreds of vehicles and aircraft destroyed or shot down. But as the

Afghans point out, more than 1.5 million of their own people lost their lives in the conflict.

As with Karmal's government, Moscow's occupation was devoid of all international support. With the exception of India, non-aligned nations were vociferous in their condemnation, and in January 1980 foreign ministers of the Organization of the Islamic Conference meeting in Islamabad demanded a Soviet withdrawal. Even violently anti-American Iran — a country that Moscow should have scored points with — called for the "lesser Satan" to leave Afghanistan. Most nations, including Canada, broke off diplomatic relations with Afghanistan.[20] At the United Nations the Soviets were able to veto any action in the Security Council, but the General Assembly voted (104 to 18 with 18 abstentions) for a resolution calling for the total withdrawal of foreign troops from Afghanistan.

President Carter warned the Soviets to stay out of the Persian Gulf on January 23, 1980, echoing the "warm-water ports" fear that Governor General Lord Auckland once voiced. Carter ended detente negotiations, embargoed all grain and high-technology exports to the Soviet Union, cut Aeroflot flights to New York, and boycotted the 1980 Summer Olympics in Moscow. When Ronald Reagan became president a year later, American aid to the mujahideen funnelled through Pakistan's military ruler General Muhammad Zia-ul-Haq intensified. In 1984 the CIA received US$30 million for covert operations in Afghanistan, the figure rising annually to $250 million in 1985, $476 million in 1986, and $630 million in 1987. The Saudi royal family replaced the deposed Shah of Iran as a provider of largesse and matched each CIA increment, supporting the Sunni Pashtuns exclusively.

War correspondents, war groupies, and white mercenaries congregated in Peshawar across the border, the most memorable being Aeroplane Annie.[21] But unlike contemporary African conflicts, this struggle would be an entirely Muslim war. The Saudis didn't discourage their own citizens from joining the insurgency, Osama bin Laden, the son of a Yemeni-born construction millionaire, being a good example. And for William Casey, the CIA chief, the attempted occupation was an opportunity made in heaven. Besides turning Afghanistan into a Russian Vietnam, the country could be used as a base from which to launch guerrilla attacks against Soviet Muslim republics like Tajikistan and Uzbekistan. After Vietnam, Central America, and Iran, the White House was quite clear about the legalities of committing u.s. troops, even Special Forces, to subvert and overthrow another government, so Casey approved a plan to launch a worldwide recruiting drive for Muslims with radical leanings to join in a jihad against the Soviets. The CIA director even made a secret trip across the Pakistani border to meet the freedom fighters.

In total more than us$3 billion in funds and weapons were pumped into the Afghan resistance as thousands of Islamic militants were recruited in Arab, Asian, and European countries and sent to training camps in Pakistan. It is conservatively estimated that between 1982 and 1992, 35,000 radicals from 43 Islamic countries passed through the camps, and many thousands more studied in Pakistani madrassas. Pakistan even authorized its embassies to issue visas immediately to anyone who professed to be a mujahideen.

Leonid Brezhnev died in 1982 as the toll in Soviet casualties and the loss of support at home and in its Muslim republics was increasingly felt in the Soviet Union. By March 1985, as the rebel organizations formed an alliance to coordinate military operations against the Soviet army and were soon advancing on Kabul and unleashing rocket attacks on its suburbs, Mikhail Gorbachev, the Soviet Union's new leader, sought to withdraw from Afghanistan with some dignity. Karmal was deposed in November 1986 and was replaced by the Parcham leader Mohammad Najibullah, the former chief of KHAD. Moscow pressed him to adopt a new constitution as a policy of "national reconciliation" as on July 20, 1987, the withdrawal of Soviet troops from the country was announced. A year later the governments of Pakistan and Afghanistan, with the United States and the Soviet Union serving as guarantors, signed an agreement known as the Geneva Accords, which the United Nations oversaw. The Accords forbade u.s. and Soviet intervention in the internal affairs of Afghanistan, and on February 15, 1989, the last Soviet troops crossed the Friendship Bridge over the Oxus on schedule.[22]

Then everything went awry. For the United States and the rest of the Western world, Afghanistan dropped off the television screen. Tragically, at that moment in time when the United States and the militants were politically close, Washington's interest in Afghanistan and the courting of Pakistan ended. With the Cold War won and the disintegrating Soviet Empire seemingly never again to be a threat, aid, weapons, and encouragement from the West for Afghanistan and Pakistan were simply terminated. As one Pakistani general bitterly said, "They used us as a condom." On their own for the first time in recent history, leaders of the orphaned Afghan resistance met in June 1987 and again in July 1990 to formulate a common policy. These meetings may have led to a united front, but ancient rivalries proved too strong and nothing positive resulted.

The brutal decade-long war left Afghanistan destitute. Farmers and herdsmen lost their fields and animals to the butterfly mines and their children to indiscriminate murder from all sides. Without a centralized authority to care for the roads and irrigation systems, the rural infrastructure broke down and farmers turned to the one cash crop for which there was a ready market — opium. The warlords seized the opportunity to divide the country among themselves. The millions of Afghan refugees in Pakistan and Iran who had been waiting for the liberation of their country from the Soviets now despaired of returning home. The war had left the countryside an ecological disaster. As bad as the scorched-earth policy, abandoned farms, and extensive sowing of land mines were, food production had almost disappeared due to Soviet mismanagement in an attempt to centralize the economy through state ownership and control. Sadly, there was no Marshall Plan or transitional policy from the West for the devastated country. Increasingly preoccupied with Iraq, Washington abandoned Afghanistan to its neighbours — the Pakistanis, the Saudis, the Iranians, and the governments of former Soviet states such as Uzbekistan, Kazakhstan, and Turkmenistan.

The Great Game now had other players who took over the arms pipeline from the Americans but aided only their own brethren. For example, the Uzbeks now found themselves courted not only by the Russian Federation but also newly independent Uzbekistan. As Shias, the Hazaras had received aid from Iran to fight the Soviets; now these funds were earmarked for use against the Pashtuns. Iran wanted the Hazaras to unite into the Hizb-e-Wahdat political party and thus obtain stronger representation in the new Afghanistan. Accustomed to being the sole purveyors of American weapons, the Pakistanis continued to support the Pashtuns but were bitterly disappointed when during the Gulf War the Afghans aligned themselves with Iraq's Saddam Hussein.

The Afghans themselves now realized they had been expendable proxies in the Great Game between the foreign powers. It was this recognition that caused the thousands of Islamic militants that the CIA had trained and armed to spread out across the world, seeking their own infidels and bringing the jihad to Europe, the United States, and even in the Dhahran and Riyadh bombings to Saudi Arabia.

Strangely enough, Mohammad Najibullah was able to retain power longer than expected, and the Afghan army held its own against all comers. When Najibullah's end came in 1992 after the collapse of the Soviet Union, it was because all petroleum imports from Moscow were stopped.[23] On April 18, 1992, Najibullah's government was overthrown as Ahmed Shah Massoud's Tajiks combined with Abdul Rashid Dostum's Uzbeks and marched into Kabul. This development was a severe blow to Pashtun (and Pakistani) pride, one the Taliban would capitalize on. Disorganized and leaderless, the Pashtuns accepted the *fait accompli* and supported the interim Islamic Jihad Council that assumed power.

The council was run by Professor Sibghatullah Mojaddedi, a moderate who was acceptable to the Americans. The plan was that he would chair the council for two months when Professor Burhanuddin Rabbani would preside over a 10-member leadership council composed of mujahideen leaders for four months. During this six-month period, the Loya Jirga would convene and designate an interim administration that would hold power up to a year pending elections. Mojaddedi stepped down on June 28, and Rabbani was elected president. Rabbani's soldiers suppressed all dissenters, especially those of Gulbuddin Hekmatyar, the Pashtun leader. From the Ghilzai tribe, Hekmatyar was well educated, having studied engineering, and had a long political career that stretched back to the rebellion against Daoud. A hero of the anti-Soviet war, he founded Hezb-e-Islami, which received millions of dollars from the CIA and the Pakistanis. Hekmatyar's radical outlook worried the Americans, but he was seen as the Saudi and Pakistani champion. Both countries had taken over supplying fuel to Afghanistan, which was seen as a further means of holding the Afghans hostage.

The son of a Herati police chief, Ahmed Shah Massoud was a true hero of the Soviet war. The " Lion of Panjshir" (his home), as Massoud was known, had the charisma to appeal to a broad base of the Afghan population.[24] Good-looking with piercing eyes and well educated (he spoke French well), Massoud studied Mao Zedong and Persian poetry equally on campaign. Like Mao, he was an imaginative guerrilla fighter, escaping assassination twice. Throughout the 1980s, ignoring his human-rights abuses against other ethnic groups, the CIA poured millions of dollars into his war chest. The Pakistanis hated this non-Pashtun, but such was his appeal that Rabbani made his fellow Tajik minister of defence, a post that gave Massoud complete licence to rape and massacre anyone he chose — and usually he chose the minority Hazaras. On February 11, 1993, Massoud's men stormed through the Hazara suburb of Afshar, killing, by local accounts, "up to 1,000 civilians, beheading old men, women, children, and even their dogs, stuffing their bodies down the wells."

Through January and February 1993, with Rabbani consolidating his position through such mass murder, and other factions jockeying for power, Kabul endured bitter house-to-house street fighting. Pakistan desperately attempted to regain control and staged the Islamabad Accord in March that made its candidate, Hekmatyar, prime minister. That Hekmatyar's Hezb-e-Islami Gulbuddin (known as HIG) specialized in kidnapping and torturing aid workers, political opponents, and journalists was bad enough, but he also ignored the next Pakistani-engineered agreement, the Jalalabad Accord, which called for the militias to be disarmed. Prime Minister Hekmatyar's army fought the forces of President Rabbani, who was only able to hold him off because of his ally, the Uzbek warlord Abdul Rashid Dostum.

The whole country was now a killing field as warring factions battled it out for control of Kabul. In 1994 the United Nations estimated that at least 25,000 civilians died in rocket and artillery attacks on the city, one-third of which was by now reduced to rubble. There was no law or order, and according to Human Rights Watch, Ahmed Shah Massoud's faction engaged in rape, summary executions, arbitrary arrest, and torture. Describing pre-Taliban conditions, an Amnesty International report in 1995 stated: "Women and girls all over

Afghanistan live in constant fear of being raped by armed guards. For years armed guards have been allowed to torture them in this way without fear of reprimand from their leaders. In fact, rape is apparently condoned by most leaders as a means of terrorizing conquered populations and/or rewarding soldiers."

The West was largely indifferent to the sufferings of the Afghans, particularly since the attention of its media was more focused on what was taking place in the former Yugoslavia. Years later, when Hillary Clinton and the wife of talk-show host Jay Leno condemned the Taliban's treatment of women and the fundamentalist movement's enforcement of the burka, a spokesman for Mullah Omar bitterly asked, "Where was Western attention then?"

Abdul Rashid Dostum was a peasant who had learned his trade in the Afghan armoured corps, and when the Soviets left, he formed his own Uzbek army to fight the Kabul government. By 1993 he controlled the traditional Uzbek homeland around Mazar-i-Sharif. Untrustworthy to both allies and patrons, Dostum continued to receive support from Russia, Iran, and Turkey because he despised two things: Pashtuns and Islamic fundamentalism. But on January 1, 1994, that didn't prevent Dostum from switching his support from the Tajik government of Rabbani and Massoud to the Pashtun Hekmatyar, causing large-scale fighting in Kabul and in the country's northern provinces. Soon all Rabbani controlled was Kabul, with local warlords running the rest of the nation. But he was still able to inflict punishment on the Pakistanis, who had supported the Pashtuns and had their embassy in Kabul sacked.

The timing couldn't have been worse for Pakistan's Prime Minister Benazir Bhutto. With Karachi, Pakistan's only port, blockaded every time there was a war with India, she planned an overland outlet to the Middle East and Central Asia. Bhutto wanted to construct a highway (or rebuild the old u.s.-built highway with power and telecommunications) from Peshawar through Afghanistan to the newly independent former Soviet countries. A stable government in Kabul, preferably Pashtun, was essential for this, but by 1994 Pakistan had lost faith in Hekmatyar, and the United States, too, tried to distance itself from his radical outlook. If instead the highway could be built to run south through Kandahar with its strong Pashtun base and then through Herat to Turkmenistan, Kabul would be bypassed physically and politically and it wouldn't matter who was in power there. Besides the Kandaharis, the group most enthusiastic for Bhutto's proposal was the truck-driver mafia, both Pakistani and Afghan. The ancient highway that ran through Kandahar now had chains across it every 45 metres as every tribe, petty government official, and local bandit "shook down" the truck drivers. With increasing commitments to carry opium to the West and return with weapons, the truck drivers were only too willing to pay for protection to one or two authorities and not all the corrupt petty government officials who preyed on them via Kabul.

For Pakistan, Afghanistan had always been the edge of the garden where the weeds and nettles grew, where wild animals foraged, and where one could dump garbage: old cars, mattresses, and surplus weapons. Kandahar was almost a suburb of Quetta in Pakistan. In fact, it had the same telephone area code. To be fair, Pakistan's policy towards Afghanistan had always been motivated by India, its giant neighbour to the east. Since independence in 1947, India had always supported whatever government was in power in Kabul. After all, a stable Afghanistan would threaten its enemy Pakistan on two fronts.

Herat was controlled by Ismail Khan. Later known as the "Minister of Darkness,"[25] the Herati warlord was a legend among mujahideen after staging the massacre of the Russian families and then fighting off the 300 tanks that the Red Army sent to level his city. Respected by his countrymen and Iranians alike, Khan governed Herat independently and well from 1992 on as crime and garbage vanished from its streets and, unfortunately, human rights, too. The city was flush with food and luxury goods imported from Iran, and Khan's personal army was well paid and equipped because of the custom duties extracted from the border trade. Bhutto (and later President Karzai) realized that Khan's support was essential to the future of the country. By November 1994, Bhutto opened negotiations with Khan and Dostum concerning the highway. The Kandaharis were another matter, though.

Kandahar, the traditional home of Pashtun fervour, had been sidelined by recent events, and its militants were irritated. The Tajiks controlled Kabul, the Heratis ruled the West, the Hazaras dominated the city of Bamiyan, and Rashid Dostum commanded all of the northern part of the country. The single Pashtun champion, Hekmatyar, was even by Afghan terms too unreliable. The Pakistani government was also in a quandary, since its prime minister, Nawaz Sharif, supported Rabbani, but Inter-Services Intelligence (isi), Pakistan's secret service, supplied weapons to Hekmatyar even as he rained rockets and shells down on Rabbani's bureaucrats in Kabul.

By 1994 even the pretense of a centralized government in Kabul had disappeared, and bandits and the private armies of warlords roamed the country. Afghanistan was more anarchic than ever, and as gun battles in the bazaars became common, no one was safe. The farmers in Kandahar Province knew that their pomegranate orchards and vineyards, to say nothing of their poppy fields, required security and stability to operate. Getting the fruits to Pakistani and Iranian markets required a road system without land mines, bandits, and chains. Without a central authority the few forests were cut down by warlords and the wood was sold in Pakistan, the deforestation bringing floods and avalanches. Chemicals used by the Soviets, and the indiscriminate planting of land mines (which daily continue to kill or maim an average of 20 Afghans, mainly women and children), had denied most of the remaining arable land to farmers.

The Kandahari students thought that the older generation of tribal leaders were too disunited and dependent on their foreign benefactors for money. Besides, they had spent too much time outside the country to be relevant. The old Marxist parties were similarly discredited, and the rural population had never had any faith in the Kabul intelligentsia. Fearing for their workers, the United Nations aid agencies began pulling out of Afghanistan, another sign that the traditional tribal structure that had existed in the country since feudal times was disintegrating. Into this vacuum stepped the one-eyed Mullah Mohammed Omar and the "seekers of truth," better known as the Taliban.

How the Taliban came to power has become the stuff of legend. There are stories that in true Robin Hood form Mullah Omar was beseeched by the poor to right injustices perpetrated against them by rapacious warlords, and perhaps there is some truth in that. A local military commander had kidnapped two teenage girls and brought them to his camp where they were repeatedly raped. Responding to the parents' entreaties, Mullah Omar collected 30 of his students, shared 15 rifles among them, and stormed the camp, rescuing the girls and hanging the commander from the gun barrel of a tank. With their children being kidnapped off the streets by soldiers, other parents, too, came to Mullah Omar for help, impressed (*shocked* would be a better word) that the religious leader didn't want any financial reward or seek power for these deeds. All he asked was that people follow the true Islamic way.

The disintegration of Afghan society had been discussed at length in shuras throughout the country, but especially in Kandahar.[26] As disillusioned Germans must have done during the days of the Weimar Republic, ordinary Afghans were willing to pay any price for peace and protection. If the truck-driver mafia, the Pakistanis, and long-suffering ordinary Afghans all wanted change, Afghan graduates of the madrassas across the border wanted it most of all. Having studied the teachings of the Prophet Muhammad, they yearned to create the ideal Islamic society in their homeland. Afghanistan would never be a land of religious purity under the disgraced leaders of the older mujahideen. The seduction of their leaders by Western influences was to blame. As altruistic as they were, the students had only known the refugee camps and not their own country, and the male brotherhood of the madrassa made them suspicious of frivolity and the opposite sex. Both were to be kept away, preferably under strict exclusion.

If the truck-driver mafia supplied the Taliban with money and mobility, the Pakistanis contributed intelligence and arms. Four years before, in keeping with the Accords, Pakistan had been forced to give up storing arms for Afghan combatants and a cache was transferred across the border to Spin Boldak. The 18,000 AK-47s and hundreds of artillery pieces and vehicles were now made available to the student army. By October 1994, the now-armed Taliban was punishing bandits and corrupt Afghan army officers who "shook down" Pakistani truck convoys. Emboldened, on November 3 the Taliban moved on Kandahar itself, capturing government posts and more arms. The opened highway not only pleased the truck drivers but provided a conduit for hundreds of Taliban to leave Pakistani refugee camps and travel to Kandahar where Mullah Omar preached. They were joined by young Pashtuns from across Afghanistan who saw this opportunity as a chance to revenge themselves against the Tajiks, Hazaras, and Uzbeks who had usurped them in Kabul.

City after city fell to the Taliban crusade, usually without firing a shot, and in February 1995, Wardak was captured, 60 kilometres south of Kabul. The capital had its own problems: it was blockaded and was being shelled by Hekmatyar, who suddenly found himself surrounded by the Taliban and Rabbani's and Massoud's armies. He fled, and the citizens of Kabul and the United Nations aid agencies fed up with the indiscriminate shelling from all sides hoped the Taliban, seen as incorruptible and broad-based, would win. But Kabul wasn't like the mud-walled villages the Taliban was used to taking, and for the first time the mob of madrassa graduates met with determined resistance.

In March 1995, when Massoud fought the Taliban to a standstill, it turned west to Herat where the warlord Ismail Khan proved as tough an adversary. Massoud airlifted battle-hardened Tajik troops into Herat, and having been on the receiving end of aerial bombardment during the Soviet war, the Lion of Panjshir made good use of the national air force to strafe and bomb Taliban encampments. Without medical or logistical support or even officers trained in military strategy, at this point the Taliban might have disintegrated and its odious regime might never have occurred — if Afghanistan's concerned neighbours hadn't stepped in.

With Hekmatyar lost to them, the Pakistani generals now took the Taliban seriously. They resupplied Mullah Omar with fresh ammunition and their convoys ferried more students from the madrassas to his frontline. More important, the ISI bribed the Uzbek warlord Rashid Dostum to cast his lot with the Taliban. With this development, Herat fell to the Taliban on September 5, 1995, and the sophisticated Persian-speaking Heratis endured a reign of terror from the Dari-speaking Pashtuns. Only the capital city, defended by Rabbani and Massoud, held out.

With the country's second- and third-largest cities in Taliban hands, the Iranians, Russians, Saudis, and Americans were forced to take notice, each aligning themselves according to faction. The Russians and Iranians aided President Rabbani, while the American State Department "rediscovered" Afghanistan yet again and (because Washington was anti-Iranian) began once more filling Massoud's bank account. The oil-rich Saudis joined with their Pakistani allies to help the Taliban. They supplied the financing for arms and transport — the ubiquitous white Toyota pickup trucks — while the Pakistanis bussed in thousands of more youths from the refugee camps to join the jihad.

The summer of 1996 was good for the Taliban as province after province fell to it, less by military strategy than through bribery and treachery. The ring closed around the capital when Jalalabad, 250 kilometres east of Kabul, surrendered on August 25.[27] When the Bagram air base was captured, the Russians could no longer resupply Rabbani by air, and it was only matter of days before the wretched citizens of Kabul suffered another pillaging. The first hint was when they woke up to discover that Massoud had abandoned the city; the guerrilla mountain fighter didn't want to become embroiled in street fighting. He also knew that the Taliban had unlimited access to men and ammunition from its foreign sources. On September 26, 1996, the Taliban entered Kabul, and Pashtuns everywhere could once more rejoice that they had retaken their ancestral city. Having survived monarchs and Marxists, the country was to enter its puritanical era.

Had the international media taken the Taliban seriously when its forces occupied Kandahar and later Herat, what now occurred in Kabul wouldn't have been a surprise. The Taliban was composed of villagers who had no experience running a semi-modern metropolis. Mullah Omar's entrance into Kabul was only the second time he had been in a city. As soon as those cities were occupied, a strict Islamic code was scrupulously enforced. Islam's basic tenets of peace and tolerance for all were subverted to the Taliban's own extreme fundamentalism.

It wasn't just that sharia law was imposed by the religious police, making the most minor offences punishable by stoning, or even that television sets and computers were smashed, hairdressing salons and bathhouses closed, and thieves' hands amputated. What affected the ordinary Afghan more profoundly was that women could no longer work. In one fell swoop the most intelligent, hardworking segments of the civil service, the educational and health systems, vanished. For a city like Kabul where more than two-thirds of the people were dependent on food, medicine, and shelter distributed by agencies such as the United Nations World Food Programme (UNWFP), the workforce to process allowances disappeared overnight. When talks broke down between the Taliban and the United Nations on the use of female workers to bake and distribute food, the organization struggled to keep its 116 bakeries open and some 300,000 people from starving. Since female doctors could no longer practise and male doctors weren't allowed to see or touch their female patients' bodies, access to medical care for women effectively ended. And most women vanished from public places, only reappearing henceforth if covered head to toe in a burka and accompanied by a male relative.

Dance, film, photography, kite-flying, non-religious music, and the display of art were also banned. Television satellite dishes and videocassette recorders were not only confiscated but hung on poles as warnings that their owners would follow them next. Men without beards were arrested as the Taliban religious police patrolled the streets and enforced sharia at gunpoint. The unfortunate flight crews of Ariana Afghan Airlines could no longer fit their oxygen masks over their beards and begged the government to make an exception for them. Punishing by public stoning and hanging in the football stadiums (they were closed, anyway) and the killing of Shia sect members by the religious police were condoned. There was no need for banks, computers, newspapers, kite-flying, electricians, lawyers, or barbers. And since Taliban soldiers weren't paid, expropriation became common. By 1997 all power was concentrated under Mullah Omar, who kept the whole national treasury in a tin trunk under his bed, doling out notes when needed.

The new era also provided opportunities to wreak revenge against the Tajiks and Hazaras still living in Kabul as *munafaqeen*, and soon long refugee columns from both tribes were making for the Pakistani border. All of this had taken place when Kandahar, Herat, and Jalalabad were overrun, but there had been little international condemnation then. This time, because there was foreign media, aid agencies, and a diplomatic community in Kabul, the world was made aware of the Taliban's excesses. Once welcomed as liberators from the warlords, the Taliban was now comparable to the Khmer Rouge in Cambodia.[28]

Only three nations — Pakistan, Saudi Arabia, and the United Arab Emirates (UAE) — recognized the Taliban and Mullah Mohammed Omar as the legitimate government of Afghanistan. All others, including the United Nations, imposed trade barriers and travel restrictions on Afghanistan. Because of this, Canada and other countries relied on the observations made during visits by their Islamabad embassy officers under the auspices of the United Nations Coordinator of Humanitarian Assistance (UNCOHA). Canadian observers in Kabul and Herat recorded the suffering of the Afghans under the Taliban. Without electrical power or fuel in the winter, residents of Kabul took to burning any wood they could scavenge to keep warm and were reduced to stealing doors and window frames to do so.

For India an Afghanistan run by the Taliban with its Pakistani puppet masters was nothing short of disaster. New Delhi expressed its indignation at the execution of Mohammad Najibullah, the former Afghan president, and then focused its support on anyone who opposed the Taliban — in this case the Northern Alliance and, on the international scene at the United Nations, Burhanuddin Rabbani.

In October 1996, Ahmed Shah Massoud and his second-in-command, Mohammad Qasim Fahim, recaptured Bagram air base, but with an inexhaustible supply of madrassa recruits, the Taliban pushed him out into the countryside. Gulbuddin Hekmatyar fled to Iran — the Pakistanis would have betrayed him to the Taliban — and by the beginning of 1997, only Abdul Rashid Dostum, entrenched in Mazar-i-Sharif, was holding out.

Dostum accepted bribes from both the Pakistanis to join the Taliban and from the Iranians so that he wouldn't, and it looked as if he had a chance when the Taliban converged on Mazar-i-Sharif. But once more the perennial Afghan faults of corruption and treachery asserted themselves: Dostum's troops were robbed of their salaries for the past five months and his generals were bribed by the Taliban to switch sides. Dostum fled on May 20, 1997, and the Taliban entered Mazar-i-Sharif and proceeded to carry out on its inhabitants the same program of persecution it had implemented in Kabul, Herat, and Kandahar. After a week of systemized humiliation, the citizens of Mazar-i-Sharif had enough and rose up in revolt, easily luring and killing the student soldiers who lost themselves in the ancient city's alleys.

That break was what Massoud had been waiting for and, joined by the Hazaras, he counterattacked. In the battles that followed, Taliban casualties numbered in the tens of thousands, and it seemed as if Kabul, too, might fall. For once this disparate group of anti-Taliban factions was able to put aside its differences, and on June 13, 1997, it formed the United Islamic Front for the Salvation of Afghanistan (UIFSA). If this military-political coalition of Tajiks, Hazaras, and Uzbeks controlled barely 30 percent of Afghanistan's population and only northern provinces such as Badakshan, Kapisa, and Takhar (thus taking Northern Alliance as its name), it had international recognition from many Western countries — and the Russians. Rabbani was made the Northern Alliance's political leader, but real power was held by Massoud who, as minister of defence, wisely gave Dostum and Ismail Khan positions within the UIFSA military command.

Throughout all of these events, without an embassy in Kabul, Canada had, like other donor nations, maintained routine contact with organizations such as the United Nations, the European Community, the Aga Khan food-aid operations, and the International Committee of the Red Cross (ICRC) that were still barely operating in the country. But the United Nations and many non-governmental organizations (NGOs) were in the process of evacuating all expatriate staff to Pakistan, and only the ICRC continued to keep its expatriates in the field. The only way that a number of aid projects remained operational was through utilizing locally engaged staff. The Taliban authorities, adept at manipulating foreign-aid agencies, formally requested that the U.N. expatriates return, conditional on a security review that its religious police would conduct.[29] However, the Taliban did give permission to the ICRC to visit prisoners without a Taliban representative present. The United Nations, though, was seeing very few new refugees arriving at its Pakistani camps despite the continuing Taliban offensive. That was because all potential refugees (mainly Tajiks and Uzbeks) were being detained at Taliban-run refugee camps near Jalalabad.

When it first came to power, the Taliban banned the cultivation of opium; after all, the Koran forbids all intoxicants. Delighted with this measure, the West hoped it would be a first step towards moderation and held out diplomatic recognition as a reward. But the cultivation of the poppy fields was far easier than growing pomegranates or vineyards — and the drug crop was far more lucrative. Upsetting the Kandahari farmers by banning opium was bad enough but taking on the truck-driver mafia that carried the contraband to Europe was suicide.

By 1999 the Taliban reinstated the cultivation of opium and controlled almost 100 percent, amounting to 4,600 tonnes. The office of the Taliban anti-drug force rationalized the announcement that opium could once more be cultivated by claiming that since it was completely consumed by Westerners, i.e., non-believers, and not Afghans, it was therefore permissible. Like governments before it, the Taliban also realized that the money brought in from heroin made it financially independent of its donors. Furthermore, such funds could be laundered through the State Bank of Afghanistan, which the Taliban now controlled.

In 2000, when the Taliban, to worldwide acclaim, once more banned opium production (triggering a rise in the market price of the drug), the value of its copious stockpiles more than doubled, to say nothing of the international goodwill the fundamentalist movement earned. The United States alone gave the Taliban US$43 million for banning the drug's production. In any case, Western countries were no longer the main recipients of the fruits of the opium poppy. New routes and markets had opened up for Afghan opium with the fall of the Soviet Union in 1991. For more than a century Russian troops had patrolled the 1,340-kilometre border between Afghanistan and Tajikistan, and continued doing so even after 1991. As Moscow pulled its legions home at the request of its former colonies, the "northern route" through Tajikistan, Kazakhstan, and Kyrgyzstan to the Russian market was now accessible to the drug cartels and truck-driver mafia of a dozen nationalities. As a result, when the last of the Russian troops departed, Russia was flooded with Afghan heroin — to the tune of US$15 billion in 2004 alone. Economists wryly estimated that only Gazprom, the Russian natural gas company, made more money.

But it wasn't only the sale of heroin that financed the war. The criminalization of the Afghan economy also contributed. The largest source of Taliban funds came from trade in commodities, not drugs. The smuggling of duty-free goods increased corruption, reduced tax revenues, and hurt legitimate businesses. The total of smuggled trade was around US$4.5 to $5 billion. The Taliban taxed this illicit trade for 60 to 70 percent of its income, and drugs accounted for the rest. Poppy cultivation replaced traditional agriculture in Afghanistan, so the country had to import most of its food products.

The hosting of training camps for militants, Islamic or otherwise, had a long tradition in several Arab countries, Libya, Sudan, and Pakistan being the best known. Those who attended these universities of terrorism came from countries as diverse as the Philippines, Algeria, Yemen, Uzbekistan, Turkey, Kashmir, and China. But nothing compared with those who graduated from camps in Afghanistan. In that country they cut their teeth on fighting and, in their view, bringing down the mighty Soviet war machine. During the 1990s, these "graduates" returned to their own countries to export jihad. Whether the funds were CIA, ISI, or Saudi, the curriculum was the same: after a century of defeat at the hands of the infidels, a new *umma* ("Islamic world") could arise from the sacrifices of martyrs such as themselves. Studying, fighting, and growing up together, these freedom fighters formed a worldwide brotherhood or network of common goals and beliefs.

The CIA had always judged that the recruits from Arab countries who arrived to fight in Afghanistan were low-grade, uneducated losers with grandiose ideas. They were equally despised by the Afghans, who used them as cannon fodder or had them dig trenches. Not so the young Saudi millionaire Osama bin Laden. With connections that went as high as the Saudi royal family, with access to private jets and engineers from his father's construction company, he was a prize for the Taliban.

Bin Laden arrived in Peshawar in 1982 and began organizing the flow of American weapons, Saudi funds, and Arab recruits into an Arab league of fighters, a group that was distrusted by the Afghan regulars as tourist amateurs. When the Soviets were defeated, bin Laden, who always claimed he personally led his men into battle, organized Al Qaeda to look after veterans of the war. He returned home and got wealthy Saudis to donate to his welfare organization. To bin Laden's horror, when Iraq invaded Kuwait, Saudi Arabia's King Fahd invited the Americans in to save his country.[30] In 1992, seeing 540,000 infidel troops based so close to the Holy Shrines, bin Laden personally attacked the Saudi ruling family as traitors to all Muslims. Banned for his actions, he moved to Afghanistan with his family, living in Kandahar in 1997 and receiving a sympathetic audience from Mullah Omar.

Soon Arab intelligence agencies were reporting that under Taliban protection bin Laden was training thousands of terrorists in a community of camps. His self-professed goal was to goad the United States into invading Afghanistan and touch off an international jihad, but so far none of the bombings had led to that. Even as the 1998 bombings of the U.S. embassies in Kenya and Tanzania took place, making bin Laden and Al Qaeda better known to the public, President Clinton only had his financial assets blocked and allowed the CIA to plan a "snatch operation" to kidnap the 1.93-metre-tall Arab.

The American dilemma of who to support was shared by every other Western nation: the cast of characters fighting the Taliban read like a gathering of commandants of Nazi death camps. Massoud's and Khan's armies were bad enough, but the rapacity of Dostum's Uzbek troops had earned them the nickname "The Carpet Robbers," and his lieutenant, Abdul Malik, practised mass executions as a matter of policy. Besides, the only "friendly" air bases and ports in the region from where air strikes or Special Forces to destroy Al Qaeda camps in Afghanistan could be launched were Pakistani. Loath to get even closer to Pakistan's Inter-Services Intelligence, President Clinton had the camps bombarded with cruise missiles from submarines offshore.

Six months after the East African embassy bombings, Al Qaeda began planning its grandest attack. It would fly a number of passenger aircraft into well-chosen targets in the American homeland — the ultimate martyrs' operation. The idea wasn't new, but the cruise-missile response had demonstrated that if Al Qaeda struck high-profile targets in the United States itself, the American counterstrike would be so great that it would cause Muslims everywhere to rise up against the West and their own disloyal governments. In February 1999 an Al Qaeda committee met in Kandahar in a building called the House of Gumad to fine-tune the aircraft plan. Present were the four future martyrs who would train as pilots in the United States. Among the targets chosen were the twin towers of the World Trade Center in Manhattan, the Pentagon in Virginia, and the White House in Washington, D.C., all high-profile, all accessible to domestic commercial flights. The funds to send the martyrs to flight school in the United States came from Al Qaeda bank accounts in the United Arab Emirates. While the plan was being worked on, just to keep the organization's name in the headlines, the U.S. warship USS *Cole*, berthed in Aden harbour, was hit with a suicide motorboat.

President Clinton repeatedly told his top national security aides that while he was prepared to work with Massoud, despite the man's record of brutality, he wasn't ready to arm the Northern Alliance. The president didn't think Massoud would ever be able to defeat the Taliban. By now governments as far away as Mauritania and Bangladesh were encountering local terrorists who had graduated from bin Laden's camps, and when the Al Qaeda leader issued a fatwa against the West, a reward of us$5 million was offered for his capture. To the dismay of the incoming George W. Bush administration, both of the closest u.s. allies in the area, the Saudis and the Pakistanis, were less than cooperative in the hunt. The Pakistanis were pleased that bin Laden had welcomed Kashmiri freedom fighters to his camps, and the Saudis were afraid the American public would find out what their security services already knew: bin Laden's connections led directly to the Saudi royal family.

In the midst of all this, the Taliban was attempting some form of respectability and was now making tentative efforts at international cooperation, meeting with diplomats from China and Turkmenistan and officials from oil and gas companies. Hoping for international respectability, the Taliban was beginning to realize it had taken a Trojan Horse into its midst. Addicted to CNN, bin Laden loved media attention for his bombings, and sooner or later, the Taliban leadership saw that his theatrics would bring down the wrath of the United States upon them. After repeated u.s. demands for bin Laden's extradition, the Taliban finally confiscated the Al Qaeda leader's cell phones on February 13, 1999, and had him removed from Kandahar. By now the stronghold was becoming too dangerous, and Mullah Omar himself narrowly escaped assassination in Kandahar on August 24, 1999, though his family members were less fortunate. On December 19, 2000, the u.n. Security Council issued Resolution 1333. It was directed at the Taliban and demanded that the fundamentalist Islamic government turn over bin Laden to the United States or a third country for trial in the bombings of the two u.s. embassies in Africa in August 1998. The resolution also called on the Taliban to close terrorist training camps and threatened trade sanctions and a freeze of Taliban assets abroad if the rogue government didn't comply.

The u.n. threat of sanctions fell on deaf ears, since Mullah Omar had other things to worry about now. In March 2001, Taliban militia acting on an edict to destroy the "gods of the infidels" dynamited the colossal Buddhas in the caves of Bamiyan. The wanton destruction of the 1,500 treasures — even Genghis Khan who had massacred the valley's population in the 13th century had left the Buddhas standing — shocked the world.[31] At the height of the Taliban's power in June 2001, even as Mullah Omar's zealots were imposing sharia law on foreign workers, too, and all female foreigners were forbidden to drive motor vehicles in the country, Massoud's forces were on the outskirts of Kabul and shelling the downtown area. The Northern Alliance was capturing towns and airfields like Bagram and now even had the means to shoot down Taliban aircraft.

But Massoud realized all too well that because of the massive aid the Taliban was getting from Pakistan, the Northern Alliance would never win. He went to Tehran and Tashkent begging for help. To eliminate bin Laden and Al Qaeda, the CIA wanted direct U.S. support for Massoud, but the outgoing Clinton administration wasn't going to risk arming any of the anti-Taliban factions or upsetting their Middle Eastern allies. The only aid the White House would allow was purposely low-tech: mortars, mules, and the endless supply of Chinese-made AK-47s. The Pakistanis were once more to be courted, if only because Clinton had been at Oxford University at the same time as Pakistani President Benazir Bhutto. After hearing her speak as a student, he remained entranced by her. The country was also essential for covert operations, especially the Predator UAV surveillance flights into Afghanistan.

Massoud refused to get involved in the hunt for bin Laden. For one thing, as a Tajik, he controlled the north and bin Laden was in Pashtun Kandahar. He also thought it was a waste of resources — his and the CIA's — that could be put to better use getting rid of the Taliban. Al Qaeda would continue to thrive after bin Laden's death as long as it was supported by the Taliban and that organization in turn was subsidized by the Pakistanis and Saudis. But capturing the terrorist leader and rolling up his Al Qaeda network was as far as U.S. policy would go. Learning from former invaders, the White House wasn't going to commit forces to Afghanistan without a legal licence from the international community to destabilize the government in Kabul and replace it with a more acceptable one.

The Lion of Panjshir was now busy pursuing his own agenda. He was wooing ethnic Pashtun rebels, especially Hamid Karzai, a former Afghan deputy foreign minister living in exile in Pakistan. Born in Kandahar, Karzai is a Pashtun of the influential Popalzai clan and hails from a family that has royalist sympathies. Educated in political science at Himachal University in India (1979–83), he had been a fund-raiser for the mujahideen during the Soviet intervention. After the fall of Najibullah's government in 1992, Karzai served as a deputy foreign minister in the Rabbani government. The Karzai family, based in Quetta, was taken in by the Taliban at first, viewing its members as traditional religious leaders who wanted to restore order, bring the Afghan king back from Rome, and break off relations with the Pakistani ISI.

After hosting meetings with Taliban leaders at his home, Karzai broke with them over their Pakistani connections, but such was his appeal that despite this the Taliban invited him to be its ambassador to the United Nations in 1996. He refused and moved to the United States, where his family ran a number of restaurants and coalesced overseas Pashtun support. When his father was assassinated by Taliban agents on July 14, 1999, Karzai swore revenge. He returned to Pakistan, and in defiance of Mullah Omar led a convoy of 300 cars to Kandahar to bury his father in the ancestral home. Well spoken, courteously Old World in manners, stylish in a cape, and called the "Gucci rebel" by his critics, Karzai was eminently acceptable to the West by 1999. He wanted arms and men to lead a rebellion in Kandahar and haunted embassies in Peshawar begging for support. Meeting with Massoud, Karzai said he was ready to begin the fight to overthrow the Taliban, but the Lion of Panjshir cautioned against going directly to Kandahar and invited Karzai to the north where his own strength lay. At last it seemed as if Afghanistan had its General Charles de Gaulle in exile.

By August 2001 the relationship between the CIA and Massoud was falling apart. The CIA (especially the Counterterrorist Center) reminded the incoming George W. Bush administration that Massoud was the best hope of capturing or killing bin Laden. His human-rights record might be dismal, but all of that was internal while bin Laden's Al Qaeda was the greater danger to the West. Not yet briefed on the Afghan situation, the Bush administration was lukewarm to any military aid. By now Massoud's officers were fed up with being badgered to mount a "Hollywood operation," as one of them put it, to capture bin Laden alive. That seemed to be the total extent of Washington's policy towards the suffering of the Afghan people, Massoud had his Washington lobbyist write to Vice President Dick Cheney, urging the new administration to re-examine its stance towards Afghanistan. He couldn't defeat the Taliban on the battlefield, he warned Cheney, as long as it was funded by bin Laden and reinforced with men and money from Pakistan and Saudi Arabia. Increasingly frustrated with the Americans, Massoud went to Strasbourg to address the European Parliament. Speaking in fluent French, he warned that if the West didn't help, sooner or later he was going to lose. "If President Bush doesn't help us," Massoud prophetically warned the European media, "then these terrorists will damage the United States and Europe very soon — and it will be too late."

In the first week of September 2001, in a routine transmission, Massoud's intelligence service informed the CIA's Counterterrorist Center that two Arab television journalists from Pakistan via Kabul had crossed Northern Alliance lines to interview the Lion of Panjshir. On September 4, when the Bush cabinet met at the White House, each member was given a draft copy of a national security presidential directive that outlined a new U.S. policy towards Al Qaeda, Afghanistan, and Massoud. Millions of dollars were to be provided, as well as everything Massoud required such as trucks, uniforms, ammunition, medicine, helicopters, and other equipment. These measures were approved by the Bush cabinet, with the more controversial covert-aid aspects, such as the use of armed Predators to hunt for bin Laden, put aside for later discussion. The CIA must have been mollified: the agency's goal of getting bin Laden hadn't changed, but at least its ally would be rewarded with all he needed to defeat the Taliban. U.S. General Tommy Franks, commander-in-chief of Central Command, was sent to talk to Pervez Musharraf, the latest Pakistani president.

Far away from Langley in the Panjshir Valley in the early morning of September 9, Massoud, who was ignorant about the U.S. turnabout, was reading Persian poetry in his bungalow. He then granted an interview to the two Arab journalists who had travelled from Kabul. One of them set up the video camera while the other went though a list of questions he intended to ask the Lion of Panjshir. Then the camera blew up, shattering the photographer's body and the room's windows as shrapnel tore into Massoud's chest. He was airlifted to a hospital in Tajikistan but couldn't be saved. The Northern Alliance was now leaderless, just as American policy had tilted towards it. Mohammad Qasim Fahim succeeded Massoud on September 13, but having no faith in the Americans, either, he went to Takjikistan to meet with the Russians for help.

On the morning of September 10, at the CIA's daily briefing to President Bush and his cabinet, Massoud's death was discussed with its consequences for the United States' covert war against Al Qaeda. Throughout that day the whole Afghan nation began to hear that the legendary Ahmed Shah Massoud was dead. Karzai had spoken to him a few days earlier and had contemplated flying into Massoud's territory, using it as a base and beginning a Pashtun uprising against the Taliban. His comment upon hearing from his brother that Massoud was dead was, as his brother later recalled, "What an unlucky country."

Watching the twin towers of New York City's World Trade Center falling on September 11, the members of both the Al Qaeda and Taliban inner circles must have been torn between exaltation and fear. As overwhelming a victory as it was, they knew that the full anger of the United States was about to descend upon them. While publicly denying any involvement in the attacks, bin Laden had succeeded beyond all expectations. He himself didn't think the towers of the World Trade Center would collapse, and he now figured that American revenge would be as overpowering as it had been during Operation Desert Storm. To his disappointment, however, the war remained covert for another three weeks as U.S. and British Special Forces clandestinely infiltrated Afghanistan from Pakistan to make contact with the Northern Alliance and organize it to overthrow the Taliban.

On September 12 the U.N. Security Council issued Resolution 1368, condemning the attacks of the previous day, offering deepest sympathy to the American people, and reaffirming the right of member nations (expressed in Article 51 of the U.N. Charter) to individual and collective self-defence. The world body also urged the global community to suppress terrorism and hold accountable all who aided, supported, or harboured the perpetrators, organizers, and sponsors of terrorist acts.

Furthermore, the United Nations stated that it was prepared to combat all forms of terrorism.

Now sanctioned to execute military action in Afghanistan, President Bush gave the Taliban an ultimatum: deliver all Al Qaeda members and every terrorist in Afghanistan to the United States; release all imprisoned foreign nationals, including American citizens; protect foreign journalists, diplomats, and aid workers in Afghanistan; and close terrorist training camps. The demands weren't open to negotiation or discussion. Stating that talking with a non-Muslim political leader would be an insult to Islam, the Taliban refused to speak directly to Bush and chose to make statements through its embassy in Pakistan. The Taliban wanted evidence of bin Laden's culpability in the September 11 attacks and proposed trying him in an Islamic court. Later, as U.S. military action became imminent, the Taliban offered to extradite bin Laden to a neutral nation. Taliban moderates met with American embassy officials in Pakistan to try to convince Mullah Mohammed Omar to turn bin Laden over to the United States and avoid impending retaliation. President Bush rejected these offers by the Taliban, deeming them insincere.

The decision to go to war was taken by the U.S. National Security Council on October 2, 2001, and the invasion began exactly at 12:30 p.m. Eastern Daylight Time on Sunday, October 7, with American and British forces bombing Taliban forces and Al Qaeda camps. Strikes were reported on Kabul (where electricity supplies were cut), at its airport, on Mullah Omar's home in Kandahar, and also in Jalalabad where the training camps were. While the U.S. government justified the bombings as a response to the 9/11 attacks and the failure of the Taliban to meet any U.S. demands, the Taliban proclaimed them an "attack on Islam." Shortly after the attacks began, Bush confirmed the strikes on national television, stating that at the same time as Taliban military and terrorists' training grounds were targeted, food, medicine, and supplies were dropped to "the starving and suffering men, women, and children of Afghanistan." The Taliban had no air force or aerial defence, and U.S. aircraft, including Apache helicopter gunships, operated with impunity throughout the campaign, while cruise missiles hammered the country. The strikes initially focused on Kabul, Jalalabad, and Kandahar, and then on the Taliban communications network. Bolstered by the intense bombing campaign, the Northern Alliance liberated Kabul on November 12–13, 2001.

The only remaining Taliban pocket was Kandahar, upon which by late November three UIFSA armies were advancing while the city was pounded by air strikes. The Pashtun force was led by Hamid Karzai and Gul Agha Shirzai, the previous governor of Kandahar, whose human-rights record was suspect. In negotiating the surrender of small groups of the Taliban, Karzai came to the attention of the international media. Ferried in by Super Stallion helicopters on November 25, U.S. Marines, the first Western combat troops to enter the war legally, set up a forward operating base (FOB) in the desert south of Kandahar. On December 5, Karzai negotiated with Mullah Omar to surrender the city and lay down all arms in return for an amnesty. Kandahar fell the next day, but Mullah Omar reneged and slipped out with a group of loyalists on motorbikes, making for the mountains of Uruzgan Province. The border town of Spin Boldak surrendered on the same day, marking the end of Taliban control in Afghanistan.

Gul Agha Shirzai seized Kandahar, while the Marines took control of the airport outside and established a U.S. base. The former provincial warlord helped himself to the booty left by the Taliban, from Toyota Land Cruisers and Pakistani-supplied arms to whole villas. In the euphoria of liberation from the Taliban, the local citizens forgot they had initially supported Mullah Omar to get rid of warlords like Gul Agha Shirzai. Overseas, in reaction to 9/11, Al Qaeda's cause had been repudiated throughout the world, even in Muslim countries. And without a sanctuary like Afghanistan to train in, the organization was now essentially dead.

Remaining Al Qaeda and Taliban forces, possibly with Osama bin Laden, soon regrouped, going underground literally and figuratively. They were said to be hiding out in the Tora Bora cave complex on the Pakistan border 50 kilometres southwest of Jalalabad, preparing for a last stand against the Northern Alliance. Tora Bora, "Black Dust" in Persian, is between two mountain ridges in a region of cliffs and forests that is difficult to reach by land. Its fortified encampments (built originally by the CIA during the Soviet war) had an extensive network of tunnels.

On December 8, General Richard Myers, chairman of the Joint Chiefs of Staff, said that Osama bin Laden was hiding out in the caves. The White House refused to consider any amnesty for bin Laden, and the United States started bombing the mountain fortress. Meanwhile CIA and Special Forces operatives encouraged (i.e., bribed) local warlords to attack the Tora Bora complex. Reports estimated that some 1,700 Taliban and Al Qaeda members were killed in the fighting by the time the cave complex was captured on December 20. There was mounting speculation that bin Laden was among them, but a videotape sent from Pakistan on December 27 and broadcast on Al Jazeera, the Qatar Arabic satellite television station, contradicted that.

The interim government of Afghanistan claimed that bin Laden and the remainder of the Taliban, demoralized and dazed, were being sheltered by supporters in Pakistan. Mullah Omar ordered his commanders to find out who had survived, hide their weapons, and remain in touch. There was a fresh generation of recruits entering the madrassas. The majority of the schools were run by the ultra-religious Jamiat Ulema-e-Islam (JUI), which had allied itself with Pervez Musharraf, Pakistan's president, to keep the popular parties of Benazir Bhutto and Nawaz Sharif from ever gaining power. The JUI endorsed jihad (as long as it took place outside Pakistan) as the Islamic struggle for the self-improvement of society (as long as it, too, occurred outside Pakistan).

That the Americans failed to send sufficient troops to Afghanistan in late 2001 was a blunder that they and the International Security Assistance Force would pay dearly for in the next few years. "American policymakers ... misjudged their own capacity to carry out major strategic change on the cheap," says Barnett Rubin, an Afghanistan expert, in a recent report. Instead the U.S. military relied on alliances with friendly warlords to exert control and help in the hunt for Al Qaeda and Taliban fugitives.

But worse was to come. As the United States moved its military and intelligence assets out of Afghanistan in preparation for the invasion of Iraq, the warlords built drug empires, engaged in widespread corruption, and undermined President Karzai. Simultaneously, the Taliban skilfully exploited the situation through intimidation and propaganda aimed at largely illiterate southern Pashtuns. From the very beginning the United States had made it clear that it had no intention of disarming the warlords or occupying the cities. The Americans had seen what had happened when the British and Soviets had tried that. Other than military objectives, there was no coherent long-term plan for the country. Since there was no accredited American ambassador to Kabul, neither the Bush administration nor the intelligence community were involved. It was the u.s. military, more specifically Central Command in Tampa, Florida, that was in charge, and in the 26 days between September 11 and October 7, it was the military that formulated a plan that was single-minded in its simplicity.

u.s. forces entered Afghanistan to secure air bases outside Pakistan from which bin Laden could be hunted down and captured in the best cowboy style "dead or alive." If sponsoring the warlords who masqueraded as provincial governors and relying on them for local intelligence facilitated this goal, so much the better. Reconstruction and support for the Karzai interim government came second to the hunt for the Al Qaeda leader. The remainder of the international community — the United Nations and later NATO — acknowledged that while the country was liberated, the security vacuum now in Afghanistan wasn't going to resolve itself and required urgent international attention. For the Afghan people the return of the warlords — the reason they had embraced the Taliban in the first place — was devastating, especially when several were welcomed into the Karzai government.

Pakistan's dilemma was that the West didn't distinguish between the Taliban and Al Qaeda, tarring both with the same brush. Islamabad did nothing to discourage Mullah Omar's recruitment from Karachi madrassas, nor did it seize the funds he was raising from Peshawar bazaars, Saudi bankers, and within the Pakistani military. The Pakistani city of Quetta, traditionally Afghan, took on a role similar to that of World War II Lisbon or Casablanca. It seethed with spies, arms dealers, and exiles, making Taliban neighbourhoods an essential part of the tour given to journalists by taxi drivers. In January 2002, taking advantage of the post-Taliban chaos and proving it had learned well from the British mapmakers, Pakistan "straightened out" the border crossing at Chaman by expropriating a chunk of Afghan territory. With u.s. approval and aid, a huge Friendship Gate was erected at the crossing, the ceremonies presided over by none other than Gul Agha Shirzai, the provincial governor. It would be easier now for him to collect tolls and custom duties — and for Pakistan's Inter-Services Intelligence to control access to its neighbour.

Even before the collapse of the Taliban regime, Afghan groups had met in Bonn, Germany, in early December 2001 under the auspices of the United Nations to develop a framework for governance of the country. The four Afghan factions taking part were UIFSA, the Peshawar Group, the Cyprus Group of refugees, and the Rome Group. On December 3 former President Rabbani accepted a list of four candidates to lead the administration until elections could be organized. The warlord Abdul Rashid Dostum (excluded from a portfolio in the government) denounced the accord as having too little Uzbek representation, as did Haji Abdul Qadeer, the governor of Jalalabad, who said there wasn't enough Pashtun representation.

On December 23, at a ceremony in Kabul, power was officially handed over from Rabbani to Hamid Karzai. The U.N. force that arrived to stabilize the situation, or "protect," the Afghans from themselves would be run by the British — and the historic connections to 1839 were obvious at the handover ceremony. As with many who had ruled from Kabul before him, Karzai's actual authority and popular support outside the capital city was so limited that he was often derided as the "Mayor of Kabul." In the provinces the same warlords whose venality had allowed the Taliban to assume power, like Kandahar's Gul Agha Shirzai, slipped back into their old ways. This time the warlords were able to settle scores by simply denouncing former opponents to the American troops, claiming they were Taliban.[32]

The agenda of the Bonn Agreement was nothing if not ambitious. It called for the installation of an Interim Administration, the holding of an emergency Loya Jirga, the appointment of a Transitional Authority, and the adoption of a national constitution prior to the holding of national elections. The agreement also ordered the 30,000 to 40,000 Afghan militia forces representing various warlords to leave Kabul. Not only did they refuse, but the warlords dictated that the U.N. stabilization force be reduced. With the Americans forging ahead with their own military campaign and the United Nations increasingly marginalized, it was agreed to put the whole operation under NATO and create the

International Stabilization Assistance Force (later to be changed to the International Security Assistance Force or ISAF).

The Loya Jirga of June 19, 2002, confirmed Karzai as the interim holder of the position of president of the Afghan Transitional Administration. The assembly had earlier approved (by a show of hands) 14 cabinet ministers of the new Transitional Administration that Karzai had presented to the assembly. He had offered vice presidencies to warlords Abdul Rashid Dostum and Ismail Khan, but both declined, their private armies still outnumbering the Afghan National Army and the foreign contingents by five to one. Karzai's cabinet succeeded in striking a balance between Pashtuns, Tajiks, and Hazaras, but Uzbeks were underrepresented as were women. There was only one female minister, Dr. Suhaila Sediq, the Pashtun health minister. The other appointments were: Vice President and Minister of Defence Mohammed Fahim Khan (Tajik); Vice President Karim Khalili (Hazara); Vice President Haji Abdul Qadeer (Pashtun); Minister of the Interior Taj Mohammed Khan Wardak (Pashtun, governor of Paktia); Minister of Foreign Affairs Dr. Abdullah Abdullah (Tajik); Minister of Finance Ashraf Ghani Ahmadzai (Pashtun, former World Bank official, former head of Afghan Aid Coordinating Agency); Minister of Education Yunus Qanooni (Tajik); Minister of Planning Ustad Mohammed Mohaqeq (Hazara); Minister of Borders Aref Khan Noorzai (Pashtun); Minister of Light Industries Mohammed Alem Razm (Uzbek); Minister of Commerce Sayed Mostafa Kazemi (Hazara); and Minister of Agriculture Seyyed Hussein Anwari (Hazara).

Having earlier gotten the support of his two rivals, former King Zahir Shah and former President Burhanuddin Rabbani, Karzai was elected head of state in a secret ballot by Loya Jirga delegates, winning 1,295 votes out of a total 1,555 valid votes cast. In his opening remarks to the Loya Jirga, the king asked the assembled delegates to work towards unity and peace in Afghanistan. In reply Karzai said that he hoped His Majesty would continue to play a unifying, if largely symbolic, role in Afghanistan as "Father of the Nation."

The country's legal system, never strong to begin with, no longer functioned. There were few trained lawyers and no physical infrastructure or record of the country's laws. With confessions extracted by torture and what judges and prosecutors who remained routinely intimidated or bribed, laws had been administered for personal or political ends for so long that the rights of individuals to a fair trial, for example, weren't even considered. Afghanistan may have signed all of the United Nations' international agreements on human rights, but that didn't prevent anyone in a military uniform, whether generals or rank-and-file soldiers, from manning a roadblock and enjoying complete impunity. Historic abuses of ethnic and religious groups and of women meant that a functioning judicial system had rarely taken root in Afghanistan, and in any case, even in the best of times, it had only really functioned in the main cities.

The country had endured 23 years of what in parts of Africa is termed "the Kalashnikov culture," in which anything and anyone could be had at the point of a gun. Within the transitional government there were Afghans who favoured a very conservative interpretation of Islamic law and those who wanted to revive the more progressive ideas in the 1964 constitution. Nevertheless, moving towards the rule of law was a vital part of peace-building in Afghanistan. The economy, all realized, would be more likely to grow if property was protected and a fair system was set up to adjudicate the many property disputes.

The Bonn Agreement of December 2001 re-established the 1964 constitution as Afghanistan's key legal document and called for the formation of independent commissions to oversee the rebuilding of the judiciary, the monitoring of human rights, the drafting of the constitution, and the selection of civil servants. But the first Judicial Commission got so bogged down in bureaucratic and political rivalries that it was disbanded after three months. Appointed in November 2002, the new commission suffered under a poorly defined mandate that allowed factions within the Transitional Administration to control the judiciary and move quickly to promote their own interests. In other words, it was hijacked by hard-liners. Faisal Ahmad Shinwari, a disciple of the Saudi-backed fundamentalist leader Abdul Rasul Sayyaf, had been appointed in December 2001 by former President Burhanuddin Rabbani. The lack of training in secular law wasn't a hindrance to the 80-year-old, who put his old religious cronies into key positions, increasing the number of Supreme Court judges from nine to 137, none of whom had any degrees in secular law, either. To the dismay of the international community, to say nothing of liberal Afghans, President Karzai reappointed Shinwari in June 2002.

Neither has the international community done anything to press for accountability of past human-rights abuses. Even at the Tokyo summit the commonly held belief was that it was more important to consolidate the peace process than stir up the past. President Karzai himself dismissed transitional justice as a "luxury the country could ill afford" until it was more settled. The lack of accountability for past crimes served only to reinforce the belief among provincial warlords and commanders of local militias that they could act as they wished with no risk of punishment.

Signs that Afghanistan was reverting to its pre-Taliban corruption era were evident by September 2003 when President Karzai visited the United States and the Shamali refugee tenements in the Kabul suburb of Shirpur were bulldozed and the squatters were cleared out by order of Mohammed Fahim Khan, the defence minister. The vacated plots were then distributed among senior government officials, including ministers, deputy ministers, governors, commanders, generals, intelligence (KHAD) administrators, and businessmen linked to Fahim Khan, Qanooni (the education minister), and Dostum. Almost immediately, each of the recipients erected extravagantly gaudy castle-like homes for themselves or to rent out.

A constitution was thrashed out prior to the holding of national elections, with another Loya Jirga in December approving it. Parliamentary elections, held on September 18, 2005, fulfilled the major conditions set out in the Bonn Agreement. On October 9, 2004, presidential elections were held, marking a watershed in Afghanistan's transition towards a democratic, self-sustaining state. President Karzai won with 55.4 percent of the popular vote, carrying 21 of the country's 34 provinces. More than 10 million Afghans registered to vote in the election, which was declared valid by a three-person panel of the joint Afghan–United Nations Electoral Management Body. Election day was a relatively peaceful event, with 6.8 million voters — 43 percent female and 57 percent male. Karzai was declared president on November 3 and sworn in on December 7. At the ceremony were Afghanistan's three surviving former presidents; that they hadn't gone the way of their predecessors — hanged or shot — augured well for the future of the country.

Afghanistan's transition to a stable and strong democracy was also marked with the inauguration of its first parliament in more than three decades on December 19, 2005. The National Assembly is composed of the 249 members of the Wolesi Jirga (Lower House), all elected, and the 102 members of the Meshrano Jirga (Upper House), some appointed. The real victory was that 12 million Afghans had registered to vote in presidential, parliamentary, and provincial elections in 2004 and 2005, with voter turnout an impressive 60 percent. "By voting, Afghans expressed their resolve to chart a democratic course," wrote Canadian Ambassador David Sproule. "Yes, the governance in Afghanistan remains a work in progress. The immediate goal for Canada and our international partners is to help the Afghan government to further extend its reach to remote areas of the country and support governance at the local level."

Less publicized but equally farsighted was the presidential decree entitled "The Establishment of a Consultative Mechanism for Appointments of Senior-Level Government Posts," issued on September 17, 2006, in which a national program for appointments was set up. It would appoint provincial governors, deputy ministers, provincial police chiefs, provincial heads of authority, and members of the Independent Administrative Reform and Civil Service Commission. The Special Consultative Board would be made up of five members appointed for five years only. All provincial deputy governors and district administrators would be appointed by the Board of the Civil Service Commission. That September, with the help of the Geodesy and Cartography Department, delineation of province and district boundaries, including the contentious borders in four provinces, was also finalized.

For ordinary Afghans the hope that their society was gradually being liberalized came not from ponderous institutions like the courts or bureaucracy but from television, the Internet, and cell phones. Proof of the electronic media's persuasiveness was never more evident than when Shinwari ordered 10 cable television operators to close during Ramadan in November 2005, and Minister of Information Sayeed

Makhdoom Raheen had privately owned television stations stop broadcasting programs deemed "Islamically incorrect," i.e., all Indian and Western films.

With 65 percent of the population illiterate, the role of television and radio stations, all of which receive considerable support from international organizations, is closely monitored.[33] Hollywood and Bollywood movies are freely available on television (or as pirated DVDs), and via text-messaging and email a generation of young Afghans, men and women, is able to interact in universities, English classes, shopping malls, and Internet cafés. Unlike the state-run station, Kabul's privately owned Tolo TV broadcasts foreign movies and music, star gossip, and secular news coverage. Its male presenters (who regularly receive death threats and travel with armed escorts) wear jeans and T-shirts, its female presenters make only desultory attempts to cover their heads, and its "Hop" dance shows stream out Madonna and Jennifer Lopez videos. The channel (Tolo means "Dawn" in Dari) claims it has 80 percent of its viewers in Kabul and plans to expand into the provinces. As liberating as it has been, Tolo's influence may be a little self-exaggerated. Even though young Afghans may seem to be culturally adventurous, they remain socially conservative.

More sinister was the approval by President Karzai's cabinet in late July 2006 of the creation of a department of vice and virtue, a plan that was expected to go before parliament when it met. Under the Taliban the former ministry with the same name had been responsible for the punishment of women who ventured outside without a male escort, and it also had men who kept their beards too short beaten. To operate under Minister of Religious Affairs Nematullah Shahrani, this department was also instructed to target alcohol, drugs, crime, and corruption.

Perhaps, as former Canadian Ambassador Chris Alexander observed, the rebirth of Afghanistan will take five generations.

2

"We Face an Enemy That Lacks a Postal Code"

"Cool spring winds blew across the 8 Wing airfield late Saturday night as the CC-150 Polaris carrying the remains of Captain Nichola Goddard taxied into position on the East Ramp," Captain Nicole Meszaros writes in *Contact*, Canadian Forces Base Trenton's newspaper. "A well-rehearsed repatriation ceremony in honour of the artillery officer was carried out at the tip of the starboard wing in sombre tradition as the 8 Wing Pipe-Major, Warrant Officer J.H. MacIntyre, played the lament 'Flowers of the Forest.' Mr. Jason Beam, Captain Goddard's widower, walked onto the tarmac with her parents, sisters and other family members who attended the ceremony. Many family members carried pink flowers, which they placed on the flag-covered casket after it was lifted by the pallbearers into the hearse."[1]

On May 17, 2006, as an artillery forward observation officer, Captain Goddard was in the hatch of her LAV when the vehicle was hit by at least two rocket-propelled grenades, one of which struck the turret. The first Canadian woman to die in combat since World War II, Goddard had been a fourth-year university student at the Royal Military College in Kingston, Ontario, on September 11, 2001, when she text-messaged her future husband that an aircraft had crashed into the World Trade Center.[2]

The road to Captain Goddard's death in Afghanistan and beyond begins perhaps on November 27, 1974, when Keith William MacLellan, the Canadian ambassador accredited to Afghanistan (but based in Islamabad), negotiated a "most favoured nation" treaty to promote and facilitate the expansion of trade relations between the two nations. This action was followed on July 5, 1977, with a treaty of development assistance granting scholarships and training awards for Afghans coming to Canada. The Soviet invasion in December 1979 ended further rapprochement, and Canada, with many other nations, withdrew its diplomatic recognition of Afghanistan. Except to contribute to U.N. refugee programs coping with the 4.4 million Afghans now in Pakistani camps, successive Canadian governments didn't view Afghanistan as a priority.

Throughout the early 1980s, stories of disillusioned Soviet soldiers hiding in the Afghan mountains who wanted to defect to the West surfaced periodically on both the CBC and American television networks. Those who had escaped from the Red Army soon discovered they had no place to go to since Pakistan wouldn't let them cross the border unless another country took them in — surreptitiously. Humanitarian motives notwithstanding, the defectors were good propaganda value both for President Reagan and the mujahideen, and the United States was able to get some of them out.

In Canada, with the "Canadian Caper"[3] still fresh in the public mind, the question being asked was: "If Canadian diplomats could get Americans out of Iran, surely they could do the same for these poor Russian boys hiding in Afghanistan?" To its credit, Ottawa had attempted to bring six defectors out in October 1984, but for various reasons that mission had been bungled and they were now sheltering with the guerrillas. But their plight had touched many Canadians, among them *Globe and Mail* reporter Victor Malarek; David Prosser, a journalist with the *Kingston Whig-Standard*; Canadian church groups such as the Holy Trinity Russian Orthodox Church; the Canadian Ukrainian Immigrant Society; and the Soviet Prisoners Rescue Committee. Each lobbied the Conservative government to bring the Russian defectors out so much that the men themselves even heard about their plight on Radio Canada's Russian-language broadcasts and were aware that Canada at least hadn't forgotten them.

What the federal government didn't publicize was that the celebrated defection of Igor Gouzenko notwithstanding,[4] Canada had a policy of never aiding and abetting defectors. Nor had Canada admitted many Afghan refugees since the Soviet invasion — barely 250 from the camps in Pakistan. The Soviet Union's KGB was also charging that because the defectors were living with the mujahideen, they had become hopeless drug addicts — hardly prime immigration material. Fortunately, the senior ministers in Prime Minister Brian Mulroney's cabinet were Joe Clark, the minister of foreign affairs, and Flora MacDonald, the minister for immigration, who also represented Kingston, Ontario. They were aware that the defector issue was so sensitive that the Pakistani government didn't want to know about it at all, something Islamabad made clear to Charles Marshall, the Canadian ambassador.

Although MacDonald wrote successive minister's permits for the six to enter Canada (provided they passed the usual medical examinations), the media and church groups were becoming convinced by 1985 that the government wanted nothing more to do with the defectors. In fact, a "Deep Throat" source within the Lester B. Pearson Building revealed to the press that the department's attitude could be summed up as: "We're not in the business of sending teams into Afghanistan at night to get ex-Soviet soldiers out, hoping the Pakistanis will look the other way." Ottawa couldn't ask the International Committee of the Red Cross to intervene in Afghanistan, since it had been expelled from the country in 1982, but at one point Canada did approach the British Secret Service (which presumably had agents there) for help.

In the House of Commons, the Liberal Opposition led by Sheila Copps berated the government for its inaction so that in April 1986 a relieved Joe Clark was able to announce that contact with the five (one had returned to the Soviet Union) had been made and that his department was now ready to work with the media to get them out. That summer a team of External Affairs officers made up of Gar Pardy (who 20 years later would be involved in the Maher Arar case), Don Saunders, and Bruce Gillies was assembled in the Lester B. Pearson Building to work the "Afghan Caper" from all possible angles. Long hours of work followed, with weekends and summer holidays sacrificed before they could get the defectors freed. In November the five were delivered across the Pakistani border to a safe house in Peshawar and then were interviewed at the Canadian embassy in Islamabad. After that they were flown (possibly by an unmarked u.s. military aircraft) to Canada and were kept at Canadian Forces Base Petawawa before being integrated into Canadian society. Twenty years later Petawawa would be the scene of another chapter in Canada's involvement in Afghanistan.

"Canadians are advised not to travel to Afghanistan. Canadians in Afghanistan are advised to leave the country." The Travel Advisory Reports from the Department of Foreign Affairs had been unimaginatively repetitious for a decade. "Canadians who choose to be in Afghanistan, despite this warning, should maintain close contact with the Canadian High Commission in Islamabad, Pakistan, or the Department of Foreign Affairs and International Trade in Ottawa, Canada. The ability of the Department of Foreign Affairs and International Trade and the Canadian High Commission in Islamabad to render assistance is severely limited." For the Canadian public, until September 2001, this warning from Consular Affairs was the extent of their country's involvement with Afghanistan.

Canada had broken off relations with Afghanistan in 1979, and unlike many other countries, didn't recognize the Northern Alliance as the legitimate government of Afghanistan, arguing that it wasn't broadly based enough or representative of all Afghan people. For the few Canadians who wanted to travel to Afghanistan, the department directed them to the nearest Afghan consulate for visas, noting that it was in New York City and represented only the Northern Alliance. "You are subject to local laws. Serious violations may lead to jail sentences or even corporal and capital punishments. Jail sentences will be served in local prisons," the travel warning continued. Emphasizing that Afghanistan was no Club Med resort, the department's advice on travel to the country concluded in graphic detail: "Corporal punishments include whipping or amputations of a hand or foot (for theft). Executions take place in public and prisoners may be shot, stoned to death, or crushed to death by the weight of a stone wall."

Yet lack of recognition or a permanent representative in Kabul didn't prevent Canada from being one of the major donors supporting relief operations in the war-ravaged country. How many Canadians knew that with their military's expertise in land-mine clearance recognized world-wide, 52 Canadian Forces (CF) personnel had been seconded in Afghanistan between 1985 and 1991, working in land-mine detection? Or that from 1990 to 2001, Canada had provided CDN$123 million in human-itarian assistance and food aid through U.N. agencies, the World Food Program, and the International Committee of the Red Cross, as well as through Canadian NGOs (Aga Khan Foundation, CARE Canada, and Médicins Sans Frontières Canada). In the depths of the Taliban excesses in 1998 and 1999, the Canadian International Development Agency (CIDA) contracted with CARE International to provide CDN$3 million in food aid directly to 11,000 war widows and households headed by females in Kabul. Even as other aid agencies pulled out, CIDA's Kabul Widows' Feeding project remained operational, albeit mainly with local staff.

Not having diplomatic relations because Ottawa didn't recognize the government of Afghanistan as being truly representative of its citi-zens might have sounded good on humanitarian grounds, but in prac-tical terms it was a drawback. The problem for Prime Minister Jean Chrétien was who to open negotiations with. On the international scene there were many who claimed to speak for the Afghan nation: the Afghan embassies in Pakistan, Saudi Arabia, and the United Arab Republics were strictly Taliban, but the Northern Alliance controlled the embassies in London and New York City. Other Afghan consulates were divided between the Burhanuddin Rabbani and Abdul Malik lobbies. When the Taliban tried to get U.N. recognition by offering the position of ambassador to the United Nations to Hamid Karzai, Ottawa didn't support the removal of the Rabbani/Northern Alliance government representative from the Afghan desk.

Canada's position on Afghanistan centred on U.N. Security Council resolutions that called for a negotiated settlement between Afghan fac-tions, a cessation of the fighting, and an end to outside interference, while Canadian diplomats called on other countries to stop intervening in or financially supporting the civil war in Afghanistan, particularly in sup-plying small arms and mines. This last directive was aimed at Russia and Iran, the main suppliers of weapons to the Northern Alliance. After 9/11, Ottawa backed the efforts of the U.N. special representative, stating officially that it "wanted to promote consensus among the Afghan people and the international community on the way forward for Afghanistan."

Come September 12, 2001, along with other countries, Canada was forced to rethink its opinion of a major player in the Great Game: Pakistan's General Pervez Musharraf. Traditionally, Canadian leverage with Pakistan had been through developmental aid, dating back to the post–World War II Colombo Plan. Like India, Pakistan was a member of the British Commonwealth, and a cornerstone of Canadian foreign policy had always been to aid members of that organization. In 1959 Prime Minister John Diefenbaker signed a treaty of nuclear cooperation with Pakistan, and six years later, just as India and Pakistan went to war, Canadian General Electric sold a 137-megawatt CANDU reactor to the Karachi Nuclear Power Plant.

Canada had already exported nuclear technology to India, and it was important that a balanced role in the region be assumed. Also, unlike India, Pakistan was a Western ally. It was only after Pakistan's testing of nuclear weapons in 1998 (and exporting the technology to Iran), coupled with General Musharraf's military coup the following year, that Ottawa belatedly imposed economic sanctions on Pakistan, restricting bilateral aid and the country's access to loans from the World Bank, the Asian Development Bank, and the International Monetary Fund. But with 9/11, despite allowing the Taliban leaders to shelter in Quetta, Musharraf was suddenly seen by the West as a bulwark against terrorism. So Ottawa eased economic sanctions and exchanged CDN$447 million in debt for CIDA-run development programs in the social sector.

Disregarding the knowledge that the Taliban was in part a creation of Pakistan's Inter-Services Intelligence, Canada now viewed Musharraf's regime as an island of relative stability in a dangerous neighbourhood — in effect, an essential ally in any large-scale action concerning Afghanistan. For one thing, Pakistan had opened three of its air bases to the U.S. military effort and Karachi was the only port through which all Coalition seaborne shipments to Afghanistan could be funnelled.[5] Prime Ministers Jean Chrétien and Stephen Harper had both made visits to Islamabad (in 2003 and 2006) as had Minister of Defence Gordon O'Connor in 2006. As it had done in Africa and the

Caribbean, Canada could offer military training assistance to the Pakistani army, especially in what Canadians pride themselves in — peacekeeping. The Pearson Peacekeeping Centre's United Nations Integrated Mission Staff Officer Course was, in fact, world-renowned. In August 2006, following calls for a special envoy to Pakistan, Prime Minister Harper appointed Wajid Khan, the then Liberal member for Mississauga-Streetsville, as his special envoy in the Middle East and South Asia. The former Pakistan Air Force pilot (shot down twice by the Indians) had a Mazda dealership and was a prominent voice in the Greater Toronto Area's Pakistani community.

If Canada was well represented in Pakistan, diplomatically it was invisible in Afghanistan. As the government of Britain's Benjamin Disraeli had learned in the 19th century, not having an accredited presence in Kabul was like driving blind, deaf, and dumb against the traffic on a busy street. Promoting Canadian interests in a complex environment and providing consular assistance to the increasing number of Canadians of dual nationality now returning to Afghanistan, to say nothing of the imminent arrival of a full Canadian Battle Group, needed an ambassador in residence and not an officer visiting three days a month from Islamabad.

This time the problem was more physical than diplomatic. There were no phone land lines or satellite communication. Kabul and Bagram airports were both pockmarked with craters and were serviced by sporadic U.N. flights from Dubai and Islamabad. And even with the use of the armoured Chevrolet Suburban from the embassy at Islamabad,[6] the roads between the Pakistani border and Kabul were too dangerous, beset as they were not only by mines but by marauding tribesmen who didn't recognize diplomatic immunity and, with U.S. aircraft bombing their country, weren't inclined to distinguish between an American or Canadian accent.

One Foreign Affairs officer who travelled frequently from Islamabad into the Taliban-run country was Glyn Berry, one of the few Western diplomats to do so. "There weren't a lot of people who went into Afghanistan, pre-9/11, since most countries like Canada didn't have embassies in Kabul," says James Wright, Berry's colleague and friend (and in 2006 the Canadian High Commissioner to London). "Glyn would go in to study the process of political development under the Taliban. Those experiences made a lasting impression on him. He saw so much poverty and deprivation. His heart went out to those people who had been suffering for so long." Berry had just been appointed to the Canadian delegation at the United Nations in New York — a "cushy" posting that gave him an apartment with a panoramic view of the New York skyline — when he heard that Canada was opening a Provincial Reconstruction Team in Kandahar. Although 59 years old, he immediately volunteered to give up his New York posting to go there.[7]

There were soon to be many military operations in the fight against terrorism in Canada's immediate future — Apollo, Athena, Altair, Medusa — but the first was Operation Support, which on September 11, 2001, provided assistance to the passengers and crew of aircraft diverted to Canadian airfields when civil aviation was grounded all over North America.[8] Rerouted travellers and flight crews were hosted at CF facilities in Goose Bay, Gander, and Stephenville, Newfoundland; Halifax, Shearwater, and Aldershot, Nova Scotia; Winnipeg, Manitoba; and Yellowknife, Northwest Territories.

Although Operation Enduring Freedom,[9] the U.S. unilateral military action in Afghanistan, was sanctioned by the United Nations on September 28, 2001, NATO Secretary-General Lord Robertson didn't announce his organization's approval under Article 5 of the Treaty of Washington until October 2.[10] Five days later Prime Minister Chrétien declared that Operation Apollo would be Canada's contribution of air, land, and sea forces to the campaign against terrorism. The mood in the House of Commons that day matched that of the nation — bellicose and one of general agreement for action against the perpetrators, whoever and wherever they were.

"On September 11, 2001, Canada and the world looked on in shock and disbelief as the deadliest terrorist attack in history was carried out against thousands of defenceless victims in New York and Washington," the prime minister told Canadians. "This was an act of premeditated murder on a massive scale with no possible justification or explanation — an attack not just on our closest friend and partner, the United States, but against the values and the way of life of all free and civilized people around the world. From the moment of the attack, I have been in close communication with President George Bush ... [and] told him that Canada stands shoulder to shoulder with him and the American people. We are part of an unprecedented coalition of nations that has come together to fight the threat of terrorism. A coalition that will act on a broad front that includes military, humanitarian, diplomatic, financial, legislative, and domestic security initiatives. I have made it clear from the very beginning that Canada would be part of this coalition every step of the way. On Friday evening, the United States asked Canada to make certain contributions as part of an international military coalition against international terrorism. I immediately instructed our minister of national defence to agree. And shortly before noon today, I confirmed to President Bush in a telephone conversation that we would provide the military support requested. Just after noon, I instructed the chief of defence staff to issue a warning order to a number of units of our armed forces to ensure their readiness."

Opposition Leader Stockwell Day agreed with the prime minister. "We know that there is perhaps no more difficult choice than to commit troops, and we support the prime minister," he said. The New Democratic Party excepted, all others in the House of Commons voted in favour of the prime minister's action. In Parliament the motion passed 212 to 10. The lone voice of dissent arguing for a peaceful U.N.-led solution was New Democratic Party leader Alexa McDonough. "To give any nation, or any coalition of countries no matter how broad, the right to act as judge, jury, and executioner when you're dealing with horrendous crime is simply not acceptable," she said.

Operation Apollo, Chief of Defence Staff General Ray Henault told the media, would last until October 2003. Canadian naval vessels making for the Persian Gulf were joined by a long-range air patrol detachment of two CP-140 Aurora maritime patrol aircraft. HMCS *Halifax* had been in the region since August and was joined by HMCS *Toronto* and HMCS *Charlottetown* in December 2001. Sometimes forgotten in the later involvement in Afghanistan was that Canadian naval vessels were rotated through the Persian Gulf and Canadian sailors hailed suspicious craft, identified them, pursued and boarded them when necessary, and searched them. With Al Qaeda fleeing Afghanistan overland into Pakistan, a naval patrol may have seemed like a "saving face" exercise when Canada had few other options. But a repeat of the suicide bombing of the USS *Cole* was feared, and "leadership interdiction operations" were conducted by the Canadian navy on merchant ships and fishing boats operating out of Pakistan and Iran. The other Canadian assets were a strategic airlift detachment of a single CC-150 Polaris transport aircraft, three CC-130 Hercules for delivery of humanitarian relief and supplies and, most important, a Canadian Battle Group working with American forces in and around Kandahar.

There were always two distinct forces operating in Afghanistan: the United States' Operation Enduring Freedom, which focused on the capture of Osama bin Laden, and the "coalition of the willing," soon to become the International Security Assistance Force (ISAF). The latter had been authorized on December 20, 2001, by United Nations Security Council Resolution 1386, and more specifically by the 6,000 troops of the Kabul Multinational Brigade (KMNB), charged with securing the capital and nearby Bagram air base. Not a U.N. peacekeeping force, the KMNB was composed of like-minded NATO members and other contributing nations and was financed by the Troop Contributing Nations (TCN).

Critics insisted that the KMNB had actually been set up to protect the transitional Afghan government from Gulbuddin Hekmatyar's Hezb-e-Islami and the armies of the Northern Alliance warlords, who were deeply suspicious of yet more foreign armies in their neighbourhood. Outnumbering the KMNB, they had nothing to fear, and it was only the threat of U.S. air power that held them in check. Command of ISAF was to be rotated among different nations on a six-month basis, and since most of the initial troops were from the United Kingdom, British Army Major-General John McColl was the first in charge. Major-General Hilmi Akin Zorlu of Turkey (the only Muslim country in ISAF) took the next rotation, and it was accepted that during this period Turkish troops would be increased from about 100 to 1,300. But with so few "boots on the ground" and a reluctance of other nations to follow, ISAF's power, like that of President Karzai, was restricted to Kabul city limits, allowing the Taliban to regroup, rearm, and return from its Pakistani sanctuaries to the rural areas of Afghanistan, especially the region around Kandahar.

After the fall of the Berlin Wall in 1989, there was a joke that the acronym for the North Atlantic Treaty Organisation actually stood for "Now Almost Totally Obsolete." Beginning in 1986, as conventional forces were reduced with the end of the Cold War, bases of individual NATO countries in Germany such as the Canadian Forces installations at Lahr and Baden-Baden were dismantled. So, with the collapse of the Soviet Union in 1991, the alliance badly needed a new raison d'être. While the 1995 Dayton Peace Accords did lead to NATO's first major expeditionary operation in Bosnia and Herzegovina, nothing equipped it to operate beyond Europe. But in the aftermath of post-9/11, the alliance bravely took up its mission to Afghanistan and on August 9, 2003, formally assumed a leadership role in ISAF. As the United States withdrew its troops to Iraq, NATO's mandate was extended to the remainder of the country: in 2004 to the north (Stage 1), in 2005 to the west (Stage 2), on July 31, 2006, to the south (Stage 3), and finally in October 2006 to the east (Stage 4). By then NATO/ISAF consisted of 32,800 troops from 37 nations, with Canada's 2,500 soldiers being the fourth-largest contingent after the United States (11,800), the United Kingdom (6,000), and Germany (2,700). However, reflecting the weakness of any multilateral entity, there were varied opinions on how to deal with the resurgent Taliban. With the exception of the United States, Britain, Canada, and the Netherlands, cautious NATO members imposed so many restrictions on their troop commitments to Afghanistan that they made them largely ineffective. For example, although outnumbering the Canadians, German soldiers were limited to patrolling the safer northern regions around Mazar-i-Sharif, Kunduz, and Faizabad.

From the start, even as the debris of the World Trade Center's twin towers settled, Canada was in the forefront of committing its forces to oust the Taliban. After Prime Minister Chrétien's speech on October 7, 2001, the country's Immediate Reaction Force (IRF) was placed on 48-hour notice to deploy overseas. Drawn mostly from the Edmonton- and Winnipeg-based battalions of the Princess Patricia's Canadian Light Infantry (PPCLI) — the same regiment that had been the first in action in World War I — it was led by Lieutenant-Colonel Pat Stogran.

Like NATO, for the Canadian army the conflict in Afghanistan was newfound vindication of its existence. The new century had caught the army "equipment- and morale-constrained," in military terms. More than its sister services, the air force and navy, it had borne the brunt of decades of government penury that dated back to the Pierre Trudeau years, while also suffering the humiliation of Somalia and the disbanding of the Canadian Airborne Regiment elite.[11] The strategists in Ottawa expected the battlefield of the future to be fast and fluid, and light infantry like the PPCLI would be too vulnerable, too lightly armed, and too slow. "The light infantry battalion was slated to go the way of the dodo bird, and there was no room for light forces," Stogran would later say. "We were totally 'mech-centric,' fighting Bosnia or the Gulf War over again. This mission came up and it demonstrated that we need a light, rapid-strike capability within the Forces."

With a photo-op on December 7, 2001, the government also demonstrated its humanitarian side when International Cooperation Minister Maria Minna herself oversaw the loading of Canadian food aid in Montreal to be shipped to Afghanistan. Some 1,200 tonnes of Canadian lentils were being sent to the port of Bandar Abbas in Iran, where the Red Crescent Society would take delivery and distribute it to Afghan refugees along the Iranian/Afghan border. "This shipment will help feed some 400,000 men, women, and children over the next six months," Minister Minna said. "This shipment, part of the 5,000 tonnes of wheat and lentils being sent to Afghanistan by the Canadian Foodgrains Bank, demonstrates Canada's commitment to stability and long-term recovery in the region." Her department had provided CDN$2.56 million through a funding arrangement that had the federal government match donations raised by the Canadian Foodgrains Bank by a ratio of four to one. The donations raised by the Foodgrains Bank came from Canadian farmers or in the form of cash gifts from the public.

Giving Canadians something to cheer about after a miserable few months, Minister of Defence Art Eggleton announced on December 19 that Canada's first soldiers were already "on the ground" in Afghanistan. Forty soldiers of the elite anti-terrorist group, Joint Task Force 2 (JTF2), had been conducting operations near Kandahar, a city still largely unknown to their countrymen back home. Later it was made known that as part of the U.S. Task Force K-Bar in actions against Al Qaeda, JTF2 strike teams had killed at least 115 Taliban and Al Qaeda fighters and had captured 107 senior Taliban leaders. The Canadian commandos had led a mountain climb to reach a high-altitude observation post in support of Operation Anaconda, and for its service its members were awarded the Presidential Unit Citation.

In January 2002, returning from their Christmas recess, Members of Parliament held a special debate on their country's role in Afghanistan, especially on how Canadian troops should treat captured Taliban. The news of the Dasht-i-Leili massacre was seeping in when New Democrat MP Svend Robinson asked Eggleton in Parliament whether Canadian troops would hand over prisoners to U.S. forces if those prisoners would face a death sentence before a military tribunal.[12] The minister assured the House of Commons that any prisoners captured by Canadian Forces would receive a fair trial and that Canadian troops would respect international law, but he added that "international law does not prohibit the use of the death penalty with respect to military tribunals." The special session was only a "take note debate," meaning there was no vote at the end. On January 29, Eggleton had to admit that Canada had captured prisoners. "This is with respect to the JTF2, so I can't go into the details other than to tell you that, as I have said, they were turned over to the United States military."[13]

The advance party of the Canadian Forces Tactical Airlift Detachment left 8 Wing Trenton on January 21 for Camp Mirage, a forward logistics base in the Persian Gulf, to prepare the infrastructure required to operate the three CC-130 Hercules transport aircraft and provide an air bridge to the theatre of operations. The location of Camp Mirage, which the Canadians were sharing with the Australian and New Zealand defence forces, was classified, but it soon became the worst-kept secret in the Persian Gulf. The media reported it to be Al Minhad Air Force Base, located near Dubai in the United Arab Emirates. The first rotation ("roto") through it took place almost immediately.

The 3rd Battalion, Princess Patricia's Canadian Light Infantry (3 PPCLI) Battle Group, which included a reconnaissance squadron of Coyote LAVs from Lord Strathcona's Horse (Royal Canadians) and combat service support elements from 1 Service Battalion, arrived in Kabul to perform tasks ranging from airfield security to combat. Because the CF had no heavy lift capability, flying them and their equipment out required hitching rides from the United States and renting huge Antonov air freighters. Although it was Canada's first deployment of an army unit in combat operations against a declared enemy in five decades, the media made much of the fact that Canadian soldiers arrived in green temperate woodland camouflage, even though the Afghan terrain was predominantly desert. The CADPAT (Canadian Disruptive PATtern) small pixellated digital pattern camouflage for arid conditions arrived in time for the next rotation.

January 2002 was historic in Afghan-Canadian relations when on the 25th, Canada officially re-established diplomatic ties with Afghanistan. The announcement was made in a joint statement by Deputy Prime Minister John Manley and Foreign Affairs Minister Bill Graham. Manley flew into Kabul to do this task personally, but his thunder was stolen by another visitor to the capital the same day — U.N. Secretary-General Kofi Annan, the first U.N. secretary-general to visit the country in 42 years. The media focused on Annan, but interim president Karzai went out of his way to welcome Canada's deputy prime minister by saying, "Two very significant trips to Afghanistan on the same day. We have not seen that for years." Since the difference in time zones meant Manley would be scooping Bill Graham's announcement in Ottawa, neither he nor Karzai mentioned the re-establishment of full diplomatic relations.

When a U.S. Air Force C-17 brought the first 25 troops (of a force of 750 soldiers) from 3 PPCLI to Kandahar on February 2, Sergeant Mark Pennie had already set up the Reverse Osmosis Water Purification Unit. Although it was originally intended to provide a clean and reliable source of fresh water to the Canadian Battle Group alone, the unit ended up supplying water to all Task Force personnel at Kandahar Airfield. Earning the gratitude of thousands of Canadians and Coalition personnel there and to come, Sergeant Pennie was awarded the Meritorious Service, the citation stating that "he also displayed great initiative in restoring the existing airfield sewage lagoon to an operable condition after many years of disuse."

Maintaining perimeter security at the strategic airfield proved to be an interesting example of the differences between American and Canadian cultures, Stogran later told an audience at Wilfrid Laurier

University. "The Americans' idea of securing the perimeter of the airport," Stogran said to the assembly, "was to climb into armoured vehicles and drive around in a 'presence patrol.' When the Canadians took over perimeter security ... in addition to a presence patrol, we went and got to know the Afghans. The security environment changed overnight. The Princess Patricia's played soccer against the Afghans every Sunday." Getting out of the vehicles and into the community "is a reflection of the Canadian way," Stogran continued, and "it won the respect of our American friends." Besides perimeter security, that month the Canadian Battle Group mounted two major combat mission sweeps as part of Operation Harpoon in the Shah-i-Kot Valley. The soldiers were searching the Tora Bora region of eastern Afghanistan for caves and evidence of Osama bin Laden and his officers. Two dozen graves were found, but if the cave strongholds had once existed, they had been destroyed by American bombing raids.

Thus far there had been no Canadian casualties, and with troops on the ground in Afghanistan, in an unusual turnabout, Canada was seen to be fulfilling its military obligations towards the international community. That the United States was especially pleased was evident when Prime Minister Chrétien met with President Bush in the Oval Office in the White House to discuss the softwood lumber treaty in March 2002. It was at this meeting that Bush greeted Chrétien by saying, "Jean, we've been kicking some real ass in Afghanistan."[14]

Sadly, the first casualties weren't from the Taliban. After Operation Harpoon, the 3 PPCLI Battle Group returned to Kandahar Airfield to train for other taskings. As there were weapons to be tested and tactics planned, an overnight training exercise was scheduled at Tarnak Farm, onetime home of Osama bin Laden and now used by Coalition forces as a practice range. A hundred soldiers from A Company were taken there for the live-fire exercise. It was early Thursday morning, April 18, 2002, and the moon at almost 2:00 a.m. illuminated the mock assaults and covering fire from the light machine guns. High above, two U.S. Air Force F-16s from the 183rd Fighter Wing were on a routine patrol. The glowing red of tracer fire was visible to the National Guard pilots. Unaware he was over a recognized training area, one pilot radioed the AWACS command-and-control aircraft for permission to fire at the tracer below. The

Canadians could hear the jets, but since this was a known training site, they weren't concerned. The AWACS controller told one of the pilots to circle the target. On his second pass, when he saw more flashes of tracer fire, he concluded they were aimed at him and dropped a 227-kilogram laser-guided bomb on them. The blast caused some of the soldiers to run to the vehicles and others to secure the area. Sergeant-Major Al Whitehall frantically radioed back to Kandahar to get the F-16s to stop firing. The eight wounded were evacuated by helicopter while the casualties were identified. Four 3 PPCLI soldiers were killed: Sergeant Marc D. Léger, 29, of Lancaster, Ontario; Corporal Ainsworth Dyer, 24, of Montreal; Private Richard Green, 21, of Mill Cove, Nova Scotia; and Private Nathan Smith, 26, of Tatamagouche, Nova Scotia.

Although no one knew it then, this incident would be the first of many such tragic exercises. In Ottawa it was 6:00 p.m. on Wednesday when the Operations Centre at National Defence Headquarters received the news. Chief of Defence Staff General Henault first heard that there were two and then four dead. His executive assistant called the defence minister's office. Ironically, both Henault and Eggleton were due to attend a dinner at U.S. Ambassador Paul Cellucci's residence in Rockcliffe, along with Deputy Prime Minister John Manley, Foreign Affairs Minister Bill Graham, and Finance Minister Paul Martin. Eggleton, still at his office in the West Block of Parliament Hill, was told to get to National Defence Headquarters immediately. There he was briefed by Henault, and at 7:30 p.m. he phoned Prime Minister Chrétien, who was spending the evening at the prime minister's Harrington Lake retreat. Almost within minutes of receiving the call, President Bush phoned Chrétien to express his condolences.

At the American ambassador's dinner the deputy prime minister was in the middle of toasting Canada-U.S. relations when Ambassador Cellucci left the table to take an urgent phone call. Almost simultaneously, Manley's pager went off, as did the pagers of the other cabinet ministers at the dinner. At 10:00 p.m. when the four victims of "friendly fire" were identified and the next of kin were notified, Eggleton's press secretary, Randy Mylyk, told journalists that four Canadians had been killed in Afghanistan. At midnight Henault held a press conference at National Defence Headquarters to break the news formally to the nation. Eggleton later convened a board of inquiry to investigate the "Tarnak Farm incident," as it is now known, and portions of the board's final report are now public.[15]

The tragedy affected Canadians profoundly. Besides experiencing the hurt of "friendly fire" from the neighbour it had gone to war for, giving rise to protests of "trigger-happy cowboys," many Canadians seemed shocked that their military was in a war zone and taking casualties. This role wasn't the traditional one of blue-helmeted peacekeeping that their troops had performed since the Suez Crisis.[16] Few Canadians had heard of Kandahar, let alone Panjwai or Pashmul. Fewer still knew what a shura was. Largely unknown before 9/11, Afghanistan was intruding into small Canadian towns and big cities alike, threatening to infect the country with its history of grief and bloodshed.

A month after the incident, on May 21, the Chrétien government announced it would bring the troops home in July and that they wouldn't be replaced. This declaration was against the wishes of the United States, but there were no soldiers in reserve to do so, Eggleton said, conceding that the Canadian Forces were now "stretched." But Canada had fulfilled its 9/11 obligations with the loss of only four soldiers — and that by an accident. To the soldiers of the PPCLI in Kandahar who feared they would be kept in Afghanistan beyond the standard six-month tour, the Canadian government's announcement brought relief. Only the JTF2 Special Forces would be replaced and the naval and air presence in the region maintained. Eggleton did hold out the possibility that Canada might send troops back in 2003.

In a final operation the PPCLI Battle Group was deployed in Zobol Province, about 100 kilometres northeast of Kandahar, between June 30 and July 4, 2002, to establish a coalition presence there for the first time. With the Afghan National Army, the Canadian troops conducted a sweep operation in the Shin Key Valley that produced information about recent Al Qaeda and Taliban activities. Several rockets were recovered, relations with the governor of the province were fostered, and blankets, food, and school supplies were distributed to local people. On July 13 the PPCLI Battle Group began preparing to return to Canada. Following a brief stay in Guam, part of the planned reintegration process, the soldiers arrived in Edmonton on July 28–30, 2002.

That summer Canada pledged CDN$250 million to the reconstruction of Afghanistan for the next two years, but the focus of attention in Kabul was on the Ottawa Treaty. The international community (and Canada in particular) met in the Afghan capital with the intention of getting Afghanistan to ratify the 1997 Ottawa Treaty banning the use and stockpiling of land mines. In an agriculture-based economy, where more than 800 kilometres of arable land were contaminated with the lethal leftovers of war (which now included unexploded U.S. bombs), where in 23 years, 200,000 Afghans had been killed or wounded by mines, where legless children and men on crutches inhabited every street corner, such a move might have seemed welcome. But while the armies of the warlords outnumbered the Afghan National Army by eight to one and the neighbouring countries were actively supplying the Taliban with arms, voluntarily destroying unused stocks of Soviet land mines was inviting suicide.

The conference authorized CDN$94 million in European, U.S., and Canadian financing towards de-mining that year alone and secured Afghanistan's agreement to the Ottawa Treaty symbolically on September 11, 2002. The three-day conference ended with the deployment of 7,000 U.N. locally engaged de-miners in their sky-blue armour, the largest non-government workforce in Afghanistan.[17] In connection with this commitment, the first high-ranking Canadian arrived in Afghanistan, but not from Ottawa. Louise Fréchette, a former Canadian Foreign Service officer and now deputy secretary-general of the United Nations, flew into Kabul on October 18, 2002; met with the ISAF commander, the Independent Human Rights Commission, and the heads of U.N. agencies; and visited a de-mining project in the Shomali Plains. (Although by 2006 much progress in de-mining had been made, because new minefields were being discovered daily, it was estimated that the goal of a mine-free Afghanistan would be achieved by 2012.)

The new year of 2003 saw the White House's focus move away from Afghanistan to an invasion of Iraq, something Prime Minister Chrétien did not want his country involved in. In February, in what must have come as welcome news to NATO, Art Eggleton's successor as defence minister, John McCallum, announced at a NATO meeting in Brussels that Canada would contribute 1,900 troops to the mission in Kabul that summer and that it would take command of the KMNB in July. Thus, when asked in the House of Commons on March 17 by Stephen Harper, the Opposition Leader, if Canada was going to join the United States in the imminent "liberation" of Iraq, Chrétien replied: "Mr. Speaker, our commitment to the war against terrorism is well-known. We have already agreed to send troops, thousands of them, next summer, to fight terrorism in Afghanistan. We will keep our duty to do that."[18] This new commitment in Afghanistan was a guilt reaction, said the cynical, for refusing to join the "coalition of the willing" against Saddam Hussein. But by sending the few troops Canada had to Afghanistan, the prime minister had chosen the lesser of two evils — or so he thought.

King Amanullah Khan built his palace in a wooded area outside Kabul in 1919, with a second palace on an overlooking hill in 1922 for his queen, Soraya Tarzi. During the Soviet occupation, both palaces were the headquarters of the Ministry of Defence and consequently were thought to be haunted by the ghosts of the many unfortunates who were tortured and executed within their walls. Once serving as the location of pitched battles between the armies of Ahmed Shah Massoud and rival Gulbuddin Hekmatyar, the former palace gardens yielded thousands of shell casings and spent ammunition rounds when Canadian engineers moved in to sanitize the area for Camp Julien.

Named in honour of Corporal George Patrick Julien, a Native Canadian soldier who was awarded the Military Medal as a private for his actions at Hill 187 in Korea, the camp, at its height, housed 2,000 Canadian soldiers. To free up its military personnel from non-core functions and make them available for frontline service, the Department of National Defence initiated the Contractor Augmentation Program in 2000. The department had long relied on private industry to support and service its CF-18s, health-care facilities, and LAVs, but with so much of its military in Afghanistan, it now wanted private industry to be there, as well. As General Rick Hillier said, "We need you there on day one, take some risks with us … as part of a team that we will build … with you supporting us." With experience in running engineering projects around the world, SNC Lavalin Pro-Fac of

Montreal was awarded CDN$200 million to construct the camp and manage its office, warehouse, laundry, maintenance, utilities, cleaning service, and food preparation. The company had over 450 civilian employees at the camp, half of whom were Nepalese. This base was the Canadian military's first large-scale camp largely run by a third party.

On July 17, 2003, at Camp Warehouse, near Kabul, Canadian Brigadier-General Peter Devlin took command of the KMNB for six months.[19] The brigadier-general's priority was the upcoming Constitutional Loya Jirga postponed at President Karzai's request from October to between December 10 and 31. The prefabricated building on the grounds of the Polytechnic Institute was soon crowded with 500 elected delegates — many of them women — assembled to approve a constitution that would pave the way for nationwide elections in June 2004. Although the Afghan military and Kabul police were responsible for security, Devlin's KMNB was on anxious alert throughout. For the troops at Camp Julien, more pleasant was the holding of a Canadian institution: the annual Terry Fox Run. When Fox succumbed to cancer on June 28, 1981, he had little idea that millions of dollars would be raised worldwide for cancer research in his name through the annual Terry Fox Run. Certainly, he would never have dreamed that Kabul would be involved in the fund-raising. As long as Camp Julien operated, the Canadian Contingent there joined the more than 2 million runners in 51 different countries in the annual run, with personnel from ISAF Headquarters being one of the biggest groups of participants from outside the camp.

By now, with so large a Canadian presence in Afghanistan, having an embassy in the country was crucial, and in June, Foreign Affairs Canada (formerly the Department of External Affairs) announced that it would open one in the Kabul neighbourhood of Wazir Akbar Khan. Comparable to Rockcliffe, the diplomatic enclave in Ottawa (if one can imagine battered yellow taxis and legless land-mine victims haunting Rockcliffe's leafy lanes), Wazir Akbar Khan was already home to the compounds of OXFAM, the International Committee of the Red Cross, the World Food Programme, and various embassies.

Setting up in the Afghan capital had its challenges, as Foreign Affairs Program Manager Peter Marshall, who was responsible for "getting it running," discovered. The department decided to take over a guesthouse being vacated by CIDA, "although the building required a major upgrade to address security, electrical, and operational needs. The international engineering company we initially worked with was not able to get the project in gear in time for the scheduled opening in July 2003, so I got the go-ahead to manage it locally. I hired a couple of local contractors with good reputations and started them off with smaller projects, like installing security grilles and a flagpole. We quickly moved on to more substantial jobs such as raising perimeter security walls, installing secure rooms and safe havens, and building a guard hut. As there was little local expertise in electrical matters, the High Commission in Islamabad volunteered its electrical experts to rewire the building and install heating and cooling units and a generator. The house's garden, once lush with grapevines, roses, and a mulberry tree, soon resembled a construction site.

"Bureaucracy proved not to be a problem; city codes and building permits were non-existent. Without any commercial banks, financing the project required a creative approach, including trips to Islamabad to bring back funds. We used cell phones for communication, but often couldn't get through for hours on the oversubscribed system. For the Internet, initially, we waited in line at Kabul's first Internet café and then purchased our own satellite dish. Unfortunately, everyone else did the same, and the satellite quickly became overburdened and slow, not to mention susceptible to sunspot activity in the afternoon.

"There was originally no central heating in the house, and in the early days we would huddle around space heaters in the hope that the creaky old generator wouldn't die during the night. City power was rare, and we didn't want to risk the flames and fumes of the kerosene heaters that were standard around town. (In 2006 city power was used whenever possible, thanks to a cable run to the nearest transformer, earning Canada the goodwill of the neighbours by improving their electricity supply, as well.) I was the only Canadian continuously on site until the welcome arrival of seven Military Security Guards in July. On August 9, after emailing pictures of our progress back to Ottawa, we were given the okay to raise the Canadian flag."

Building the new chancery, official residence, and staff quarters would cost an estimated CDN$41 million with CDN$ 9.2 million in annual costs to keep functioning.

Career diplomat Christopher Alexander was appointed Canada's first ambassador to Afghanistan on July 3, 2003. He had joined the Canadian Foreign Service in 1991 and served in Moscow from 1993 to 1996. The Canadian embassy was opened on Friday, September 5, by Bill Graham, the foreign minister, who said, "A firm diplomatic presence is important in enabling us to work closely with our Afghan partners ... and to ensure that the country doesn't again become a haven for terrorists." To Peter Marshall, now en route to a posting in Hanoi, looking at the embassy gardens for a final time "once more green and lush," it had been all worthwhile. A full diplomatic staff was in place by the end of August 2003, and by 2006 it doubled to 20 Canadians with 34 locally engaged personnel, necessitating the purchase of a second and third compound farther down the street.

Of the many postings considered "hardship" for Foreign Affairs staff, the embassy at Kabul was the most difficult. The recreational amenities locally available were limited. The Russian-built Olympic pool had been drained by the Taliban, not only for puritanical reasons but because its high diving board was used to push captives off. And the Royal Kabul Golf Course was still littered with unexploded ordnance — the fairways had seen several battles, none of which involved balls or nine irons. When attending a social event outside the compound's walls required an escort of Canadian Military Police, when an escape from Kabul meant flying to Dubai or Islamabad for four days (knowing that colleagues at the British embassy had the "six weeks in, two weeks out" option to go to London or anywhere else), the feeling of being hemmed in was inevitable. Oprah Winfrey's talk show might be beamed in by satellite, home contact via the Internet and the latest in fitness equipment in the Canadian Club (the gym in the compound) might be available, but living in close quarters with colleagues, especially for three meals daily, made for a long two-year posting.

The trials and tribulations of a Kabul posting paled, however, when compared with one at Kandahar Airfield. To the military commander at the base, Foreign Affairs assigned a political officer, who was required to provide political advice and analysis to the military on the impact of the local, national, and international political environment. The officer also worked in close consultation with the Canadian ambassador in Kabul,

A monument to the Russians: conservative estimates are that the Soviets lost 147 tanks and 1,314 armoured personnel carriers in Afghanistan. Photo by Lieutenant-Commander Robert Ferguson, Strategic Advisory Team.

A monument to the Taliban: built by the Russians, the Olympic-size swimming pool in Kabul was drained by the Taliban, which used it to push captors off the diving boards. Photo by Lieutenant-Commander Robert Ferguson, Strategic Advisory Team.

In May 2002, an Afghan woman permits a photograph during a visit to her village near Kandahar by a Civil Military Cooperation team from the 3rd Battalion, Princess Patricia's Canadian Light Infantry Battle Group (3 PPCLI BG). Photo by Master Corporal Danielle Bernier, Combat Camera.

Soldiers of 3 PPCLI Battle Group hike through the mountains east of Gardez at 3,000 metres above sea level in March 2002, resting frequently to adjust to the oxygen-poor atmosphere. Photo by Corporal Lou Penney, 3 PPCLI BG.

A CC-130 Hercules aircraft from 8 Wing Trenton, Ontario, arrives in May 2002 at Kandahar International Airport with the Canadian flag flying from the co-pilot's window. Photo by Corporal Lou Penney, 3 PPCLI BG.

Members of HMCS *Regina*'s naval boarding party make their way in a rigid hull inflatable boat to a suspect vessel in the Gulf of Oman in April 2003. Photo by Master Corporal Frank Hudec, Combat Camera.

Sergeant Laurent Morin (left), Private Mathieu Champagne (driving), and Private Stephane Ayotte (rear) from B Company, 3rd Battalion, Royal 22nd Regiment Battalion Group (3 R22ER Bn Gp), drive their Iltis to the assembly point prior to departing for patrolling in Kabul during Operation Halle in June 2004. Photo by Corporal John Bradley, 3 R22ER Bn Gp.

In February 2003, Defence Minister John McCallum (right) meets with NATO Secretary-General Lord Robertson to promise Canadian troops to Afghanistan. Photo courtesy of NATO.

Canadian Forces Bison armoured vehicles sit in a compound at night in July 2003 at the Canadian International Security Assistance Force (ISAF) camp in Kabul. Photo by Sergeant Frank Hudec, Combat Camera.

Canadian soldiers in a LAV III drive past the ruins of the king's palace in Kabul in July 2003. Photo by Sergeant Frank Hudec, Combat Camera.

Minefield sign and inert land mine at an ISAF camp in Kabul. Afghanistan is one of the most heavily mined countries in the world, and the land mines left over from the country's nearly three decades of war still claim more than 100 victims a month. Photo by Sergeant Frank Hudec, Combat Camera.

In October 2003, Prime Minister Jean Chrétien takes a moment to play foosball with Master Corporal Miller of the 3rd Battalion, The Royal Canadian Regiment Battalion Group (3 RCR Bn Gp), during an informal visit to the Junior Ranks Mess at Camp Julien in Kabul. Photo by Master Corporal Brian Walsh, 3 RCR Bn Gp.

Bombardier Marie Robert, serving with the Unmanned Aerial Vehicle (UAV) Troop of 2 Royal Canadian Horse Artillery Regiment, Petawawa, in November 2003, guides the Sperwer UAV as it is hoisted onto the catapult ramp prior to launch. Photo by Corporal Doug Farmer.

The first 18 of 60 Mercedes-Benz G-Wagons land at Kabul's airport on March 5, 2004. Photo by Corporal Chris Connolly, Operation Athena Roto 1.

In May 2004, Christopher Alexander (right), the Canadian ambassador to Afghanistan, meets senior fire officials at the opening of a refurbished fire hall in the Khoshal Khan Meena district of Kabul. Photo by Corporal John Bradley, 3 R22eR Bn Gp.

In April 2004, Nejabad, a soldier with the Afghan National Army, guards TV Hill, an observation post in Kabul, along with Canadian soldiers with ISAF. Photo by Sergeant Frank Hudec, Combat Camera.

In Kabul an inukshuk stands on top of a bunker familiar to the troops in front of the king's palace prior to the transfer in late 2005 of the Canadian Forces' Camp Julien to the Afghan government. Photo by Master Corporal Robert Bottrill, Combat Camera.

Corporal Eric Hjalmarson, after returning to Camp Nathan Smith from a three-day patrol in Maiwand District, Afghanistan, in April 2006, cleans equipment, including the LAV that he and his crew were travelling in. Photo by Sergeant Carole Morissette, Task Force Afghanistan Roto 1.

Sergeant Jeff Simourd of Halifax guards the Sperwer UAV after landing, following its first flight around Kabul in late 2003. Photo by Corporal Doug Farmer.

In December 2005, young Afghan children in Kandahar look through the new backpacks filled with school supplies given to them by members of the Canadian Provincial Reconstruction Team Signals Section. Photo by Sergeant Jerry Kean, Department of National Defence.

the Provincial Reconstruction Team political director, and senior Afghan officers. Contrary to the public image of diplomats flitting about the cocktail circuit, this posting required long hours of work in a war zone.

As relative newcomers to Afghanistan, Canadians were struck by one of the most obvious shortcomings of the situation: there were hundreds of old Soviet tanks, artillery systems, and other heavy weapons rusting around Kabul, either abandoned or in private hands. "They were literally sitting in garrisons loyal to factions, often determined by ethnic affiliation, led by commanders who were in one way or another loyal to the warlords," recalled a Canadian at the embassy. "As long as the heavy weapons remained in their hands, the leverage, the influence, the impunity of these warlords would remain large. We raised the issue: shouldn't some sort of cantonment take place? And the answer came back from friends and allies who have been here longer than we had. They thought 'it might be a little ambitious for the time being,' and 'not sure if the traffic can bear it,' or it 'might be destabilizing,' and 'these people are quite attached to their weapons.' We had to go back ... several times over, and to be fair there were a few people in town who liked the idea and wished they had thought of it themselves.

"It took weeks and months to build a small international consensus that this was a policy initiative to pursue. And then it took until the end of the year [2003] to get the first heavy weapons moving. But when it happened, it was highly symbolic. It helped to put flesh onto the bone of this idea of demilitarization — that people could and should be asked to disarm after 25 years of war. And that by shrinking the space occupied by military forces ... you could rebalance power inside the country and give the economy, social sectors, civilian sectors of life a shot in the arm. Eighteen months later, 9,000 heavy weapons around the country were all in cantonment."

The first Canadian prime minister to visit his country's troops overseas was Robert Borden. In June 1915 in great secrecy he took a train to New York City and caught the White Star's *Adriatic* to Britain. The *Lusitania* had been sunk the month before, the u-boat scare was at its height, and Borden thought taking a ship belonging to a neutral country from a neutral port was a good security measure. When the media and the Opposition discovered that the prime minister was unwilling to suffer the same dangers many thousands of Canadian soldiers who embarked from Quebec City or Halifax did, the outcry in the House of Commons and newspapers was memorable. Canadian prime ministers have flown overseas to review their soldiers since Prime Minister Mackenzie King suffered a flight in a Liberator bomber in World War II. Since it was the first time he had ever flown, King took the precaution of consulting by a seance former Prime Minister Wilfrid Laurier and his mother, both deceased, about the flight.

Prime Minister Jean Chrétien was the first Canadian prime minister ever to enter Afghanistan, arriving in Kabul from Islamabad on October 18, 2003. Chrétien met with President Karzai and Lakhdar Brahimi, the U.N. secretary-general's special representative for Afghanistan. Ever the politician, Chrétien also managed to get in a game of foosball in the Canadian Forces Junior Ranks Mess at Camp Julien. While there the prime minister spoke about the rocket attack that had taken place on the camp on September 11 (the Chinese-made 107 mm rocket hit a sea container near the kitchen) and then left for the airport.

Captain Richard Little, responsible for the planning and integration of the unmanned aerial vehicles (UAV) and Artillery Hunting Radar (ARTHUR) site, related what happened next. "The PM had just left Camp Julien for KAIA [Kabul Airport] when the call came from a radar. There was a mortar attack going in on HQ ISAF. The PM's route went right through that part of town. The point of origin came from a part of town known for not liking ISAF, and in fact the location of the base plate was a soccer pitch, in other words, a perfect mortar site. We managed to get the word to the PM's motorcade to make their way post-haste to KAIA. At HQ ISAF no sounds of impacts were reported. Thirty minutes later, the PM was in the air on his way to Islamabad, HQ ISAF secure, and the area where the mortar was had soldiers clearing it. The report probably stemmed from a helicopter flying overhead, but one could never be too sure, especially when the PM is involved."

On Remembrance Day 2003, a monument was unveiled at Camp Julien to the six Canadians who had lost their lives — the four in Operation Apollo and the two in Operation Athena. Flanking a two-tonne boulder taken from the mine strike that had killed Sergeant

Robert Short and Corporal Robbie Beerenfenger on October 2 were a pair of marble plinths etched with the inscription "Dedicated to Those Canadians Who Gave Their Lives in the Service of Peace While Serving in Afghanistan." After a two-round salute from an LG1 Howitzer, Lieutenant-General Rick Hillier spoke for all when he said, "Many books and volumes have been written about what needs to be done to change our world. The people I see before me today are actually doing it." That day the Canadians were served Boston Pizza at lunch. Donated by the company, a refrigerated container of ingredients to make 2,200 pizzas was flown 11,167 kilometres from Trenton.

The comedy of Wayne and Shuster and the big band music of Captain Bob Farnon and His All Soldier Canadian Band had entertained the World War II grandfathers of Canada's military personnel in Afghanistan. In this war the music was Stompin' Tom Connors's "The Hockey Song" and Amanda Stotts's "Chasing the Sky." From November 17 to December 2, 2004, the CANCON show played at Camps Mirage, Julien, and Warehouse. Those in the audience from other countries might not have understood Dave Broadfoot's jokes, but whatever the nationality, they appreciated "Rock, Paper Scissors" (Diana Frances, Brad MacNeil, and Drew McCreadie) followed by "Jana Jana" (Jana Berengel) accompanied by her dancers Melissa and Lowela. The CF Show Tour had been arranged by the Canadian Forces Personnel Support Agency, which had a long tradition of providing show tours to CF members serving overseas and in isolated locations at home like Alert on Ellesmere Island in the Arctic. Some of the performers on this tour had played for the Canadian soldiers in Bosnia, and Annette Ducharme (doing the French content) had even performed during Operation Eclipse in Ethiopia.

Other tours played Kandahar Airfield in later years. In "Stand-Up in Kandahar" two years later, as Lieutenant-Commander Kris Phillips was introducing the show, two Taliban rocket attacks forced everyone into the bomb shelters, giving the comics some new material. "Saturday night! Well, hello Taliban!" shouted Shaun Majumder from the television show *This Hour Has 22 Minutes*. Over the course of a six-month major mission, a CF Show Tour was usually held at the midpoint (third or fourth month) of the rotation.

The Canadians were just getting used to the news that Paul Martin had become prime minister on December 12 when a reminder about how dangerous the country was took place five days later. A local came to Camp Julien and asked that ISAF troops accompany him to remove a large amount of ammunition from his home in the Chahar Asiab area of Kabul. There the Canadian Explosive Ordnance Disposal Team discovered the largest weapons cache to date. Among other items, it included some 289 82 mm shells, 228 75 mm shells, and 59 82 mm mortar rounds. In total more than 4,736 different kinds of munitions were removed from this site weighing 5,142,670 kilograms and blown up with C-4 explosive. One of the hazards the Canadian explosives de-fusers endured was that to prevent children from playing with ordnance, the elders usually buried them in the communal toilets.

"Back in February we attended a luncheon at the home of the *wakil* ['village elder'] of Police District Seven [PD 7]," Captain Martin Anderson said. "And when we were done he asked if we would like to visit a room in his home where he had opened a small private school for disadvantaged children." Looking into the unheated, one-room school, the Canadians were surprised to see that the 30 shy, smiling children were sitting on the cold concrete floor because the school had no desks. Unfortunately, commented Captain Mark Gough, the public-affairs officer with Task Force Kabul, this situation wasn't uncommon throughout Afghanistan. What touched them was that someone had opened their house to provide a place of learning. "This is a very poor village, many of the students are orphans or have lost their fathers during the fighting," said Fata, the *wakil*'s son.

"They can't go to the government schools because many have to work to help their families. We are trying to build a relationship between education and the lives of the children in PD 7," Captain Anderson, president of the camp's Humanitarian Club, told the club's other members. "We see hundreds of old metal desk frames throughout Kabul. The Humanitarian Club purchased these discarded desks, and the club members refurbished and donated them to schools in need, like this one." Within a month, 10 desks, pencils, exercise books, and a wide variety of school supplies (as well as several soccer balls) were delivered to the *wakil*'s home by the members of the Camp Julien Humanitarian Club.

Driving in Kabul was nothing short of chaos. One of the Canadian Strategic Advisory Team posted to the city, Lieutenant-Commander Robert Ferguson, said that there were "No rules and, by default, the most aggressive and largest vehicles take the right of way and all others yield or face the consequences. This can create quite a unique flow of traffic, since small Corolla taxis cannot hope to compete with armoured U.N. SUVs. Compound this by the fact that the U.N. drivers aren't worried about dinging their vehicles, and you start to get the picture. Just for fun, throwing in a few thousand pedestrians and the odd peddler of goods standing or even sitting in the middle of the road makes the adventure much like a game of human 'Frogger.' The consequences are all too real, though, and it makes for a heightened sense of driving when you are concentrating on not hitting anyone or anything while at the same time scanning for that possible attack at every turn. It is something that is very difficult to describe unless you have actually been exposed to it. My only worry on arrival back in Canada will be trying to break my life-essential driving habits of Kabul before I get a reality check from the men in red."

The year 2004 began well for Canada. As commander-in-chief of the Canadian Forces, Her Excellency, Governor General the Right Honourable Adrienne Clarkson, visited her troops in Kabul in December 2003–January 2004, making her New Year's address from the city (the previous years she had spent Christmas aboard Canadian ships in the Persian Gulf, and the year before that at a CF base in Kosovo and Bosnia).

On February 9, Lieutenant-General Rick Hillier took command of ISAF for his six-month tour of duty. With over 2,000 men in Camp Julien, Canada was now the largest contributor to the ISAF force. To some, their country was wading deeper and deeper into the morass of Afghanistan without a clear mandate, something retired Major-General Lewis MacKenzie blamed on the fact that "the deployment was never debated in Parliament, nor was it explained to the Canadian public. As a result, there is a high level of confusion throughout the country regarding the mission, which makes it all the more difficult for families to cope with the loss of their loved ones. (The military had strongly recommended against a large contribution to ISAF in Kabul due to lack of resources.) But Prime Minister Chrétien announced to the collective surprise of the House of Commons that Canada would take over the running of the mission in Kabul. Major-General Ross, who had researched the 'doability' of such a role and concluded that we did not have the resources to carry it out, resigned. The prime minister, to his considerable embarrassment, soon discovered that General Ross was right and proceeded to plead with other countries to join Canada as 'partners' (a euphemism for 'we can't do what we said we would do; would you please help us out'). NATO, which was ... downsizing its mission in the Balkans, fortunately agreed to step in and run the ISAF mission. Canada, which three months earlier had said it couldn't find 850 troops to replace the 3 PPCLI Battle Group serving with the U.S. forces in Kandahar, ordered its army to prepare 4,000 troops for security duties in Kabul over a one-year period."[20]

Defence Minister Bill Graham announced on February 13, 2005, that Canada would be doubling the number of troops in Afghanistan by the coming summer, and that they would also be leaving the relative safety of Kabul for the former Taliban stronghold of Kandahar where Canada would run a Provincial Reconstruction Team. Unique to this conflict, a PRT was a military formation combined with small components of diplomacy and development. But that wasn't all ...

On the Ottawa winter afternoon of March 21, 2005, just before Paul Martin's first meeting with U.S. President George W. Bush and Mexican President Vicente Fox in Waco, Texas, the prime minister's closest advisers convened in Room 323-S in Parliament's Centre Block. They were joined by General Rick Hillier, hand-picked the month before by Martin to be chief of defence staff and transform the military. On the agenda were several foreign policy issues for the prime minister to take with him to Waco. But these issues were outflanked by Hillier, who wanted permission to move a complete battle group to Kandahar. Many of the people present were wary of Canada leaving the multinational ISAF umbrella and relocating to Kandahar, which was exclusively run by the United States as part of Operation Enduring Freedom.

The prime minister, who had inherited the war in Afghanistan from his predecessor, didn't think the country was "a natural fit for Canada." Peacekeeping in Haiti and Darfur was more within Canada's capabilities. Former Foreign Service officer Jonathan Fried, now

Martin's foreign policy adviser, reminded everyone that Canadian troops had been in Kandahar before — in 2002. Others present were leery of Canada taking the initiative. Even the British and Dutch, the other two NATO allies most committed to ISAF, hadn't allowed their troops into the volatile Taliban-run south. The Canadians could choose to garrison the restive city of Herat instead, where 1,800 Italian troops would soon be. But Hillier saw things differently.

In the mid-1990s, Canada made significant troop contributions in Bosnia and Croatia, in the Adriatic and from Aviano, Italy, but they had been so deeply embedded in multinational command structures that they were practically invisible. "We never did get full credit for those contributions because of the way we put them out of the door," Hillier later told *Jane's Defence Weekly*. "We did not have a decisive influence or decisive effect that led to good influence for Canada in the Balkans. We had no major leadership positions, we did not have a chair at the table." Hillier found it infuriating that despite being one of the major contributors of forces on land, sea, and air to the multinational peace support force, Canada had been left out of the five-nation contact group for Bosnia. "What we're looking for is the chance to have sufficient profile … sufficient credibility that gives us the opportunity to get leadership appointments and to influence and shape regions and populations in accordance with our interests and in accordance with our values."[21]

The Canadian military had never produced a Dwight Eisenhower or a Bernard Montgomery or even a George Patton from its officer corps. But here was, wrote a military analyst, "a Canadian version of General Douglas MacArthur, the high-profile American commander who in the 1940s and 1950s made a career out of ignoring direction from political masters and charging ahead with his own agenda."[22] For a senior military officer to candidly tell an appreciative media that anyone who thought Canada didn't need more troops should be tarred and feathered and ridden out of town on a rail was an "American" style and not part of the national psyche.

Until that winter afternoon the war in Afghanistan had been palatable to the Canadian public — if any deaths could be said to be that. Holed up in Kabul, ISAF was in "risk aversion" mode with few casualties. The patrols through the city streets were as close to the traditional role of peacekeeping as possible, yet high-profile enough to be part of the anti-terrorism campaign. But all that was about to change. As the most popular, most articulate military leader Canada had ever had, Hillier was also the most controversial since the crazy, bigoted Sam Hughes. When he called the terrorists "a big ball of snakes" and "scumbags" in July 2004, many of his supporters were embarrassed, even before the number of ramp ceremonies climbed. Member of Parliament Carolyn Parrish shot back that Hillier was "testosterone-fuelled." But he spoke his mind, saying what most Canadians believed. As author Peter C. Newman said, here was a general who didn't talk like Dr. Phil. And though Hillier managed to alienate three of the most influential professions in Ottawa when he said it was the soldier not the journalist who guaranteed freedom of speech, that it was the soldier not the politician who guaranteed democracy, and that it was the soldier not the diplomat who was the tangible expression of a nation's willingness to extend its values worldwide, such words had no effect on his career and, in fact, helped him earn the nickname of "Teflon General."[23]

While Hillier professes non-involvement in politics, those who know the general aren't fooled. "He's played an extremely political role," says Peggy Mason, a former U.N. disarmament ambassador who worked for Hillier. "I would say that he has a clear political agenda and he's been very successful at advancing it for some time now." (If that is true, the general would be wise to remember how Douglas MacArthur ultimately fared.) But on March 21, 2005, speaking without notes, Hillier was focused and persuasive. He got his battle group for Kandahar with the "chance to have sufficient profile." Camp Julien would be closed — the decision was made in May — and the focus of Canada's military involvement in Afghanistan would move to Kandahar.

While it wasn't a case of "cry havoc and let slip the dogs of war," there were some who wondered if Canadians were unprepared for the possibility of their troops suffering a high number of casualties.[24] The decision made that March afternoon would cost the lives of more than 40 Canadian soldiers and billions of taxpayers' dollars. Within a year the Canadian public would discover why, apart from the Americans, British, and Dutch, no other NATO ally wanted to be in Afghanistan's south.

The first Canadian troops to drive from Camp Julien to Kandahar in June 2005 were from the Force Protection Company (FP Coy). Private Michael Freeman wrote of the journey: "It was 0400 hours as we rolled through the gate of Camp Julien and headed off into the unruly regions outside of the capital. As we headed westward with the sun rising at our backs, the huge snow-capped mountains of the Hindu Kush lit up with a spectacular golden glow. The countryside of central Afghanistan is marked by incredible geographic contrast. The convoy passed through regions of scorching desert marked only by lonely dust devils weaving their way across the limitless sand. The area greatly resembled southern Alberta. One obvious difference, however, was the hundreds and hundreds of wild camels that were grazing all along the route. All around us now were endless grassy plains and lush, gently rolling hills, all framed by the majesty of the mountains. At frequent intervals we passed through checkpoints manned by soldiers of the Afghan National Army. The trip from Kabul to Kandahar ended up taking 15 hours to complete and the soldiers in our convoy were very happy to finally arrive." To Freeman the facilities on the base were impressive, and he noted fast-food outlets such as Burger King, Pizza Hut, and Subway, as well as two gymnasiums and a mini-bus transit system with more than 20 stops. He found it hard to believe "that they were still in war-torn Afghanistan."

On June 29, 2005, Canadian soldiers began deploying to Kandahar Airfield (KAF), the headquarters of the Multinational Brigade for Regional Command South. Home for approximately 9,000 soldiers, airmen, and civilians, KAF also possessed expensive military aircraft such as Black Hawk and Chinook helicopters and British Royal Air Force Harriers. Perhaps that was why the base's defence was handled by the RAF regiment. The Taliban hid in the nearby farming communities from which they could launch rockets at night, taking advantage of the fact that to avoid the scorching heat during the day, Afghans worked their fields at sunset. Another security threat were the 1,500 Afghans who entered the base daily to work for the Coalition. Although each was searched and put through biometric scanners at one of the base's three gates, more than 150 were suspended monthly for suspicious activities.

Canada unsuccessfully tried to sell Camp Julien to other NATO countries operating in the Kabul area, but it was considered too isolated from downtown and especially from the airport. The Norwegians, Hungarians, Turks, Italians, and other tenants of Camp Julien were given notice to leave in July since the tent city was scheduled to close by December. The " teardown" involved sending 90 vehicles, 100 sea cans (containers), and miscellaneous pallets and truckloads of construction supplies, wire, and concrete barriers to Kandahar. General Rick Hillier confirmed that Canada would never again build a base as elaborate, expensive, and confined as Camp Julien. Because the Kandahar region was relatively more dangerous than Kabul and the Department of National Defence wouldn't put its civilian contractors at risk, SNC Lavalin's involvement ended and the CF decided to use the U.S. Army's civilian contractor, Kellogg Brown & Root, which was already in place at Kandahar. Canadians weren't abandoning Kabul completely, said outgoing camp commander Colonel Walter Semianiw, since officers would remain at ISAF Headquarters and the National Training Centre detachment. Through five six-month rotations more than 6,000 CF personnel had been through Camp Julien before Operation Athena ended on October 18, 2005.

David Sproule was appointed ambassador to Afghanistan in October, replacing Chris Alexander, who left to join the United Nations. Prior to the appointment, Sproule had been Canadian High Commissioner to the Republic of Bangladesh, and before that while in Ottawa he had been director for human rights and deputy agent for Canada in the case concerning the legality of use of force in the International Court of Justice. Over the years ambassadorial positions had attracted their share of prima donnas and worse — "jobs for the boys," i.e., political appointees — but here was an inspired choice. Because of his outreach program of speaking tours across Canada and interviews with journalists, Sproule became the diplomatic face of Canada in Afghanistan. Unfortunately, much of his time in Kabul was taken up with greeting every Ottawa politician who arrived for a quick tour of CIDA projects and the requisite photo-op of handing out maple-leaf-decorated school bags to local children. A reminder of how dangerous a posting this was for a Canadian diplomat came a week after Sproule's arrival when a rocket hit the embassy building. Luckily, there were no injuries, unlike an earlier incident on March 28 when a roadside explosion destroyed a Canadian embassy vehicle, wounding a passenger, a locally engaged security guard.

The ambassador's Foreign Service colleague, Glyn Berry, was killed on January 15, 2006, when an explosives-laden car swerved into the G-Wagon taking him from a meeting with an Afghan political leader. It was soon common knowledge among the local community that Berry's death, coming just after Canada moved into Kandahar, was a warning from the Taliban — and perhaps Pakistan's Inter-Services Intelligence. At Berry's funeral in London, Deputy Foreign Affairs Minister Peter Harder told mourners that weeks before the attack that killed him, Berry had been seconds away from a bomb attack on a convoy. Yet he chose not to leave. "Nobody could have been more dedicated to the people of Afghanistan," Harder said. Berry believed, he said, that "the principal challenge is not peacekeeping but peace-building [which requires] … people on the ground that can deliver the goods."

Among the mourners were Berry's two sons, Gareth and Rhys. The latter said, "My father used to say, 'Whatever you do in life, make sure you're happy and make damn sure you've got a good story at the end of it.' My father lived by that in everything he did."[25]

The Afghan National Police immediately "fingered" Pir Mohammed in Berry's murder. His Toyota Town Ace minivan had been at the scene of the explosion, and when they raided the suspect's home, the police said they found weapons, documents, and photos of a reputed Taliban leader. The murder of a Canadian diplomat was a high-profile one, and on the strength of the evidence, the Afghan National Police reacted with uncharacteristic efficiency, arresting the 30-year-old Mohammed a day later. But on January 18, after less than two days in custody, the suspect walked calmly out of prison, going back only to ask for the return of his confiscated cell phone. The Canadian authorities, who wouldn't be arranging a board of inquiry into Berry's death until February 6, had been unaware of the arrest or the release.

Operating room technician Master Seaman Bill Pritchett left Canada on February 8, 2006, and wrote in his diary:

> The flight was all right. The contour flying was okay.
> It was kind of different having to put on your PPE

[personnel protective equipment]. When I arrived, I was eager to get going. When you got there, you usually had the AAG [Arrival Assistance Group] with assorted things like phone cards, etc. I could not wait to see the hospital. When we broke for lunch, I ate quickly and went to the hospital to show my face. I was the last of the OR team to arrive. I had heard that the other members hit the ground running. I wanted to be part of it. I did not want to miss anything. Some of them had to delay their AAG procedures by one day because they had cases to do. While walking to the hospital, I was thinking, I cannot believe I am here in Afghanistan. I was very glad that I was. We were assigned our temporary accommodations, "weather havens." They were okay. I was glad the really hot weather did not come before the AC was installed.

REALITY OF BEING THERE. I remember the first time I realized that we were in a war zone. We were doing a skin graft on a local civilian. Then we got the word that there had been a firefight with four KIA. I thought, KILLED IN ACTION, this is the real thing, and this is what I have been training for. It just seemed to me that you wanted to do as much as you could and then more. This was another reality check for me that Canadians were going to get hurt and Canadians were going to die.

Suicide attacks dramatically increased in the summer of 2006 as the Taliban changed tactics. When Lieutenant-Commander Rob Ferguson arrived in Kabul in June as the newest member of the Canadian Strategic Advisory Team (SAT), he and his colleagues were very aware of suicide improvised explosive devices (SIEDs). "Despite the best intelligence information available, there is really no way of predicting when or where an attack might happen," Ferguson wrote. "The best that one can hope to do is to make it difficult for a potential bomber by blending in, altering your habits, and driving fast. It is surreal to arrive at work, sit down at your desk, and be rocked by the force of an explosion that shakes your building and its windows. After an initial response of 'that was a big one,' your training kicks in and you quickly conduct a fan-out of the team to ensure that everyone is safe. Chances of actually being caught by one are relatively small, though, and there is a strong determination among the team to conduct business as usual regardless of the threat. To do otherwise means that the terrorists win and that is simply unacceptable."

When the first Canadian troops left to fight in the Boer War, they were seen off at Ottawa's Union Station en route to Quebec City by throngs of well-wishers. As bands played and flags flew, the soldiers, all of whom were volunteers, were showered with gifts from private donors and commercial corporations and embarked laden with games, books, boxing gloves, 2,722 kilograms of tobacco, and 20,000 cigarettes. Speeches and newspaper editorials of the day described them as "ideal Canadian manhood" and "as pure as the air of the sunlit north." At the port of Quebec City the 1,039 men were then crammed into the Allan Line's old cattle boat *Sardinian* for the voyage to Cape Town. There were too few lifeboats, not enough bunks (20 stowaways were later discovered), and drinking water was rationed throughout the voyage. Fortunately for them, the British had asked that Canada send only infantry (despite the reputation of the hard-riding Boers), so horses and artillery weren't crammed in, as well.

In Canada's war in Afghanistan, Trenton, Ontario, home of 8 Wing's Polaris transports, was the scene of all departures and arrivals. The Canadian equivalent of the USAF Dover Air Force Base in Delaware, it soon became familiar to the public when yet another flag-draped coffin emerged from the belly of a Polaris. "One day the 8 Wing Trenton flight line is sombre with the homecoming of another Canadian soldier killed in Afghanistan," wrote Lieutenant Pierrette LeDrew, watching one of 19 flights deliver the next rotation in August 2006, "while the next is filled with soldiers kissing their loved ones goodbye as they head off to Afghanistan for their six-month tour of duty. Some soldiers were pacing nervously, others sat stoically, waiting for the boarding announcement that, for some, could not come soon enough, and for others, would come too soon. Most were putting on a brave face, trying to reassure someone who cares for them, and possibly themselves, as well, that everything would be okay. Soldiers played with their small children and hugged their spouses one last time; parents, whose children were leaving for the harsh reality of military service in Afghanistan, held on to them as long as they could as they accompanied them to the departure gate. There were a lot of smiles, but also a lot tears. A lot of laughter, but also a lot of serious moments. Whether it was with a last shared cigarette, a family picture, or an extended hug and a kiss, people tried to hold on to each other and each other's memory as long as they could, in the hope that it would carry them safely through the next several months. Finally, the call for boarding came...."

An eight-hour flight to Zagreb, Croatia, followed, the refuelling stop holding unhappy memories for some Canadians. "Upon stepping out of the plane I felt a huge acidic lump in my stomach," remembered Captain Richard Little. "The airport had not changed one bit from when I landed there a few years earlier as a peacekeeper in Bosnia. I had attended two ramp ceremonies there." The Polaris arrived at Camp Mirage after a six-and-a-half-hour flight, and Little remembered: "It was now hotter than 35 degrees. At 0230 we mustered the 'chalk'[26] (for the Hercules flight to Kabul), ensured that everyone had their armour and helmets ready. Everyone had signed for the ballistic plates (I had mine from Gagetown) and we were ready to go. We were briefed, and at 0330 we walked to the plane. We loaded, put in our earplugs, sat down, and awaited takeoff. We took off and the plane immediately became like an oven. After three hours of flying, we were ordered to don our armour and helmets. At the 45-minute mark before landing, the plane started doing some serious banking and turning. This wild roller-coaster ride proved thrilling yet frightening at the same time. When we landed at Kabul International Airport (KAIA), it was a relief. The loadmaster lowered the ramp partially. I've been on enough Hercules to know that usually when the ramp gets lowered the fresh air comes in and cools off the interior quite rapidly. However, when this ramp was lowered, the air remained hot. In fact, I believe that it even got warmer."

When Little's group disembarked, Brigadier-General Peter Devlin and Regimental Sergeant Major (RSM) CWO Wayne Ford were there to greet them. "Once inside the terminal we were given weapons and one mag and organized into vehicles. In the belly of a Bison, we rode to the newly constructed Camp Julien. Once there we were given briefings all day, containing some theatre-specific information, and spreading of some interesting urban legends. The temperature during the briefings was a stifling 46 degrees. Towards the latter part of the afternoon we remounted into a Bison and headed out to Camp Warehouse, my home for the next six months."

When Stephen Harper was sworn in as prime minister on February 6, 2006, his office received congratulatory calls, emails, and letters. There was some criticism about the seal hunt and also about David Emerson, the prime minister's choice for trade minister, but none of the mail concerned Afghanistan. A month later that changed. Although the number of letters about the seal hunt were still greater, more and more callers and writers were critical of Canada's deployment to Afghanistan and wanted the troops brought home. Officially called "Stabilization," the Canadian strategy had been encapsulated into the buzz words of "Defence, Development, Diplomacy." The CF might now be facing an asymmetrical conflict between state military forces and belligerents who engaged in activities regardless of the traditional laws of war or international humanitarian law, but to the Harper government the conflict wasn't considered "a war" and none of the new cabinet members were allowed to refer to it as one.

No Canadian prime minister, not even the globe-trotting Pierre Trudeau, had ever been to Kandahar until March 2006, the same month as President Bush's visit. On March 10 the Ottawa media were told to assign their correspondents for a prime ministerial journey. Since it was Prime Minister Harper's first flight outside Canada, the speculation was intense. But the Prime Minister's Office gave nothing away, except that the media were to report to the government hangar at the Ottawa airport. The Canadian Forces Polaris took them with the prime ministerial party to Islamabad with a refuelling stop at Zagreb. Safely in the air, Harper revealed to the press that the Afghanistan trip had been planned for a while, admitting that he was making it to build support for the mission at home. Sixteen hours later the Airbus landed at Islamabad, where in the heavy, superheated atmosphere a Canadian Forces CC-130 Hercules waited to fly everyone to Kandahar. That they were going into a combat zone was made clear to the journalists when they were issued with helmets and flak jackets. The prime minister flew in the cockpit of the Hercules, which landed at Kandahar Airfield in a dust storm. General Rick Hillier, the architect behind the controversial move to Kandahar, was on the tarmac to welcome the prime minister. Harper toured an operations centre, and the next day he made his "You can't lead from the bleachers" and "Canada won't cut and run" speech.

Although it wasn't an official bilateral visit, there were Afghan government officials who felt slighted because the Canadian prime minister had come to their country but didn't meet with them. Harper did shake hands with the old regional war hero, Mullah Naqib, but the meeting was a salutary lesson in Afghan politics. Pir Mohammed, the Kandahar police's only suspect in the Glyn Berry murder, belonged to the powerful Alokozai tribe, and in a country where membership (whether religion or tribe) had its privileges, Mohammed had friends in high places, in this case, Mullah Naqib.

A legend among Soviet war mujahideen, Mullah Naqib had personally shot down three Hinds with CIA-supplied Stingers. After the war, he embraced non-violence and, unlike most of his countrymen, even returned the remaining SAMs to the Americans. His Alokozai warriors then fought the Taliban, welcoming Karzai back to Kandahar in 2001. Revered locally, Naqib was designated by Karzai to accept the Taliban surrender and then assumed the governorship of Kandahar. Unfortunately, Gul Agha Shirzai, who had been told that only the airport was his, pre-empted Naqib's appointment and took Kandahar City, as well, spreading rumours among the Americans that Naqib had been one of the Taliban. Ready to believe they had caught someone close to Al Qaeda, the U.S. Special Forces even escorted Gul Agha Shirzai to the governor's palace in Kandahar City, and it was only Hamid Karzai's personal intervention that saved Naqib from an American prison.

With Pir Mohammed's arrest, the respected Naqib knew that the Kandahar police detachment, infamous for its corruption and Pakistani links, was intent on framing one of his tribesman for the diplomat's murder. Given enough time, the police could even torture a confession out of Mohammed. Naqib went to see Ahmed Wali Karzai, the younger brother of President Karzai, to plead his case. Now the godfather of the clan, Ahmed Wali Karzai called the local governor who called the police chief, and Pir Mohammed walked out of prison and disappeared.[27] The Afghan

National Police, which thought it had practised due diligence in pursuing the investigation, knew that continuing to investigate somebody so well connected was a waste of time and effort. At the time of Harper's visit Berry's death was still unresolved. As for Mullah Naqib, the prime minister invited him to visit Canada.

Harper had already said he would unilaterally extend the mission in Afghanistan at least until February 2008 if he failed to get the support of Parliament to do so until 2009. Polls taken just after his visit to Afghanistan showed that a 55 percent majority of Canadians supported sending troops. Now, having earned his right to talk on the subject, back home, on May 17, Harper introduced a motion in the House of Commons asking the Members of Parliament to support the government's two-year extension of Canada's deployment of diplomatic, development, civilian police, and military personnel in Afghanistan with the provision of funding for this extension. News of the death of Captain Nichola Goddard, the artillery officer with the 1st Royal Canadian Horse Artillery who was killed in a Taliban ambush, had put Afghanistan back on every television screen in the country. Goddard was the first Canadian woman to be killed in action while serving in a combat role. Now the conflict was beginning to dominate the correspondence received by Harper's office. In May 2006, of the 1,453 letters and emails, two-thirds called for the prime minister to pull the troops out of Afghanistan, with 114 phone callers telling him to do the same.

But after six hours of debate in the House of Commons, Harper's motion narrowly passed 149 votes to 145. The New Democratic Party, the Bloc Québécois, and a few Liberals tried to block the non-binding motion, saying Harper hadn't provided them with enough information about the new mission. Liberal Opposition Leader Bill Graham, whose party had originally launched the mission in 2001, grumbled that many MPs felt they "had a gun put to our heads and without knowing all the details of why a two-year prolongation is being made at this time."

The decision was a lot easier for General Hillier, who asked, "Would Canadians be content to allow, because of inaction partly on our nation's part, the Taliban to resume control of Afghanistan, with all their extreme ways, and with the whipping of women because their heels click when they walk on asphalt? I think the answer's a resounding 'No.'"

Canada's greatest asset in Afghanistan was unknown to most Canadians. When, as minister of defence, John McCallum announced that a Strategic Reconnaissance Team (SRT) had departed for Kabul on March 22, 2003, few Canadians had understood or appreciated what that meant. Reconnaissance was crucial to the planning of Operation Athena, the Canadian contribution to ISAF in Afghanistan, and the SRT morphed into the Strategic Advisory Team (SAT) later on. "We are not here to push Western beliefs," Lieutenant-Commander Rob Ferguson explained. "SAT is not in Afghanistan to pursue its own personal agenda or derive personal profit. Quite simply, SAT is here to help Afghanistan in the ways that Afghanistan determines is the best for its future. And what could be more Canadian than that?"

Mandated by President Karzai personally to go anywhere in the country and investigate anything, the first SAT had arrived in September 2005 and was made responsible for monitoring Afghanistan's progress against its benchmarks. Personally invited by President Karzai to work at the ministerial level across all ministries and deal with the United Nations, the World Bank, key donor nations, and NATO/ISAF on almost a daily basis, this small group of Canadians, all adept at leadership and management and possessing strong organizational skills, was able to interact in the local community and get around the city and surrounding areas much more regularly. They lived at a compound located in the same block as the Canadian embassy and CIDA, both of which they had strong relationships with.

Ferguson was attached to the Afghanistan National Development Strategy (ANDS) Working Group and essentially worked for the senior economic adviser to the president. "We are exactly the type of people Afghanistan desperately needs," he said. "Most Canadians are aware of the military operations that Canada is involved with in the province of Kandahar. What they may not be aware of are the activities that Canada has supported, other than fighting. The SAT has been extremely proactive within the Afghanistan government, involved with developing capacity in several key ministries and organizations at the strategic level." The team members are or were involved in the president's office, the Civil Service Commission, the Ministry of Rural Rehabilitation and Development (MRRD), ANDS, and the Ministries of Transport and

Justice. They are further supported by members of the team with specialist analytical skills and communication expertise.

How had Ferguson gotten this position? He had worked in the United Kingdom with the Royal Navy and had trained with the NATO Allied Rapid Reaction Corps as an information operations officer in the deployed headquarters. On his return to Canada in 2004, Ferguson had helped draft the Defence Capability Plan and had come to the attention of the director-general of strategic planning, Lieutenant-General Andrew Leslie (now chief of the land staff). "I mentioned to Lieutenant-General Leslie that I would be looking for another challenge," Ferguson said, "and he immediately offered me the opportunity to deploy in support of the SAT mission."

This small but punchy team has had a significant impact on the development of Afghanistan. SAT members assisted ANDS in developing the Afghanistan Compact, whereby the United Nations' Millennium Development goals were expanded and customized according to Afghanistan's needs. SAT members drafted the Afghanistan National Development Strategy as well as the process by which the strategy would be implemented. Public administration reform was jump-started by SAT expertise, and the team continues to work closely with the government to develop key strategic messages for the people. The team also continues to work closely in developing plans for rural development. Most important, SAT has completed these tasks alongside its Afghan colleagues, teaching and guiding, providing advice, and building future indigenous capacity in the process.

SAT has a number of significant advantages over other types of organizations that provide assistance. First, the team is able to draw from a highly proficient field of experienced officers. Therefore, it is highly flexible and responsive to Afghanistan's needs. Being military, SAT members are trained to operate in environments that are less secure. Therefore, SAT is able to work consistently under austere conditions. When some organizations shut down and retreat behind their compound walls due to threats, SAT members continue to show up for work alongside their Afghan colleagues. Additionally, the less-restrictive force protection rules that SAT members operate under allow them to go out into the community and the country to get a much better feel for

Afghanistan's progress. This fact isn't lost on the Afghans, who have great respect for Canada as a result of SAT's perseverance and dedication. And SAT doesn't have its own agenda and doesn't have any strings attached to its assistance. Its goal is to simply provide the best support and advice it can to help Afghanistan determine what Afghanistan requires. Therefore, the opinions and assistance of SAT members are actively sought throughout government.

Ferguson was eventually exclusively employed by the Afghanistan National Development Strategy Working Group, a temporary organization that was established to serve two specific functions: the development of a poverty-reduction strategy for Afghanistan, and the monitoring of the Afghanistan Compact Benchmarks. This organization liaised regularly with all of the ministries of the Afghan government, as well as with key donors and international organizations. Essentially, Ferguson explained, "it is the hub for all of the development work that is being conducted in Afghanistan to meet its goals. In this respect, no other country is as strategically placed as Canada with respect to influencing Afghanistan's development."

Ferguson's team was made up of 16 people: a commanding officer (colonel), a chief of staff (lieutenant-colonel), two team leaders (lieutenant-colonels), six majors/lieutenant-commanders split among the teams, one civilian defence scientist, one civilian development expert, one public-affairs communications specialist (lieutenant-commander), one administrative support (warrant officer), one chief (chief warrant officer), and one force protection specialist (master corporal).

"Each team is likely to be slightly different as the support that's provided evolves in concert with the Afghanistan government's needs," Ferguson said. "SAT members possess a wide variety of operational experience and academic credentials. We can work individually or as part of a team and can flex our support as required, which makes us unique. All this is to say that everyone has their own story about how they were selected, but two things are consistent and considered mission-essential for this task. First, the individual must have credentials both operationally and academically so that they will be able to contribute from the first day. Second, and what I consider to be most important, is character. SAT members must be extroverts. They must be willing to take chances and have a solid track record of building relationships and supporting a team. It is definitely not a job that everyone can do. Lack of either of these capabilities would hamper the mission. Personally, if I had to choose which was more important, I would choose the latter, as relationships in Afghanistan are critical to mission success. That is what makes this job so interesting."

"Several months ago our president and CEO, Paul House, received a call from General Rick Hillier on behalf of the troops stationed in Kandahar," explained Doug Anthony, Tim Hortons' director of business development. "They had told the general that the one thing they would really like on the base is a Tim Hortons."

On July 1, 2006, at 10:00 a.m. Kandahar time, the Canadian Forces Personnel Support Agency (CFPSA) officially opened the first Tim Hortons outlet at a deployed mission outside Canada. The 12-metre trailer was well situated on the Boardwalk rectangle, KAF's shopping mall, and joined Pizza Hut and various souvenir concessions. It was an ideal way to celebrate Canada Day as CFPSA Chief Executive Officer Major-General Doug Langton, commander of Task Force Afghanistan (TFA), Brigadier-General David Fraser, and Doug Anthony cut the ribbon to Tim Hortons coffee, iced cappuccino, doughnuts, muffins, cookies, and Timbits. "This is about serving you as you continue to do the outstanding job Canada asks of you," Major-General Langton told the soldiers. "We hope this little piece of home will make your lives in Afghanistan just a little bit easier." The outlet is run by CFPSA, though Tim Hortons staff stayed a few weeks initially to help. CF personnel pay prices comparable to those in Canada, and profits made within this project are reinvested in morale and welfare programs for CF members.

Ninety years before in the very same month, Canadian soldiers attacked German positions on the Somme. That battle lasted from July 1 to the end of November in 1916, and while the summer of 2006 in Kandahar couldn't compare, it was the bloodiest few months to date in Canada's involvement in Afghanistan. The causes were many. Hundreds of Taliban insurgents were said to be massing outside Kandahar in a district called Panjwai to take advantage of the changeover of the American troops to

NATO, i.e., the Canadians. For Asadullah Khalid, the new governor of Kandahar, the answer was simple: "They chose Panjwai and Zhari about seven months ago and began to build up bases. Why these districts? Because it was close to Kandahar, close to Helmand, close to the border with Pakistan." The completion of the poppy harvest in May had freed able-bodied men to join the Taliban where they earned CDN$400 a month.

The region itself had always been a mean one, home of the Nurzai, a surly tribe that nursed its historic grievances against the ruling Durrani. All the local jobs and contracts from the Americans and Canadians, it was said, were going to the Durrani. The Nurzai had, in their eyes, always gotten the short end of the historic stick, and the fact that the government in Kabul, controlled by Karzai's Durrani, was now using foreigners to eradicate their poppy crops only confirmed their suspicions. However exaggerated or delusional these perceptions were, when the Taliban, the drug lords, and local landowners offered the Nurzai good reason in the form of intimidation or money to fight the foreigners, it was hard to argue against it. With their convoys of armoured vehicles, the Canadians were no different from the Americans or British or Russians.

The convoys were resupplying the Provincial Reconstruction Team at Camp Nathan Smith (CNS) where about 220 Canadian Forces soldiers and officials from Foreign Affairs Canada, the Canadian International Development Agency, and the Royal Canadian Mounted Police worked. Another resupply destination was Forward Operating Base Robinson, a desert outpost in the Sangin district of Helmand Province that overlooked a suspected opium-smuggling route. Protected by an inner sand berm and an outer line of razor wire, FOB Robinson housed about 170 Canadians. On June, 10, 2006, Canadian troops unveiled a new forward operating base near El Bak, about 200 kilometres north of Kandahar. Built on a rocky base, overlooked by mountain slopes, and surrounded by villages loyal to the Taliban, FOB Martello was almost indefensible.[28] But because it was in the middle of a Taliban transit-and-smuggling route into the south, it was strategically located. Another new FOB, situated at Spin Boldak and close to the Pakistani border, would prove to be the most dangerous base of all after Canadian troops replaced French Special Forces there.

After being in Afghanistan for a while, Canadian Forces Master Seaman Bill Pritchett made the following lists:

Things That I Look Forward to When I Get Home
- Drinking coffee early in the morning in the backyard with my wife, Peggy.
- Walking my dog.
- Seeing the kids.
- Swimming.

Things That I Discovered I Missed
- Feeling the rain on my face.
- Lying on the grass looking at the sun.
- Going to the toilet and not having to get dressed to do so.

Things That I Won't Miss
- Ramp ceremonies.

Most of the Canadian volunteers who went off to the Boer War were young, urban, poorly paid, white-collar or skilled blue-collar workers "bent on escaping," Pierre Berton writes in *Marching as to War*, "the strictures and stifling boredom of Canadian life." They went for love of adventure as much as for love of empire.

In the war in Afghanistan, the young men and women who volunteered and died there had strikingly similar reasons. They had watched (some as teenagers) the aircraft slam into the World Trade Center and didn't want terrorism to come to their hometowns of Edson, Alberta; Sackville, Nova Scotia; or Conception Bay, Newfoundland. "He loved being there," said Corporal Matthew Dinning's father when the 23-year-old was killed on April 22, 2006. "He was a proud Canadian. He believed in what he was doing." For 22-year-old Private Kevin Dallaire, killed in combat on August 3, 2006, it was travel. The only place he had ever seen, said his father, was his home province of Alberta. On the other hand, 42-year-old Sergeant Robert Short, killed on October 2, 2003, had served in

Cyprus and Bosnia and had done three tours in the Balkans. "He was a professional soldier … always trying to do the best he could," remembered his brother. Master Corporal Timothy Wilson, who died on March 4, 2006, age 30, "was champing at the bit" to join the fight in Afghanistan, said his father.[29] Before being killed by Taliban mines or RPGs, they had, as Lieutenant-Colonel John McCrae wrote more than 90 years earlier in his poem "In Flanders Field," "felt dawn, saw sunset glow,/Loved, and were loved." They had also worked at Northern Telecom, played hockey, written poems to their six-year-old daughters, driven Pontiac Firebirds, and married high-school sweethearts.

"Sadly, I have been involved in far too many ramp ceremonies," wrote Major James Bradley of the Multinational Medical Unit at Kandahar Airfield. "So far I have seen off 25 Canadians, six Americans, and 15 Brits. One thing that has been amazing is to see the resiliency of our Canadian soldiers. When they are injured, they want to get back to their comrades as quickly as possible. I had supper the other day with a guy who had been shot in the hand and the shoulder. I remembered him because I was in the operating room for part of his surgery. He essentially refused to be sent home. The doctors relented, and his unit found him a job where he could remain in camp and still be useful. In another incident last month, a soldier stepped on a mine and had his foot blown off. He was one of the soldiers who had been in our facility during the mass-casualty incident of September 4, 2006, when the American A-10 strafed Charles Company. Upon seeing one of our nurses, he said, "Remember me? Well, I am back.""

Four Canadians were awarded the Victoria Cross in the Boer War (and four at the bloodbath of the Somme in World War I alone). Their actions — going back under heavy fire to rescue their comrades without regard for their own safety or holding off the enemy in desperate rearguard actions — were eerily similar to official citations more than a century later.

"Sergeant Michael Thomas Victor Denine, MMV, CD Edmonton, Alberta, was awarded the Medal of Military Valour. Deployed with 8 Platoon, C Company, 1 PPCLI, on May 17, 2006, Sergeant Denine while sustaining concentrated rocket-propelled grenade, machine gun and small-arms fire, the main cannon and the machine gun on his light armoured vehicle malfunctioned. Under intense enemy fire, he recognized the immediate need to suppress the enemy fire and exited the air sentry hatch to man the pintle-mounted machine gun. Completely exposed to enemy fire, he laid down a high volume of suppressive fire, forcing the enemy to withdraw. Sergeant Denine's valiant action ensured mission success and likely saved the lives of his crew.

"Master Corporal Collin Ryan Fitzgerald, MMV Shilo, Manitoba, and Morrisburg, Ontario, was awarded the Medal of Military Valour. Master Corporal Fitzgerald, deployed with 5 Platoon, B Company, 1 PPCLI Battle Group, is recognized for outstanding selfless and valiant actions carried out on May 24, 2006, during an ongoing enemy ambush involving intense, accurate enemy fire. Master Corporal Fitzgerald repeatedly exposed himself to enemy fire by entering and re-entering a burning platoon vehicle and successfully driving it off the roadway, permitting the remaining vehicles trapped in the enemy zone to break free. Master Corporal Fitzgerald's courageous and completely selfless actions were instrumental to his platoon's successful egress and undoubtedly contributed to saving the lives of his fellow platoon members.

"Awarded the Medal of Military Valour, Private Jason Lamont, MMV Edmonton, Alberta, and Greenwood, Nova Scotia, was deployed with the Health Support Services Company, 1 PPCLI Battle Group, on July 13, 2006, when part of the reconnaissance platoon came under heavy enemy fire and was isolated from the rest. During the firefight, another soldier was shot while attempting to withdraw back to the firing line and was unable to continue. Without regard for his personal safety, Private Lamont, under concentrated enemy fire and with no organized suppression by friendly forces, sprinted through open terrain to administer first aid." Private Lamont's citation could have been a dispatch from Beaumont-Hamel in the Battle of the Somme in 1916 except the action took place in Helmand Province, Afghanistan, in the 21st century.

"Sergeant Patrick Tower, SMV, CD Edmonton, Alberta, and Victoria, British Columbia, won the Star of Military Valour. After an enemy strike in the Pashmul region on August 3, 2006, which resulted in numerous casualties, Sergeant Patrick Tower led the platoon medic and a third soldier across 150 metres of open terrain, under heavy enemy fire, to render assistance. On learning that the acting platoon commander had perished, Sergeant Tower assumed command and led the successful extraction of the force under continuous small-arms and rocket-propelled-grenade fire."[30]

On August 1, 2006, the Canadian military in Afghanistan transferred from the u.s.-led Operation Enduring Freedom to NATO. Under the Americans (with their focus on anti-terror combat operations), it was thought that reconstruction efforts had been sidelined. For the Canadians the summer just got bloodier. Master Corporal Raymond Arndt, 31, was killed and three other Canadians were injured in a traffic accident on August 5, 2006. The soldiers were travelling in a resupply convoy on Highway 4, carrying medical supplies to the forward operating base at Spin Boldak, when their G-Wagon was involved in a head-on collision with a civilian truck. A suicide bomber detonated an explosives-laden pickup truck near a NATO resupply convoy heading north from Spin Boldak on Highway 4 on August 11, 2006, killing Corporal Andrew James Eykelenboom, a Canadian medic in a G-Wagon. The 23-year-old corporal, "Boomer" to fellow soldiers, had already saved the lives of many in combat and was the first Canadian military medic killed in action since the Korean War. A suicide bomber drove an explosives-laden car into a Canadian resupply convoy on August 22, 2006, killing 27-year-old Corporal David Braun in a LAV III and wounding three others. About two hours later a 10-year-old Afghan boy was killed and a 17-year-old injured when a Canadian soldier fired at a motorcycle that had raced through the security cordon around the bomb site. On September 3, 2006, Warrant Officer Richard Francis Nolan (39), Warrant Officer Frank Robert Mellish (38), Sergeant Shane Stachnik (30), and Private William Jonathan James Cushley (21) were killed and as many as seven were wounded in a battle to oust insurgents from the area around Pashmul village. The insurgents launched a series of well-organized ambushes that killed the Canadians as they attempted to cross the dry Arghandab riverbed.

Given the casualties from the previous weeks, the staff at the Role 3 Multinational Hospital hoped that Labour Day 2006 would provide a respite. For a generation that had grown up on the television series *M*A*S*H* where a bubble-canopied helicopter dropped casualties off at the Mobile Army Surgical Hospital, this was very different. As there is no frontline in Afghanistan, and thus no need to keep moving, the hospital at Kandahar Airfield is in a building, not a tent. It is also well equipped with nine ward beds, three intensive-care beds, two operating rooms, a CAT scan, an ultrasound, x-rays, digital imaging, and a blood bank. While the wounded are still brought in by helicopter — now Chinooks and Black Hawks — technological advances mean that the trauma team is already prepared before they arrive.

"Those who die tend to die before they reach hospital," said trauma surgeon and Canadian Forces Major Dr. Homer Tien. "If they arrive alive, generally they survive. We have had a few Afghans die in our facility, as well, but we then transfer them to their families. Rather than fly out of camp, the families will pick up the bodies in their own car or van. We had one guy make his final trip home in the trunk of a taxi."

That Labour Day they needed all of their resources, thought Major James Bradley, the deputy commanding officer of the Multinational Medical Unit at Kandahar Airfield. "Just before 0530 hours, on September 4," he said, "an American A-10 strafed Charles Company, Task Force Kandahar.[31] A report of 'mass casualties on our hands' came from the unit. Within 10 minutes it was known that there were at least eight casualties and that two helicopters were required. By 0545 hours, the casualties were reported as six Priority 1s, six Priority 2s, and at least 16 ambulatory. A few minutes later we were informed about the KIA. At 0550 hours the duty doctor declared a facility MASCAL [Mass Casualty Evacuation]. Over the next half-hour the number of casualties went up. We were now at six Priority 1s, 13 Priority 2s, and 13 Priority 3s.[32] All Role 3 personnel reported to their place of work and started preparing for the high number of casualties. We discharged a few patients and moved some less-severe patients over to the minimal-care ward.... Major Crispo, the physiotherapist, organized the stretcher bearers, and Master Warrant Officer Lamirande coordinated with the Military Police for traffic control outside the facility. The British Air Staging Unit, which is located immediately outside our facility, sent over all their personnel to be litter bearers and assist in the trauma bays. Six ambulances were sent to the tarmac to transfer casualties.

"The first Black Hawk helicopter arrived at 0647 hours, carrying three litter and three ambulatory patients.... Thirty-four minutes later a Chinook arrived with 11 litter patients. A Black Hawk with three more litter and two ambulatory patients followed eight minutes later. Once off-loaded, the Chinook departed to pick up another load. Due to the numbers of casualties, it was decided that some of them would be sent to the Dutch Role 2 Enhanced in Tarin Kowt. Major Taylor [an American physician], Chief Warrant Officer St. George, and Master Warrant Officer St. Croix conducted a triage on the tarmac with the downwash from the Chinook blowing over them. Six casualties were transferred to two waiting Black Hawks for the trip to Tarin Kowt. Finally, at 0801 hours, the Chinook returned with four litter and 10 ambulatory casualties. Somewhere along the line the fog of war came into play, because the above number adds up to 36 casualties, yet we ended up with 37. Throughout, the ambulances, led by Sergeant Chamberlain (United Kingdom), were busy shuttling casualties from the flight line to the back door of the Role 3.

"Normally, the facility has six trauma bays. For this incident we set up two more and added four additional beds on the ward. The activities in the trauma bays showed the true nature of this multinational unit. There were Canadians, Americans, Britons, Dutch, Australians, and Danes working together in perfect harmony. Although the CTV news report said that it was absolute chaos, the reality was anything but. Everyone worked at a hectic pace, but it was all well coordinated, and in the end, everyone was cared for by the best staff in the best hospital in Afghanistan. The laboratory conducted more than 60 procedures. Diagnostic Imaging did more than 160 x-rays and CT scans. The surgical teams performed eight surgeries. There were countless bandages and sutures, and throughout, the staff remained upbeat and reassuring to the patients. Of the 37 casualties we saw that day, six went to Tarin Kowt, we admitted 16, and the remainder were treated and released. Although we have a 19-bed capacity, we had 24 patients in the ward that night. The following morning we evacuated eight patients to Landstuhl [in Germany]."

For Bradley this tour was nothing like any before — an opinion shared by anyone who had done previous missions. "This is war," he said. "It is real combat, and I see the results of that here every day. Canadian wounded are only a small fraction of what we see. Most people in Ottawa don't appreciate the number of casualties we see on a regular basis." His first three tours were in Bosnia. "They proved to me that

U.N. stands for 'Useless Nations.' It was my tour that had the 55 hostages taken by the Serbs, and then our camp in Visoko was surrounded by the Muslims, and we had what I would describe as criminal rules of engagements issued by the U.N."

Worse was to come: "Monday, September 18," Bradley said, "saw another busy day for the Role 3 Multinational Medical Unit in Kandahar. A suicide bomber had attacked a platoon of dismounted Canadian soldiers in the Panjwai area. The bomb was laden with ball bearings and there were numerous casualties with serious injuries to legs in particular. We received the initial report at 0925 hours. Within 20 minutes it was obvious that this would be a MASCAL. Everyone was called in, and the British and Australian Role 1s sent staff over to help. The first Black Hawk arrived at 1036 hours with two litter cases. That helicopter picked up Master Warrant Officer Ralph of Role 1 to take him to the scene. A second Black Hawk with three litters arrived at 1043 hours. Finally, 26 minutes later, a Chinook landed with six litter patients and two walking wounded. One more casualty came in later by Black Hawk, and finally some of the less-severe wounded came into Primary Care after returning to the camp by convoy. There were a total of 22 casualties from the incident. This doesn't include the four soldiers who died.

"Although this MASCAL had fewer casualties than the Labour Day incident, the severity of the injuries was greater this time. Also, just prior to the MASCAL we had received three local national casualties from a separate incident. The multinational team is very slick at responding to MASCALS. All sections prepared for the onslaught. Patients were moved out of the ward to the overflow beds in Primary Care, supplies were readied, an additional trauma bay was set up, stretcher bearers were briefed, and additional personnel were dispatched with the ambulances to assist with triage at the flight line.

"The ambulance teams were a mix of Canadians, Americans, and Britons. They off-loaded the casualties from the helicopters and then loaded them into the ambulances. The ambulances moved to the back door of the facility, and the stretcher bearers, mostly coming from the British Air Staging Unit, brought the casualties to the trauma bays. The bays filled up quickly, so we used two beds in the ward for a total of 10 trauma bays. The trauma teams were made up from all nationalities.

There would be an American doctor with a Canadian nurse, a Danish specialist, and a Dutch medical technician. Each trauma bay had a different mix. We had eight Norwegian nurses in the facility to assist with Operation Medusa. They saw more trauma on this one day than they had seen in six months in their facility in Mazar-i-Sharif.

"It was quickly established that we would send some casualties to Tarin Kowt (the Dutch Role 2 Enhanced facility). Unlike the previous MASCAL, the injuries were too severe to simply off-load the Chinook and reload onto a Black Hawk. This time everyone was brought into the facility, life- and limb-saving interventions were initiated, x-rays were taken, IVs established, wounds redressed, and the patients packaged for transfer. Three patients were loaded into Black Hawks and sent to Tarin Kowt. Although they were supposed to go to the Dutch facility, they ended up in the American Forward Surgical Team (also in Tarin Kowt). The Dutch felt short-changed for not being able to help. They were asking us to send them some other casualties to them.

"Back in our facility, the Canadian and Danish surgical teams quickly got to work. Each team worked for 12 hours. There were nine surgical patients requiring a minimum of three procedures each. Warrant Officer Gagnon's diagnostic-imaging team saw 20 patients, each requiring between eight and 20 procedures. Sergeant Côté and her laboratory technicians were equally as busy. The patient administration cell, with help from the clerks, was busy collecting names and personal information as well as the patients' clothing and weapons. As they were removing some personal effects from some clothing, they discovered a ball bearing inside the top left pocket of a combat shirt. It had penetrated the flak vest, bent the guy's dog tags and a St. Christopher's medallion, smashed his dosimeter, and embedded itself in a plastic sleeve holding some papers.

"After such a traumatic event, many of the soldiers, including those who weren't injured, needed someone to talk to. The Mental Health team and padres were busy, and sometimes it was the nurses such as Lieutenant Jen Lalonde sitting on a bed holding a soldier's hand while he told her his story. You know morale remains high when [we] … were betting Tim Hortons ice cappuccinos on the location of the latest attack. Despite the heavy workload that day, when asked what we would do if there was one more Priority 1 patient, Lieutenant-Commander Kao's response was: 'Hey, we're at war. Bring it on.' Of course, that quote wasn't as good as one from Corporal Hamelin on the Labour Day MASCAL. He was keeping people away from the facility when a Dutch officer came by for sick parade. Corporal Hamelin told him, 'Unless you have a bullet in you, you're not coming in here.'"[33]

President Karzai visited Ottawa and Montreal from September 21 to 23, 2006, barely a week after four Canadians had been killed and 17 wounded in a suicide bombing. With 29 Canadian soldiers killed from IEDs and fighting the Taliban in the nine months of the year so far, Karzai thanked Canada for its contribution, praising the country's sons and daughters who had made the ultimate sacrifice, "so that we in Afghanistan may have security ... and to ensure the continued safety of their fellow Canadians from terrorism." Taken immediately after the Karzai visit, a poll showed 57 percent of Canadians supported the country's efforts in Afghanistan, an all-time high.

Even when the Taliban wasn't involved, Major Bradley and the staff at the Multinational Medical Unit were busy. "On the evening of October 2," he said, "we experienced a MASCAL that was, in the words of Private Fulford, like a scene from the movie *Dawn of the Living Dead*. Across the airfield from our facility is a cement factory. Some local national workers were trying to heat up asphalt in order to prepare it for the runway extension. Their safety standards are not the same as in Canada. They poured gasoline on the asphalt and used a blowtorch to light it. The fire became uncontrollable so, thinking they would be able to snuff it out, they closed the lids on the container. As they did this, they created a fuel/air bomb that exploded and sent flames and burning gasoline onto the workers.

"The explosion was 400 metres from the hospital and was seen by some of our staff. Initially, it was believed it was just another rocket attack, but then the call came in for us to send an ambulance. As the ambulance departed the facility, a minivan arrived.... Master Seaman Eric Thiboutot, a medical technician, described the scene as something out of Michael Jackson's video *Thriller*. The casualties were walking around looking for help — skin, hair, and clothing dripping off their bodies. Master Seaman Thiboutot quickly directed the casualties to the trauma bays, which at the time was devoid of people. He went to the duty officer and requested assistance.

"Not knowing the source of the burns, Master Seaman Thiboutot and Captain Lévesque, the charge nurse, ushered all the casualties to the facility shower room, essentially making it an improvised decontamination room. As the casualties emerged, they went back to resus [resuscitation] for assessment and initial treatment. Prior to the arrival of more senior staff, Corporals Deveault and Parker did a stellar job of initial treatment. In the meantime the ambulance that had been dispatched to the scene came back with three additional casualties. There were now 11 casualties from this incident, the duty physician declared a MASCAL, and the recall of personnel was initiated. The seven trauma bays were filled and we quickly put up two more. Saline solution and water were poured on the patients in an effort to cool them down. Bandages and saline were used at an incredible rate. The smell of burnt flesh and gasoline filled the entire hospital. The floor was covered in water, dressings, clothing, and charred flesh. Many of the patients were going into shock.

"By now less than 20 minutes had passed since the arrival of the first casualties. As with previous MASCALs, the multinational flavour of the unit could be seen in each trauma bay. There were six severely burned patients; each with between 45 and 90 percent burns to their bodies. Canadians, Americans, Brits, Dutch, Australians, and Danes worked together at a frenetic pace. It was obvious that our facility couldn't handle so many acutely ill patients, so we arranged to send two to the Dutch Role 2 Enhanced in Tarin Kowt. They were incubated, bandaged, and had IVs inserted. They were then taken by ambulance to a waiting Black Hawk helicopter.

"The specialists, led by our internist, Lieutenant-Commander Kao, determined the best course of action for all the remaining patients. Nine patients were admitted to the ward. Only two of these could be considered minor cases. Three of the burn patients plus an American civilian drug overdose patient who had arrived just prior to the burn victims were intubated and mechanically ventilated. The ICU beds were now full.

"The next morning we transferred two stable patients to Tarin Kowt. The Canadian and Danish surgical teams started debridement and changed dressings. This carried on for many hours. Later in the day we were able to release three patients and transfer one to the civilian hospital in Kandahar City. The three worst patients remained in ICU. Lieutenant Commander Kao and the critical-care nurses worked non-stop on these three patients. Major Tremblay, the head nurse, juggled schedules in order to provide critical-care-nurse coverage for the burn patients. The norm in Canada is to have one nurse per ICU patient. Here we had two nurses for three beds.

"Just as we had discharged and transferred most of the burn patients on October 3, we heard about a mortar attack on Patrol Base Wilson. There were reports of casualties and two Canadians killed. For the second day in a row we were to receive 11 casualties from one incident. The casualties were a mix of Canadians and Americans. Four required surgery and had to be admitted to the ward.

"On October 4 we prepared the two American and one Canadian patient for evacuation to Landstuhl. Meanwhile the burn patients remained in the ward. All three required one-on-one nursing care. For three days we tried to find a civilian facility that could take them. Finally, the Italian NGO hospital in Kabul said it could take two of our patients. On October 5 we prepared two of the patients for transfer to Kabul. Our last burn patient, the most severely wounded, had no chance of survival. We were able to transfer him to the civilian hospital in Kandahar City so his family could be with him before he died. In all, four of the burn victims from this incident died. Fortunately, no new patients came in and they were all able to have a full day of rest."

In an interview on CBC Radio on the weekend of September 17, 2006, Prime Minister Harper finally acknowledged that Canada was fighting a war in Afghanistan. Until then Defence Minister O'Connor and other government leaders had denied that Canada was at war at all. Whatever it was, in monetary terms alone the conflict had cost Canadian taxpayers CDN$2.3 billion, which included the CDN$466 million for development that the Canadian International Development Agency had spent. Maintaining the troops there until 2009 would take another CDN$1.25 billion. The final bill, according to the figures released by the Harper government in the House of Commons on September 22, 2006, in reply to a question asked by NDP defence critic Dawn Black, was

CDN$3.5 billion. Critics thought the figure was purposely "low-balled" to make it more acceptable to the public.

If that was the government's intention, it didn't work, since demonstrations were held across the country on October 29, 2006. "Support Our Troops, "Bring Them Home Now," "Canada Out of Afghanistan," said the signs. "Health care, day care, anything but warfare," chanted the thousands who turned out in cities across Canada. A week later an Ipsos Reid opinion poll conducted for CanWest News showed that the level of support among Canadians for their country's military mission in Afghanistan had fallen to 44 percent, down 13 percent over the course of a month since President Karzai's speech. Only 41 percent now supported staying the course until 2009, and 58 percent, a clear majority of Canadians, expressed opposition.

It didn't help when that month the British Royal Statistical Society published some chilling statistics. The society noted that the fatality rate among Canadian and British troops in Afghanistan from May 1, 2006, to August 12, 2006, was higher than Britain's fatality rate in Iraq. When adjusted for the relative size of troop commitments, a Canadian soldier in Kandahar was nearly three times more likely to be killed in action than a British soldier and four and a half times more likely than an American soldier in Afghanistan. A Canadian soldier in Kandahar was nearly six times more likely to die in hostilities than an American soldier serving in Iraq. The war in Afghanistan was far deadlier than the conflict in Iraq, despite the commonly held notion to the contrary. If, in 2002, Prime Minister Chrétien had committed Canadian troops to Afghanistan as the lesser of two evils, four years later the choice made had backfired.

Sheila Bird, vice president of the Royal Statistical Society, wrote in the September 9, 2006, issue of *New Scientist* that the risk to NATO forces in Afghanistan was approaching the level faced by the Soviets, who had abandoned their war there after 10 years. A study made by the Canadian Centre for Policy Alternatives determined that if the current rate of military deaths since February 2006 remained unchanged until the end of the mission in January 2009, the Canadian Forces would sustain another 108 deaths. While he grieved at the death of every Canadian in Afghanistan, Chief of Defence Staff General Rick Hillier was realistic.

"We are soldiers," he said. "This is our profession. This is who we are and what we do." The move to Kandahar and the battle group that Hillier had argued the Martin government for, remained, in his view, essential to the mission. There could be no aid or reconstruction without security, and the Afghan National Army and the Afghan National Police were in no position to provide it, so Canada had to.

For Major Bradley at the Kandahar Airfield military hospital, "The Christmas of 2006 in Kandahar was pretty good, considering I was so far away from family. On Christmas Eve we did a unit barbecue. Other than the wind, it was quite enjoyable. After the meal, we went to the headquarters tent where we did the gift exchange. The number of parcels from Canada was incredible. Indeed, it was too much. By the way, does everyone in Canada think we have a hygiene problem here? The volume of toothpaste, toothbrushes, shampoo, and dental floss could sink a ship. Our party went on for about five hours, not bad considering we could only have two beers each.

"Christmas Day was quiet, but that evening we had a fantastic concert put on at the new Canada House. The chief of defence staff was brilliant. He made special note of the medical staff. We received quite the ovation from everyone there. Mary Walsh and Rick Mercer were great, then there was a soloist and a rock band — a great evening for everyone. The best Christmas present for us in the Role 3, however, was that for the first time on our tour the ward was empty. At 1215 hours on December 24 we discharged two patients. For the next 72 hours no one came in — amazing timing."[34]

Unwittingly, Major Bradley was echoing German novelist Erich Maria Remarque's historic conclusion to another war: "It was, as on a day that was so quiet and still on the whole front, that the Army report confined itself to the single sentence: All quiet on the Western Front."

3

"Where Security Means Not Dying"

"Afghanistan is the largest recipient of our aid, so it's really important to me to see my people ... and to encourage [them] in their efforts," announced Josée Verner, the Canadian international cooperation minister, when she arrived in Kandahar on October 22, 2006. The minister responsible for the Canadian International Development Agency (CIDA) had been sent on a public-relations offensive to counter the drop in support by the Canadian public from 57 percent to 44 percent. Ipsos Reid Senior Vice President Darrell Bricker explained the figures: "There's no good news on Afghanistan. The only thing we hear ... is about ... what Canadian got injured or killed today. There's no sense of progress."

While Canadian military efforts had grabbed the headlines, little of the reconstruction efforts had done so, and Verner's surprise tour was designed to remedy that.[1] But held in the middle of Eid (Afghanistan's major religious holiday) when all the CIDA projects had shut down for the week of celebrations, the minister's ill-timed tour didn't allow her to see anything Canada was funding, though she did attend a photo-op with selected school girls and handed out school bags. Worse, the media reporters who accompanied her complained they couldn't get specific details about the 300 schools or the "93 projects, completed or in progress" described in official handouts. The media labelled the visit tokenism, but undaunted the minister flew on to Kabul for a quick three-hour stopover where she dispensed CDN$14.5 million to create community-based schools for girls and to train female teachers and forked over another CDN$5 million to help 1,500 Afghan women earn a living through tending home gardens.

The federal government was under pressure to show that its humanitarian mission in Afghanistan hadn't been hijacked by conflict. Ottawa's promise of CDN$100 million a year for 10 years (with CDN$6 million being lavished on Kandahar Province alone) was being spent on items and programs as diverse as kites, soccer balls, vaccinations, garbage trucks, textbooks, a generator for the Shrine of the Prophet Muhammad's Cloak, the fortification of flour, 100 bicycles, de-mining programs, women's wellness sessions, and small loans for entrepreneurs. Minute when compared with the money dispensed by the United States Agency for International Development (USAID) and less comprehensive than the funds distributed by Bangladesh's famous BRAC, with its micro-financing and women's education programs, Canadian aid is mainly channelled through several agencies.

These agencies range from the World Bank and the International Red Cross to very Canadian organizations such as CARE Canada (looking after the oldest Canadian aid program — the Kabul Widows), Corrections Canada, the Aga Khan Foundation Canada, the Mennonite Economic Development Association, and Breaking Bread for Women. Micro-financing, well digging, and 50 kilometres of power lines are some of the projects funded in Afghanistan, which is the largest recipient of Canadian aid. CIDA's commitment to social development, adopted in 1997, had moved from physical development to capacity building. The organization had earmarked CDN$9 million for Afghanistan's justice system, with a CDN$6.35 million contract with the International Development Law Organization (IDLO). Based in Italy, IDLO trains judges, prosecutors, and legal-aid lawyers with the aim of increasing protection for women and children. But despite the appearance that Afghanistan is awash in billions of dollars in aid money — and it is true that since 9/11 donors at international conferences have pledged US$15 billion — few have anted up. The consensus is that Afghanistan is being rehabilitated "on the cheap." Figures from the International Monetary Fund show that US$67 a year per

Afghan was spent, compared with other nation-building exercises like Bosnia (US$249) and East Timor (US$256).

"We need to accelerate quick-impact reconstruction projects," General Rick Hillier told the *Toronto Star*. "Saying to the district elders: 'What is it, actually, that you want? What are your priorities here?' Because what we've found is that, in the south, where we're operating, when the elders or the shura take responsibility, when they say this is what we need and now we're going to make sure that the conditions are right for you coming in to help us, they then protect it. Where that's occurred, less than 1 percent of the built stuff will ever be destroyed by the Taliban. Where we, as the international community, go in and just sort of build something without consultation, the Taliban are much more successful at destroying it or blowing it up."

On October 13, 2005, Hillier and Defence Minister Bill Graham presided over a ceremony to bestow the name Camp Nathan Smith on the compound that houses the Canadian Provincial Reconstruction Team outside Kandahar. (Private Nathan Smith of the 3rd Battalion, Princess Patricia's Canadian Light Infantry, was killed on April 17, 2002, at Tarnak Farm.) Taken over from the Americans, the enclosed complex of buildings once housed a jam factory dating back to the Soviet era. The concept of Provincial Reconstruction Teams, or PRTs, originated in the Coalition Humanitarian Liaison Cells that U.S. military forces in Operation Enduring Freedom established in early 2002. The small outposts, dubbed "Chiclets," were staffed by a dozen U.S. Army Civil Affairs soldiers who assessed local humanitarian needs, implemented small-scale reconstruction projects, and established relations with the U.N. Assistance Mission in Afghanistan (UNAMA) and non-governmental organizations already in the field.

Conceived as a way to integrate diplomats, development experts, police officers, and "military assets," the PRT provided a stabilization package that blended security and aid and initiatives to promote governance. The earliest PRTs were in the south under U.S. command and in the north under the British, who opened their first in May 2003 in Mazar-i-Sharif, and a second, smaller PRT, in Meymaneh. Further PRTs were established in Faizabad and Baghlan by Germany and the Netherlands. In 2004, ISAF gradually assumed command of PRTs in both the north, the west, and the south. As of March 2006, there were 23 PRTs in Afghanistan (14 still under Operation Enduring Freedom and nine under ISAF).

Major Ron Leibert was 38 years old, from Manitoba, and an infantry officer with the Princess Patricia's Canadian Light Infantry, originally from 1st Battalion Edmonton. When in Bosnia, he coordinated the distribution of humanitarian supplies and basic services for the U.N. mission. His role in Afghanistan varied only in the details. "In 1999," he said, "when the Serbian forces withdrew, there was no law or services, so we basically helped the locals administer the area. We took care of every detail, from issuing birth certificates to dealing with property issues for the locals. So the Canadian Forces have a long-standing experience in dealing with these sort of issues, usually learned the hard way."

Leibert explained what his PRT did. "It combines four federal government departments — Foreign Affairs, DND, CIDA, and the RCMP under one roof. Despite the name, we aren't strictly centred on reconstruction. The focus is primarily on development in the broadest possible sense. It is a multi-faceted organization that promotes the main areas of concern, which are governance, development, and security. With governance issues we draw on the experience of Foreign Affairs and CIDA in terms of how to govern in an inclusive and democratic manner. In development we are trying to provide the government of Afghanistan with the tools to provide basic services to the public. The Afghan government attempts to provide health care, police security, and good roads, and what we do is bring together here the departments that can help them. Governance is one issue and security is another. The PRT helps with their police — the RCMP officers here work closely with the Afghan National Police to provide mentoring, training, and support.

"The Afghan National Police has not received the same attention and support that the Afghan National Army has, and it faces significant challenges because of that. Glossed over in the media is the tremendous toll in casualties taken by the Afghan police, especially in a combat function, which it is not trained to do. That is not the role of the police. We here in the PRT are trying to help them overcome some of those challenges, such as institutionalized corruption or bad organization, to produce tangible results. We assist in the coordination of police forces and the army so that the former can focus on more policing functions rather than military operations. We are also attempting to professionalize the Afghan police's conduct towards an international standard.

"The PRT is the primary interface between the various Canadian departments here, and we provide the protection to allow them to coordinate on the ground. For example, CIDA's program "Confidence in Government" is designed to strengthen government legitimacy by allowing its representatives to project services into areas that do not have them. The program allows us to put services into areas that, though not completely lawless, are places where the Afghan government has so far been unable to provide basic services. And the military provides CIDA with the facilities, protection, and transport to do so.

"I should mention that while we provide the security, the participation of the Afghan people provides a degree of security in itself. People aren't going to burn down projects they have invested their own time and capital in, so through encouraging this process we basically protect the project itself. It is very difficult to measure success, and it is very hard to judge from one day to the next if the PRT is making any kind of progress. What I can say since I have been in Kandahar is that there has been considerable economic improvement. For example, there is already a lot more commercial activity than when I arrived here six month before. There are improvements in the police force, and a recent command change in this area in police chiefs. The new one is very professional and competent. So we are making progress. Remember that we are working to a timeline that is completely foreign to North Americans. This project we have undertaken is going to take at least 10 to 20 years to produce tangible results. It's an ongoing process that is going to require long-term commitment by the international community.

"What we are attempting to do is really to change ideas. A lot of the problems here are attributable to the conflicts that existed during the Soviet era and during the post-Soviet conflict of the Taliban days — troubles that empowered illegitimate groups to destroy the infrastructure. In destroying traditional leadership structures especially at the district level, they destroyed public confidence in local government. At the same time they empowered warlords, criminals, et cetera, because those sorts of people thrive in such insecure times. Have we done things properly in the past? Certainly not. We have learned the hard way through trial and error. We have taken some wrong turns in the past. Here we are in Afghanistan and we are trying to avoid mistakes by using the lessons learned in the past and make a positive impact."

Captain Tony Petrilli is a CF reservist, which means that not only does he volunteer for general military service but also for a specific mission when positions are open to reservists. His personal reason for accepting the PRT challenge was that he could combine his 20-plus years of civilian experience as an engineer with his 18 years of military experience. Captain Petrilli believed that this blend of skill sets could be used to support the mission in the PRT as a member of the Civil Military Cooperation Detachment (CIMIC Det). One of the teams of the CIMIC Det deployed to Afghanistan with Task Force Orion, the CIMIC team at the PRT consisted of three four-person teams under the operational command of each of the rifle companies. One team was co-located with PRT CIMIC for most of the "Roto," but the remaining two resided at Kandahar Airfield.

"This proved problematic in that we were not able to coordinate our efforts and pass on our learnings," Petrilli remembers. "Regrettably, we could have been that much more effective by the simple act of all being located in one place. This shortcoming was identified and corrected by the next Roto. Within the walls of the PRT, we have Canadian representation from the Department of National Defence, Foreign Affairs, International Trade Canada, the Canadian International Development Agency, the Royal Canadian Mounted Police, and other Canadian police forces, which during my tour was an officer from the Charlottetown Police Force. A constant partner was USAID. During my stay, we had a return of the U.K. Department for International Development [DFID UK, the British. agency that is a counterpart to CIDA] for a period of time, and expressions of interest from Corrections Canada, the U.S. Secretary of State, and the government of the United Arab Emirates. The challenge that the PRT has is to spread prosperity over a large area quickly with limited resources and all within an uncertain and difficult security situation."

What follows is Captain Petrilli's own account of his experiences with the Provincial Reconstruction Team.

The Experiences of CIMIC Within the PRT

The aim of CIMIC is to support the mission through three core functions: liaison with civil actors, coordination of civil support to the military force, and coordination of military support to civil actors. Effects-based operations (EBO) was the focus of CIMIC. All CIMIC activities were measured against a desired effect. The effect categories were governance and justice, security and stability, and development. Higher headquarters set the effect categories.

Much of our ongoing work was with a diverse set of civil actors. This ran the full range from those who had a local interest to national representatives with everything in between. The CIMIC Det also met with district, tribal, and community leaders throughout Kandahar Province. To give a flavour for the diversity of those who visited, here are a few examples: our neighbours who would often call upon us for assistance with water, power, and roads; citizens who came from all parts of the province requesting assistance of all types and magnitude (no scheme was too farfetched, and because we sought to reinforce the authority of the government, we would refer people to local shuras, which were encouraged to engage the government); those who wanted funding to start a private business (circus, eye clinic); NGOs (for example, Afghans for Civil Society run by Rangina Hamidi); international organizations (UNAMA, for example, where we had regular contact with Sonja Bachman, who was the deputy for southern Afghanistan, and Nazia Hussain, who was the human-rights officer); and provincial and local politicians as well as the occasional national official such as the female MP who represented Kandahar Province at the national assembly (Farida Ahmadi).

CIMIC has regular liaison with key individuals in leadership roles in Kandahar and with key institutions that have an important role in the well-being of the population. These included Mayor Osman of Kandahar City and provincial directors of key Government of Afghanistan ministries. Chief among them was Director of Higher Education Dr. Saifi in his capacity as chancellor of Kandahar University; Director of Education Rafiki, who we tried to support as much as possible given the enormity and critical nature of his duties; Director of

Public Health Dr. Pochla, who had Mirwais Hospital under his area of responsibility; and the Ministry of the Interior through Colonel Hussain, who resided at the PRT and provided liaison duties in connection with our focus on Security Sector Reform and the training of the Afghan National Police.

Often individuals or groups of individuals came to our gate. Taking the time to meet and having access to us resulted in a number of opportunities to help, at times, at no cost. A chance meeting between the president of the Kandahar University Student Union and the OC CIMIC Det established a trusting relationship. This relationship was further developed when the 13-member student council was invited to the Kandahar Provincial Reconstruction Team (KPRT) by the commander for a briefing on Canada and Canada's mission in Afghanistan. Some students later came forward to provide information to specialists at the KPRT. Furthermore, liaison with the chancellor of the university identified a need for a water system and a backup power generator. These two projects were underway before our Roto departed. Liaison with the director of Kandahar Technical College led to the identification of projects that received Canadian Expeditionary Force Command (CEFCOM) approval for funding.

Liaison with civil actors is a core function of CIMIC, and liaison played an important role in the early months of the mission. As the focus changed in the latter months to more kinetic operations, the shortage of force protection resources made it exceedingly difficult for CIMIC operators to carry out the same level of liaison. We were fortunate that many came to us at Camp Nathan Smith, but many meetings that should have been carried out were not. We assisted with humanitarian assistance, though we are not in that business. As a military force, we were sometimes the only ones who would travel into an area — and then tentatively. Many of the IOs and NGOs rarely strayed from Kandahar City. Thus we organized Village Medical Outreaches (health clinics) and Women's Wellness Sessions to provide basic education to women as well as pass out material goods such as foodstuffs, clothing, and farming implements that made the life of villagers a little easier.

My primary duty, as the CIMIC projects officer, was to carry out projects using public money and any no-cost initiative that furthered the mission. Projects are not a core function for CIMIC, but they were certainly my focus as an adjunct to the CIMIC aims of civil support to the military force and coordination of military support to civil actors. The commander of the PRT had a sum of money under his Commander's Contingency Fund (CCF), and this was most of the money that I spent as the CIMIC projects officer. One of our goals was to have as much local participation in projects as possible. Every project was carried out using local contractors and labour. That was how we provided economic benefit and expansion to the local economy. Most of the Canadian-funded projects dealt with our focus on short-term security as part of our role in Security Sector Reform. This included the building and upgrading of police stations, the purchasing of equipment and vehicles, the provision of a mechanical repair facility for vehicles, et cetera. Some of the projects were focused on longer-term security that resulted from good health and strong educational institutions. A list of projects and initiatives appears later. I also had multiple duties while staffing short-ages existed and leave-induced shortfalls were experienced. Then there was the bane of my existence — being a duty officer, an undesirable by-product of being an officer. The first months I was triple-tasked: proj-ects officer, CIMIC second-in-command, and duty officer.

The CIMIC Det had the responsibility for all civil military operations in Kandahar Province. To coordinate and "de-conflict" the efforts of all CIMIC and civil affairs teams from other nations, the CIMIC Det carried on with the biweekly CIMIC synchronization meetings established by our predecessors. In these meetings were the other government depart-ment (OGD) partners — CIDA, Department of Foreign Affairs and International Trade (DFAIT), Department for International Development United Kingdom (DFID UK), and USAID — as well as the Japan International Construction System (JICS), the Japan International Cooperation Agency (JICA), UNAMA, the World Health Organization (WHO), and several NGOs.

As Task Force Orion assumed responsibility for the entire province, other national CIMIC organizations began to wind down their operations. The Dutch and French CIMICs withdrew and the U.S. Civil Affairs downsized. In addition to sharing information, the CIMIC syn-chronization meetings were a forum where development ideas could be identified and furthered. One such case was when the CIMIC Det brought to the meeting the needs of Kandahar Technical College. This prompted UNAMA to offer to have the college's syllabus updated by consultants, UNICEF to commit to provide resources for new dormitories, and DFAIT to agree to seek ways that its resources could be applied. CEFCOM initially approved a CCF budget of CDN$100,000 to reconstruct a college building that had been battle-damaged but was meant to house automobile repair and electrical shops.

The need for reconstruction and development was apparent from the outset of the mission. Although, as I have said, projects are not considered a core function of CIMIC, it was clear that in the insurgency environment of Kandahar, CIMIC was the only agency capable of delivering projects in the short term. Much of the focus of the CCF was on Security Sector Reform such as new police stations, renovations to existing police stations, and police equipment. In an effort to broaden the scope of the CCF to more visible projects, the CIMIC Det sought and received CEFCOM approval to conduct projects at Kandahar University, Kandahar Technical College, and Mirwais Hospital. Time and time again when we engaged leaders at the various levels they wanted to see "concrete" results that bettered the lives of the average Afghan. Small projects were targeted at the communities surrounding the KPRT, but this was the proverbial drop in the bucket.

After the experience with managing charitable donations for the palliative care of the young Afghan boy Namatullah, the CIMIC Det wrote the constitution and bylaws to create a Non-Public Fund (NPF) trust account. The fund was called the Matériel Assistance to Afghanistan (MAA) Fund and provided another source of funding, with charitable donations to be used for small humanitarian projects. Before departing, we were able to purchase furniture for classrooms and the staff lounge at the Dand High School after Sergeant Julian Syme of Task Force Orion CIMIC identified the need. The purchase was made with the generous donation of Mr. Race, who gave the CDS a CDN$10,000 cheque and wanted to see it used to help Afghans.

A final source of funding was CDN$70,000 provided from an Information Operations (IO) budget. These funds were used for Village Medical Outreaches (VMOS) to bring basic health care to villages where there was none, Women's Wellness Sessions and the repair of Afghan National Police vehicles in a program called the Maintenance Repair Operation (MRO) project. Finally, a portion of the CCF was set aside for Quick Impact Projects (QIPS) primarily to assist remote areas where the manoeuvre elements operated. Little was achieved in these remote areas due to the ongoing conflict and the lack of contractors willing to operate in the insecure areas.

Support to kinetic operations was a major task of CIMIC in the latter part of the deployment. KPRT CIMIC was tasked to support all VMOs by providing civilian doctors, dentists, and veterinarians in order to put an "Afghan face" on the activity. Requests for village kits of Matériel Assistance (MA), from supplies received from CJTF-76 (Division), to support Task Force Orion were assembled at the KPRT. A village kit consisted of two tri-walls of essential goods such as food, coal, gardening tools, stoves, school supplies, medical supplies, et cetera. These village kits were created to support the rifle companies in their post-kinetic activities, leader engagements, and mitigation of combat operations. Management and organization of the four sea cans of MA at the KPRT fell to Plans Officer Captain Frank Provencher and the two CIMIC drivers. Support for damage control and battle-damage re-mediation became significant due to the numerous operations. To mitigate battle damage, CIMIC had a role in gathering information to allow for the damage to be repaired in due course.

A Day in the Life of CIMIC at the PRT

My personal routine varied and depended on patrols and duty commitments. If it was a typical day, I got up early, went to the gym, and had a run before breakfast. Running was excruciatingly boring because the circuit was short and became repetitive. The official day started at 8:00 a.m. when we had our CIMIC meeting. At 8:30 a.m. (except for Fridays and Sundays when it was skipped or came later respectively) our leadership attended the Commander's Update Briefing (CUB), which later became known as the PUB (PRT Update Briefing) once the PRT was moved to brigade command. The CUB or PUB was the general forum for the daily threat briefing.

The typical day when on-site involved preset meetings (both internal and external) and unannounced drop-in visits. Meeting times with locals were on approximate timings and on Afghan Time. As Westerners, we set our meeting times strictly and often tightly scheduled. Some understood the concept, especially the contractors I dealt with, but many did not. As a result, between the unscheduled meetings and erratic timings, a state of fluid chaos existed. Another on-site activity was duty, which was an after-hour commitment. If we left the camp, every movement from CNS involved a patrol. These had their own tempo. Patrols could be cancelled, delayed, or modified while underway due to operational requirements. Lastly, there were the unknowns, those that were related to being in an active insurgency and being prime targets of that effort.

Shuras were organized for geographic districts or the *ulema* or religious scholars. We attended and participated in as many shuras as possible as a way of understanding the issues. My meetings revolved around various aspects of project administration. Anyone with a shovel was a contractor. In spite of that and the general absence of building codes and standards, there were some very capable contractors. As a result, the capacity to do construction projects existed, especially in the Kandahar City area. There were yet others who I refer to as the "logistics providers," those who could find, purchase, and deliver to the area just about anything money could buy. It could be frustrating to work with the local contractors, but at the same time they were very resourceful.

Alerts were ever-present. There was always a Toyota Corolla that was being used by a suicide bomber to be on the lookout for. Towards the end of our tour there was a volume and consistency of walk-in traffic warning of an imminent attack on CNS. Kandahar Airfield was rocketed regularly, but we managed to be more or less free of this phenomenon, though we were closer to the populace and hence more vulnerable to an attack without the buffer of space KAF had. The neighbouring compound occupied by our local security force had a grenade attack that resulted in four injured. Other than this incident and nearby shots fired on Thursday nights (weddings are celebrated on Thursday and often with shots fired) we managed to stay uneventful and safe within the camp. This I attribute to both our security force, which lived in and knew the surrounding area, and the good relations we kept with the neighbours. Some of the projects and activities that we did were intended to improve the lives of our immediate neighbours. This included having a number of them as employees.

The days collided into one another except for an event that reminded us of what particular day of the week it was. Fridays are the equivalent to our Sundays. Because we did not receive visitors on Friday, we used that day to get caught up with any activity that was falling by the wayside such as the endless paperwork. We arrived at the PRT short-staffed. Furthermore, CIMIC took casualties early on in the tour. We were slowly brought up to strength. Staff fluctuations and leave cycles meant that CIMIC was never at full complement. This meant long, full days.

There were a number of strange bedfellows at the PRT. This came about as a result of the security situation. The PRT had among its residents counter-intelligence staff. Their job was to screen anyone who might be allowed unescorted access to the camp. They also received walk-in traffic that had intelligence information they wanted to pass on. Human intelligence operators who might have more specific interests occasionally visited us. CIMIC had constant interaction with locals, and we turned over any information that we gathered. Our information collection role was a passive one, though. There was, however, one regular supplier of information who was passed on so others could develop the relationship more fully. I called him our CIMIC spy. Other strange bedfellows were the security force led by Colonel Tor Jon that protected the camp and USP&I. The latter was a private security firm that operated in southern Afghanistan, and we kept in touch because it was to our mutual benefit.

There was constant interaction with local nationals, both visitors and employees. This was in contrast to KAF where local nationals were few in number relative to the military population. Much of a typical day was spent meeting with locals. Some made an appointment, but many would just show up at our gate. Those who did call ahead functioned on Afghan Time, in other words they were not as particular about keeping an appointment or arriving on time.

The PRT had at its peak six civilian police officers who, in conjunction with the Military Police Platoon, provided the Afghan National Police with advice and training in cooperation with Colonel Hussain.

He was the representative from the Afghan Ministry of the Interior, which is responsible for police activities. Five were from the RCMP and the sixth was from the Charlottetown police. The civilian police are on year-long tours.

There was a steady stream of VIP visits. This was disruptive but was a break from the everyday. Some of our visitors were the following: President Karzai; Prime Minister Harper; generals and admirals, including the chief of defence staff and CEFCOM commander; ambassadors (Canadian ambassador to Afghanistan and the Japanese ambassador to Afghanistan); and Members of Parliament from Ottawa.

Above all, the PRT was a military unit operating in a hostile environment. Our reconstruction efforts sometimes took a back seat to the military realities. This became very evident when a Special Forces operation was taking place, particularly when it was controlled from our Operations Centre (OC). Those of us on duty had ringside seats. That same sense of priority also came to the forefront when there was a contact in southern Afghanistan and it was blaring over the radio in all its life-and-death drama.

We received donations from all sources. Sometimes they were not appropriate such as foodstuffs that contained pork or baseball caps advertising beer. There was a steady stream of donated school supplies. These low-value shipments did not make much sense from a practical viewpoint but were positive in that they showed that Canadians at home were behind the mission. It was more preferable to send money because, using the school supplies as an example, we could buy a lot more for the money in Kandahar, have a local economic impact, and avoid the shipping that we were often asked to provide. Air-movement capacity was at a premium. We always welcomed high-value/low-volume shipments, as became the case with a donation of medical equipment for Mirwais Hospital. It seemed that most donors wanted some kind of indication that the donation had made it to its destination as opposed to giving to a large charity where one did not know precisely if the donation had actually had an impact. We were able to provide feedback with an email and most often a photo. This direct feedback was highly appreciated.

The PRT would support military operations. This included using our Quick Reaction Force (QRF) to assist where needed. Our mechanics would go out and recover vehicles if they were close to us. We were a secure area that patrols could come to if they needed a place to stretch. Our Military Police would pick up persons under custody (PUCs) for further processing. One PUC who came to us struck me as being no different from any of the contractors I would meet daily. He was well dressed and clean. They had obviously taken him into custody for a reason, and it drove home to me the point that in an insurgency anyone you shook hands with could be the enemy.

Prior to the return of CIDA and DFAIT, their three locally employed initiative officers reported directly to OC CIMIC. They proved to be an invaluable resource, and consideration should be given to allow the CIMIC Det to hire similar knowledgeable resources. With the Terps (interpreters), they provided continuity that was necessary to keep the momentum in an operation when there is turnover every six months as the rotations come and go. We worked closely with the Terps who attended all our meetings and were out on every patrol. They understood the workings of the government where it was functional and took great pains to help us understand their society and how it all came together. We had a particularly difficult time when one of them was struck by an RPG that ultimately resulted in the loss of both his legs below the knee. (Niaz was not only one of our Terps but he was also the son of Colonel Hussain. Colonel Hussain was a shadow of his former self, walking around the camp with a hollow, defeated expression. In time he came to understand that Niaz would recover and remain a productive member of society. We essentially redesigned the PRT to include sidewalks and ramps so that Niaz could move freely within the PRT.)

Patrols were an important part of our getting to know our Area of Responsibility (AOR). As kinetic operations increased, our ability to get out decreased. I was fortunate in that many of my projects involved the police. Captain Drew Greenaway, CO of 1 MP Platoon, had the ability to patrol and proved invaluable in the end as our patrolling resources diminished. Because we had common aims (supporting the Afghan National Police), we worked closely and were able to get things done.

We worked hard at the PRT but made time for recreation. It was easy to lose that balance in an intense environment such as Kandahar City.

Impressions

These are some of my impressions of the KPRT and Afghanistan gathered throughout the time there. The most obvious difference between the Canadian- and U.S.-run PRTS was that we wanted to put an "Afghan Face" on reconstruction efforts. The Americans pretty much handed everything out. People came to the PRT asking for things as if we were Santa's Workshop. Our approach meant that we were there to help Afghans solve their own problems as opposed to having us do it for them. Afghans have to develop the capacity to do it themselves. There is no point in making them dependent on us, since we will eventually leave. By working through their government, we wanted them to develop confidence in their government. This we did by working with various directors of government departments to identify their needs. Unfortunately, there is a deep mistrust of the Afghan government because of its corruption. This is a point the Taliban makes, giving it some legitimacy — that the government is corrupt and that makes them bad Muslims. The Taliban wouldn't still be around if there weren't aspects of its message that resonated with the locals.

Everything was a little more difficult to attain given the key limitation set by the reduced mobility that the security situation imposed. Whether going across the city or 100 metres outside our gate, the need to have force protection slowed things down. I personally had never known such a lack of mobility. In my business life, going to the other side of the world is as easy as making travel arrangements and getting entry visas when required.

Security was the first priority. CIMIC had a role in security by developing relationships with the local nationals and carrying out projects that contributed to short-term security and longer-term stability. The need to conduct operations securely included not only the soldier but extended to our employees. Many of our interpreters went to great lengths to hide the fact that they worked at the PRT. Some had their families well away from Kandahar. They dressed in a more Western way when they were out — for example, wearing ball caps and slacks to look less Afghan. Rightly so. A bus full of employees going to KAF was targeted, with 12 killed and many more injured, including children. Several were family members of our head Terp.

The level of violence in this part of the world is hard to understand from our Canadian frame of reference. Shortly after my return to Canada, the shootings at Dawson College in Montreal took place. I remarked to my colleagues at work that in Kandahar this was a routine occurrence. A Canadian newspaper reported the numbers of Canadians and Afghans killed in Kandahar. For every Canadian killed, approximately 10 Afghans died. In the West we try to live as long a life as possible while maintaining a certain quality of life. In other parts of the world, including Afghanistan, a life is always ready to be ended in martyrdom.

The PRT and CIMIC projects had a Security Sector Reform focus. The prior Roto had made much progress in a short period and had started a significant number of projects and initiatives. Along with the RCMP, the CIMIC Det worked with the Afghan National Police leadership to further advances in Security Sector Reform through the professionalization of the local police. Several projects completed by the CIMIC Det assisted in this endeavour.

The camp was as accessible to Afghans as possible, given the security situation. The camp also provided facilities for meetings. We ran what I called the best restaurant in Kandahar. It was not too difficult to get attendance at a meeting that included a meal afterwards. At times my estimate was that 30 to 40 percent of the daytime occupants of the PRT were locals either directly employed by us or working as contractors. Providing jobs was by far the best way of rebuilding Afghanistan.

The generation that grew up in the madrassas of Pakistan were indoctrinated in hatred and narrow-mindedness. Younger children approached us with smiles and exuberance. They were very open and genuine and wanted to engage in conversation and score the odd giveaway item. The future of Afghanistan rests with the children. Education will figure prominently in the solution. Education will open their minds, provide a genuine choice, and distance them from traditional narrow views of the world. There are those who believe that only boys need to be educated and then only in the Koran, which they insist (sometimes with violence) has all the answers. The road to a better future will be difficult, but there is hope with the children.

The PRT could be effective in this counter-insurgency operation if resourced correctly. If it is equipped with the tools to do the job and a streamlined bureaucracy, it can make a difference. We have to be willing to make the effort and pay the price. Afghanistan is not Disneyland nor will it be resolved in a time frame that makes it understandable to us, be it a rotation, this year in time for Christmas, or before the next election.

Tour Events

Just as I returned from leave prior to my deployment to the PRT on January 16, 2006, we learned about the death of Glyn Berry in a suicide bombing the previous day. Mr. Berry was our Foreign Affairs representative and senior diplomat. This was a significant event for our tour as we came to appreciate later. It resulted in turmoil for the OGDs because it caused Ottawa to re-evaluate the risk to employees other than those working for the Department of National Defence and the RCMP. The final product of this exercise was that the commitment to the rebuilding effort was impaired due to the lack of permanent staffing.

The most significant event for CIMIC was the death of Lieutenant Bill Turner. He was not only a colleague we had trained with intensely but was Canada's first CIMIC fatality. When Niaz was injured, Corporal Eykelenboom was one of the medics on the same patrol. He saved his life. A few short weeks before the tour ended, Corporal Eykelenboom lost his life to an IED attack that targeted the patrol he was riding with near Spin Boldak. This was one fatality that had me thinking hard. Perhaps it was because we were all closer to home than we had been in seven months. Perhaps it was the pain of the family that was so visible when we saw the repatriation and funeral on TV. Perhaps it was that he was committed to helping others, including anyone who meant him harm, as is the duty of any medic in a combat situation who treats friend and foe. Perhaps it was the gruesome end that he met.

Initially, operations were focused on Kandahar City and Gumbad. IEDs dominated the first part of the tour but eventually the focus was on kinetic operations, especially what we now call the Battle of Panjwai. The shift had a pronounced effect on the operations we were able to carry out. Resources were scarce, and simple matters like getting out of the camp were unattainable.

Kandahar PRT Projects and Initiatives

The PRT pursued a number of projects. Most of the Canadian-funded projects were done using Department of National Defence funds. I make a distinction between a project and an initiative. A project is where public monies are being spent. An initiative is pursued at low or no cost except for the time and effort of the individual involved. Every project had to have an Afghan Face. This meant that we wanted the Afghans to be seen to be the ones who successfully concluded the project. The purpose was to have Afghans gain confidence in their government and to get into the habit of turning to it when they had a need. This was accomplished by identifying projects in cooperation with the appropriate director of the government department involved, using local contractors and in the end having a public ceremony to inaugurate the beginning of the project with local government officials. Afghans tend to turn to aid agencies and other social welfare agencies such as their tribe far more quickly than the government. This happens because the government generally lacks a presence, especially in the rural areas, and when it is present, it is under-resourced and typically corrupt.

Completed Projects

The projects listed below were completed. The CCF funded all but the Governor of Kandahar LAN Project, which was funded by DFAIT:

- Enhancements were carried out on existing ANP Substations Numbers 3, 4, 5, and 8. The ANP called them substations, but we would refer to them as police stations. In any event, we stuck with the confusing terminology. The projects consisted of various upgrades to make the police substations more secure. These had been built by the United States, but a number of improvements were identified, for example, the addition of detention cells so that the RCMP could train the ANP in the handling and processing of detainees.

- The construction of the 100 Call Centre located at ANP HQ. Afghanistan has a 100 number that is similar in concept to our 911 emergency call centres. We configured a room in the police HQ and handed it over to the RCMP, which coordinated with the Germans to add the equipment and provide the training.

• Also at ANP HQ was a project to construct an ammunition and weapons storage point to give the police a place to store their weapons and ammunition. Weapons and ammunition are abundant and not well accounted for in Afghanistan. This project made it possible for the ANP to put some order in its house. The construction of the ammunition consolidation point at Camp Shirzai secured ammunition formerly stored at ANA 15 Div. More about that project later.

• In cooperation with the RCMP, basic policing equipment was purchased, including clothing. This was distributed to police officers who were registered and had undergone basic training at the Regional Training Centre, a facility created to train the ANP. This project was known as the ANP Equipment Fielding Project.

• The purchase of a prisoner transport van for the Ministry of Justice was undertaken after a request from the ministry. This was used by the Kandahar City jail to bring prisoners to court and to bring them to Mirwais Hospital when the prison clinic could not treat them.

• Kandahar City did not have the means to remove solid waste. As a result, Mirwais Hospital piled it on-site with obvious health risks. The purchase of a solid-waste-removal dump truck for the hospital was identified by the hospital as its top requirement, even more of a priority than the purchase of medical equipment and supplies. Although this was an urgent need, no one stepped up to the plate. The PRT commander used the CCF to purchase the truck.

• The Kandahar Fire Department Equipment Fielding Project served a purpose similar to that of the ANP Equipment Fielding Project. The fire department is part of the ANP. One fire station in Kandahar City with 20 firefighters and one working truck was expected to cover the entire province. We purchased some basic firefighting equipment as a start to address this badly resourced organization.

• Kandahar University has medical students doing practical training at Mirwais Hospital. Information technology equipment was purchased such as computers and furniture, and Internet connectivity was provided to give the students the ability to go online to research various treatment options.

• When the generator at the Shrine of the Prophet Muhammad's Cloak failed, we were approached to purchase a new one. This we did willingly.

• The power supply in the province was particularly unreliable, which prevented students at Kandahar University from attending to their studies. A generator to provide more reliable power was bought.

• Basic water services were lacking at the Kandahar City Prison to supply a number of areas, including the Women's Detention Area. Plumbing was provided to assist with basic sanitation.

• The governor of Kandahar lacked the means to communicate with the directors of each government department that administered the province. The LAN Project included the installation of networked computers with Internet connectivity and the hiring of a network administrator to support the network.

• Twelve new ANP patrol vehicles were purchased to improve policing abilities. These were equipped with the basic policing equipment to allow the police the mobility they required to do their work.

Various small projects were carried out to improve water, power, and road facilities in the neighbourhood. We referred to the neighbours as Boraka Village, but that was inaccurate in that there were many villages around the camp that benefited from the projects. The following CCF-funded projects were underway at the end of the Roto:

• The construction of ANP Substation Number 9 was started in January 2006. This station was situated to improve control over one of the northern entrances to Kandahar City. Our bureaucratic ineffectiveness resulted in this project being stalled.

• The construction of ANP Substation Number 7 was started during our Roto. This station was situated to improve control over the western entrance to Kandahar City.

• A number of improvements were carried out to enhance the Kandahar University campus. Power from the grid was sporadic. The backup power generator previously purchased was given a building as part of this project. Water had to be trucked in, since they lacked a potable water supply. The water supply on the university side was not potable, but the water from the mosque was, so we obtained permission to access the mosque water for the students of the university. There is justice in using water from the mosque (founded by Mullah Omar, a person dedicated to keeping people ignorant) to help provide education and enlightenment to the students of Kandahar University.

• The purchase of Light Up the World (LUTW) solar lighting packages was done to stimulate some economic development, especially among the most disadvantaged. The LUTW Foundation is an initiative by a University of Calgary professor to bring light to remote and underdeveloped parts of the world. The units consist of a photovoltaic solar panel, a battery, and LED lights that are highly efficient. They are intended to be affordable. Solar power is viable in this part of the world, and there is room for additional applications such as solar panels for street lighting and well pumps.

The following Information Operations–funded projects were underway at the end of the Roto:

• The ANP is hampered by a lack of mobility necessary to carry out basic patrolling tasks. Part of the shortcoming is a general lack of vehicles. However, another aspect is the ANP's inability to keep the vehicles it has roadworthy. The ANP Mechanical Repair Operation (MRO) exists to provide mechanical repair abilities that are not organic to the ANP. Located at the Kandahar PRT, the MRO provides the ANP with the external capability to keep its vehicles in good working order so that they may be available to support the ANP's operational needs. The PRT provides the following: facilities and tools; operation staff with non-dedicated CF management and supervision; dedicated locally employed mechanics to carry out repairs; procurement and financial administration support; and a rented vehicle to deliver assemblies to specialty repair shops and pick up parts and materials.

Village Medical Outreaches were conducted to provide basic medical care. They were often combined with the distribution of matériel assistance:

• Women's Wellness and Information Sessions were carried out to provide women with education on basic needs. This included fundamentals such as hygiene.

A number of no- or low-cost initiatives were also completed. Providing gifts for local employees during important Afghan holidays demonstrates respect for Afghans. Nowruz is the celebration of the new year and coincides with the spring equinox (March 21). Although it originated in ancient Persia and is not an Islamic festival, it continues to be celebrated because it is the natural calendar celebration of the renewal of life. The PRT has recognized significant events in the Afghan calendar by purchasing a food basket for each employee. This was done in the past for such events as the Eid al Fitr, which is the celebration that follows Ramadan. We also identified, with the help of the local mosques, 100 or so of our neediest neighbours and put together a similar food basket for them.

The donation of foodstuffs to the Ministry of Public Health's Supplementary Feeding Program at the polyclinic for pregnant and nursing mothers was an opportunity to use some of our surplus foodstuffs for a good cause. Our kitchen had a surplus of food that was left over from the rotation that we were taking over from. That, in addition to other non-perishable foods that CIMIC had in storage, was sent to the polyclinic in Kandahar. The Supplementary Feeding Program is aimed at women who are pregnant. Afghanistan has one of the highest mortality rates of children dying at childbirth and mothers dying during childbirth. The program targets this unfortunate demographic. We had approximately 13 tri-walls (cardboard boxes that sit on a standard pallet) that required two Jingle Trucks to move.

In order to collect information gathered in the province, a CIMIC database was developed and maintained. This allowed us to capture and pass on information about Kandahar so that succeeding CIMIC Detachments would have a resource to refer to.

The donation of school backpacks to Qabayelo School was an example of the support provided to the province's director of education. This was part of an ongoing effort to build up school supplies for the students and teachers of the province so that they had the basic means to gain an education. The story of Qabayelo School is illustrative of the repression practised by the Taliban.

The PRT donated gifts and food to the attendees of International Women's Day celebrations. Celebrating International Women's Day in this part of the world is an advanced concept.

Early in the mission, the CIMIC operators at the KPRT met with the Industrial Association of Kandahar, which led to the development of a good working relationship and brought about a no-cost recycling contract with one of its member companies and the KPRT. We collected plastic bottles, aluminium cans, and Styrofoam sheets for recycling. Investigations were started to see if this could be introduced to KAF.

The encouragement of education in the face of the Taliban's efforts to deny it was an important effort. It took the form of the donation of bicycles to recognize academic achievers. One hundred bikes were given to the director of education so that he could reward students who had achieved academic excellence in the province.

The Matériel Assistance to Afghanistan Fund was created to offer a way for Canadians to donate money to assist the mission in Afghanistan. A Task Force Afghanistan Committee comprised of personnel from the PRT and the task force manages it. The money can be spent on matériel that can help improve the quality of life in Afghan communities. For example, more than $US7,000 was spent to purchase furniture for a high school in the Dand district.

A teacher was provided to the women and children detained in Kandahar City Prison using private donations. These donations came from a group of individual soldiers who saw the need to help a group of people who would not get help otherwise.

Highways 1 and 4 were in need of security improvements to make them safer by increasing the police presence. We provided project management support in the form of liaison with the ANP and our engineering service provider. This project was at its initial stages and preliminary work was started.

Similar solid-waste-disposal issues existed at the prison as those that transpired at the hospital. A cooperative agreement was entered into between the Ministry of Public Health and the Ministry of Justice to use the solid-waste-removal dump truck at Mirwais Hospital to remove waste from the prison. Another similar cooperative agreement between the Ministry of Religious Affairs and the Ministry of Higher Education was signed, this time to use the existing water supply at the Eid Gah Mosque for the university. As part of the arrangement, an ablution facility was built for the mosque's faithful.

The resources the fire department possessed to carry out its duties were insufficient in general, but the current station was particularly lacking. Conceptual drawings for a new Kandahar City Fire Station were commissioned. Efforts were started to get a basic design to approach potential funding sources. One source approached was the New York Fire Department because of the link between the September 11, 2001, attacks in New York City and the Kandahar connection to Osama bin Laden.

Various donors were supported in the local distribution of donated goods. The sources were varied. Books with Wings donated textbooks for Kandahar University; the City of Langford Fire Department contributed firefighting equipment; and others gave medical equipment (Alberta), hospital bed linen (Camp Mirage), soccer jerseys, et cetera. All addressed the vast needs of Kandahar.

We carried out coordination with U.S. CERP (Commander's Emergency Response Program) to nominate various projects to this funding source. The CERP teams had a better ability to get projects done and greater funding. Some needs were addressed by passing the projects to our U.S. counterparts.

Captain Demiray (also referred to as Imam or Padre) is currently the only Muslim padre in the Canadian Forces. He was part of our Roto and did outstanding work by establishing relationships with local clerics. We purchased a number of Korans for presentation by Captain Demiray. The gift of Korans and the fact that we had our own imam were gestures of respect that demonstrated our understanding of the importance of religion to our hosts.

Securing Sources of IEDS

The Afghan New Beginnings Program (ANBP) is an Afghan-led effort with significant support from the United Nations Development Programme (UNDP). The program consists of two thrusts: the Disbandment of Illegally Armed Groups (DIAG) to disarm and reintegrate former combatants, and the Ammunition and Technical Section, which focuses on securing the large amount of ordnance that is freely available in Afghanistan. The CIMIC team at the PRT secured funding from the CCF to build an Ammunition Consolidation Point (ACP) at the Afghan National Army's Camp Shirzai to secure ammunition formerly stored insecurely. Once secure, the munitions at the ACP could be accounted for and distributed to legitimate users such as the army and police. The bulk of the munitions consolidated were stored at the 15 Division location situated in the northeast part of Kandahar City.

While there were other participants, Canada contributed most of the materials and labour to construct the ACP. These included the engineering drawings for the facility, labour provided by our engineers to level the site and fill the HESCO barriers, funding a contractor to string barbed wire on the HESCO barriers, and the purchase and delivery of the sea containers used for the actual storage of the ammunition. This CCF-funded project provided a safe, secure, and centralized storage site for more than 40 truckloads of ammunition. The project resulted in the removal of a significant source of explosives that was known to be used to create IEDS that threatened the lives of our soldiers and the local population.

At an approximate cost of $CDN60,000, it was arguably the most effective money spent to buy security for our troops and to safeguard the local national lives that were typically lost when our troops were targeted. It was noted in a discussion with UNDP that the ammunition stored at 15 Division was the largest single accumulation of unsecured ordnance in southern Afghanistan. This project never did make it onto the public radar. No matter. The right thing got done. Many good stories such as this one took place but were never reported.

The Public Project: The Story of Little Namatullah Zaman

This story is about a six-year-old boy named Namatullah Zaman who showed up at our gate on February 18, 2006, with his grandfather, looking for urgent medical assistance. Captain Adrian Norbash, our camp doctor, diagnosed him with terminal cancer with approximately one month to live. One of the soldiers (Corporal Brian Sanders) contacted his church (North Edmonton Christian Fellowship or NECF), which raised CDN$10,000 literally overnight. We had most of the Canadian media at the PRT at that time. That was before fighting got underway. CTV's Lisa LaFlamme and Steve Chao produced stories that brought Namatullah's plight to the attention of Canadians. It was a big story in Canada that resulted in an outpouring of generous donations. I only became aware of the reaction in Canada because my sister brought it to my attention. Ironic, since the story was happening a stone's throw from my workplace, but that was what the intensity of our days was like.

Namatullah headed out early one morning, and the media was there to see him off, such was the empathy this little boy's plight stirred in Canadians. Included was the arranging of foot surgery for Taj Mohammad, the attentive grandfather of Namatullah who remained with him throughout his stay in the hospital in Lahore, Pakistan. The church identified a hospital that was able to provide the necessary care. As the CIMIC representative, I was tasked with getting Namatullah to Shaukat Khanum Hospital in Lahore where he received palliative care at a facility that specialized in cancer treatment and possessed Western medical standards. CIMIC supported the needs of Namatullah and his family by identifying an NGO that could provide someone to act as a patient-care attendant and assist the family members who accompanied Namatullah.

Along the way fund transfers were arranged to provide money for medical treatment, living expenses, transport, and ultimately for the funeral. Namatullah only lived for one month before succumbing to the cancer. He returned to Kandahar when it looked as if he was in remission. In the end, we didn't catch the cancer early enough. We suspected this all along but set out to make his remaining days comfortable and relieve him from his state of constant pain as he made his final journey. Namatullah's legacy was that he sensitized Canadians to the poor state of health care in this part of the world.

The Information Operations (IO) Battle

There are two military groups whose function is to communicate the events that take place in the operational zone. They are Public Affairs and Psy Ops. Public Affairs is responsible for keeping those at home informed, and Psy Ops has as its audience the local population. IO is tasked with the coordination of efforts that involve information.

We communicate using a full spectrum of media outlets to the local population. Peace Radio, Peace TV, and the Peace Paper are used by the Coalition to get key messages out. These were run by CJTF-76, the Operation Enduring Freedom divisional command, and were taken over by ISAF when we transitioned over to NATO command. Radio is, by a fair margin, the most popular medium. An educated guess would be that 80 to 90 percent of the citizens of Kandahar Province listen to radio, and this seems to be true of both men and women. In the city and surrounding districts, there are local FM stations with a strong listenership. In the more remote districts, there is a reliance on shortwave stations such as BBC World Service. Also, radio ownership on a household basis is fairly high.

Kandahar City has a government-run television station, and there is a fair degree of television viewership in the city, though the degree of ownership on a household basis is relatively low. Lastly, there is the print media. There are two major newspapers in the city, one of which is owned by the government and is produced every other day, and a private

From right, Prime Minister Stephen Harper, Defence Minister Gordon O'Connor, Chief of Defence Staff General Hillier, Ambassador to Afghanistan David Sproule, and Commander Regional Command South Brigadier-General David Fraser address the media at Kandahar Airfield during the first official visit to Afghanistan by the prime minister and defence minister in March 2006. Photo by Sergeant Roxanne Clowe, Combat Camera.

The RG-31 armoured patrol vehicle is the newest acquisition of the Canadian Forces. It made its first appearance in Afghanistan in March 2006. Photo by Sergeant Carole Morissette, Task Force Afghanistan Roto 1.

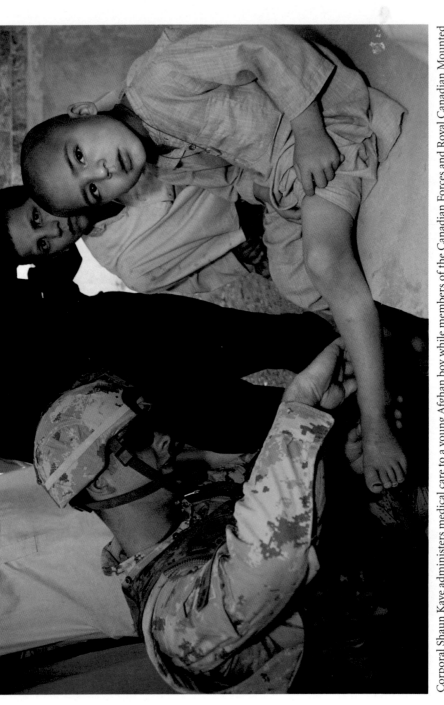

Corporal Shaun Kaye administers medical care to a young Afghan boy while members of the Canadian Forces and Royal Canadian Mounted Police conduct a presence patrol in Arghandab in April 2006. Photo by Sergeant Carole Morissette, Task Force Afghanistan Roto 1.

Superintendent Wayne Martin of the Royal Canadian Mounted Police attends a meeting in May 2006 with Kandahar Province Chief of Police Abdul Malik Wahidi. The occasion marks the official handover of the newly built ammunition and weapons storage point located within the compound of Afghan National Police Headquarters. Photo by Sergeant Carole Morissette, Task Force Afghanistan Roto 1.

Foreign Affairs Minister Peter MacKay takes part in the dedication of the Glyn Berry Room at the Camp Nathan Smith Kandahar Provincial Reconstruction Team in May 2006. Photo by Sergeant Carole Morissette, Task Force Afghanistan Roto 1.

Newly arrived Canadian soldiers with ISAF listen to a threat-assessment briefing at Kabul International Airport in July 2003. Photo by Sergeant Frank Hudec, Combat Camera.

Aided by an American Chinook helicopter, members of A Battery of the Royal Canadian Horse Artillery from Shilo, Manitoba, practise lifting one of their new M777 guns at Kandahar Airfield in April 2006. Photo by Master Corporal Doug Desrochers, Task Force Afghanistan Roto 1.

The Kandahar Provincial Reconstruction Team's Captain Julie Roberge converses with Qayum Karzai, an Afghan parliament member, during a press conference of five governors of Afghanistan's southern provinces in Kandahar City in April 2006. The meeting was about security, reconstruction, and unity of effort. Photo by Sergeant Carole Morissette, Task Force Afghanistan Roto 1.

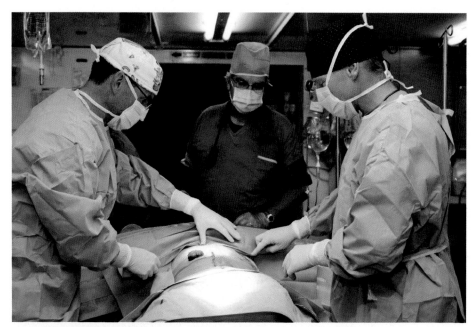

In April 2006 medical staff at the Canadian-led Multinational Medical Unit at Kandahar Airfield provide care to an injured Afghan National Army soldier who received a gunshot wound. Photo by Sergeant Gerben van Es, Task Force Afghanistan Roto 1.

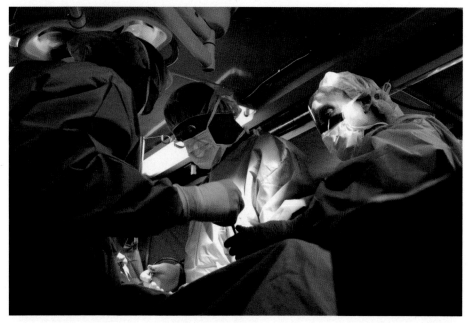

From the left, Canadian Forces Dr. Major James Wagg, Danish Dr. Major Berth Larson, and operating room technician Master Seaman Bill Pritchett perform surgery in the Canadian-led Multinational Medical Unit at Kandahar Airfield in June 2006. Photo by Master Corporal Robert Bottrill, Combat Camera.

Major Andy "Cookie" Cook, aircraft commander of a Canadian CC-130 Hercules, enjoys a Tim Hortons iced cappuccino in July 2006, minutes before takeoff from Kandahar Airfield. Photo by Master Corporal Robert Bottrill, Combat Camera.

Ramp ceremony at Kandahar Airfield in August 2006 for Master Corporal Jeffrey Walsh, who was with the PPCLI from CFB Shilo in Manitoba. Photo by Master Corporal Doug Desrochers, Task Force Afghanistan Roto 1.

Canadian soldiers pay tribute to fallen comrades Warrant Officer Frank Mellish, Warrant Officer Richard Nolan, Sergeant Shane Stachnik, and Private Mark Graham during a ramp ceremony held at Kandahar Airfield in September 2006. Photo by Sergeant Lou Penney, Task Force Afghanistan, Operation Athena.

The remains of Sergeant Shane Stachnik are received during a solemn repatriation ceremony on the ramp at 8 Wing/CFB Trenton on September 6, 2006. Sergeant Stachnik, a member of 2 Combat Engineer Regiment, based in Petawawa, Ontario, was killed on September 3, 2006, fighting against Taliban insurgents west of Kandahar City. Photo by Corporal Simon Duchesne.

At a parade representing the authority transfer in the summer of 2006 from Coalition to NATO/ISAF of the southern provinces of Afghanistan, four military men salute as the parade and colours are presented: from left to right, Abdul Rahim Wardak, Afghanistan's minister of defence; Lieutenant-General Karl Eikenberry, commander of Coalition forces; Lieutenant-General David Richards, commander NATO/ISAF; and Major-General Benjamin Freakley, Coalition operational commander. Photo courtesy of NATO.

Two young girls are curious about Canadian Private Jason Taylor, a member of 5 Platoon, 2 Section, as he patrols the outskirts of the Provincial Reconstruction Team site in Kandahar in August 2005. Photo by Sergeant Jerry Kean.

A Leopard C2 tank from Charles Company Combat Team, 1st Battalion, The Royal Canadian Regiment Battle Group (1 RCR BG), rolls out of FOB Ma'Sum Ghar en route to Howz-e-Madad in Kandahar Province in December 2006. Photo by Captain Edward Stewart, Joint Task Force Afghanistan, Operation Athena Roto 2, 1 RCR BG.

Left to right: Prime Minister Stephen Harper with Vaira Vīķe-Freiberga of Latvia and NATO Secretary-General Jaap de Hoop Scheffer in Riga in late November 2006 at the NATO Summit. Photo courtesy of NATO.

Triage on the flight line: a Royal Air Force Chinook delivers Canadian casualties. Photo by Major James. Bradley, deputy commanding officer, Role 3 Multinational Medical Unit, Kandahar Airfield.

Soldiers of Bravo Company, 1st Battalion, The Royal Canadian Regiment Battle Group (1 RCR BG), receive Christmas greetings on December 24, 2006, from their company officers and the battle group commanding officer before getting their food served to them by Chief of Defence Staff General Rick Hillier at Strong Point West in Kandahar Province. Photo by Captain Edward Stewart, Joint Task Force Afghanistan, Operation Athena Roto 2, 1 RCR BG.

newspaper that is produced weekly. With an urban literacy rate around 40 percent (much lower for women) and a rural literacy rate of 15 to 20 percent, these papers have a very small circulation of between 1,500 and 3,000 per issue. That being said, this type of media is valued among the elites. One of the clever items that we give out is a radio, and at a cost of $US20 each, we can pass out a significant number to the local population. They are battery-powered and solar-powered and can be cranked to provide dynamo power. The radios have AM, FM, and shortwave capabilities. The front of the radios has the Peace Radio frequencies screened on for quick reference. These radios are highly sought after, and we pass out as many as we can to help get out the message.

Canadian media were embedded throughout the operation. They reported events to the Canadian public within the boundaries set by operational security. "The infidel comes to Afghanistan to suppress Islam." That was the accusation made by Mullah Dadullah Lang on the front page of the *Globe and Mail*. Nothing, in my opinion, epitomizes what novices we are at the IO game more than this episode. Our actions on the ground said otherwise, but who will know unless we proactively communicate what we are doing. There were a notable number of projects that assisted religious institutions as described under the projects' heading. We have a lot to learn about IO. The Taliban are experienced practitioners of IO.

In the summer of 2006, RCMP Superintendent Wayne E. Martin was the police adviser at the Kandahar PRT. When Superintendent Martin arrived in Kandahar, he was amazed to see local police officers patrolling Kandahar's streets in flip-flops. On January 15, 2006, Martin was in the convoy hit by a suicide bomber who killed Glyn Berry. The PRT's conference room was named in Berry's honour. Martin's job was to train between 600 and 700 Afghan police officers, and he likened the task to building a house, with he and his men at the "foundation stage." What follows are his thoughts on the PRT.

"The RCMP," Superintendent Martin says, "was brought here by the Canadian government to deal with the local police situation. Our role, as part of the Kandahar PRT, is to assist the Afghan police. We offer them some training programs and are here to advise, mentor, and monitor their activities, and finally we also equip them to a limited extent. We work in concert with other countries in this. The Germans have the lead through a bilateral agreement and have a long history of working here. The Americans bring a big development budget to the law-enforcement table and are heavily involved.

"Currently, we are six on the ground, including one member of the Charlottetown municipal police. I emphasize that the RCMP doesn't work alone. We are the conduit, if you will, of international police development. The programs that work well are those where we can interact with the Afghans themselves. The ones that give you the most satisfaction are the training programs, and we have a number here. They vary all the way from training in firearms to motorcycle riding, which we did in cooperation with CF personnel. Also, we provide training in basic rudimentary safety tips. We have also done patrol tactics and small-unit tactics. An important partner in this is the CF military police, which has a strong presence here. They give us the mobility with air patrols that allow us to get around, as well as provide their expertise in small-unit tactics. In the Western world, at least, civilian police patrols rarely get attacked by RPGs. That's a routine occurrence here, an almost daily event for the Afghan police. The ultimate goal is to have a police force civilianized, but in order get to that state, they do need small-unit military tactics to survive.

"Other things we do is train them how to operate checkpoints, how to conduct vehicle searches, how to conduct personnel searches in the cultural environment you have here. Also how to handle IED situations. Afghans tend to be very cavalier in their handling of unexploded bombs. We teach them how to cordon off the area and wait until the experts arrive.

"There aren't that many female police here in the country. I have interacted with a couple of them at ANP headquarters where they perform office duties, though there's one involved in forensics. Women working outside the home is so new here, and policing is a traditional male role. It isn't a career that's traditional for females in this society. It will take time for that to change.

"We don't get involved with salaries or promotions. [Attempting to centralize authority in Kabul, the Afghan government has given control of the ANP to the Ministry of the Interior instead of the provincial governors.] That's up to the Afghan government. There has been a recent initiative to increase them. The German government has the lead in police reorganization here and are working on pay and rank structuring with them. [Now ANP officers can collect their salaries from a bank rather than from the local governor. Kabul is working on banning bonuses paid to the police by the governor/warlord.] They are also working on reform in rank — like how many generals you need here and how many constables you need at this station, that sort of thing.

"We have built a local police station with the Commander's Contingency Fund using dollars out of the Canadian Forces. It's north of the PRT in an area of the city that's been troublesome for the local citizens. The station abuts near the mountains and is an entry point not for insurgents but criminals, as well. We located it strategically on high ground on a main road where it gives a good overview of the north end of the city. We intend on using it as a training detachment. Canada has 12 new police trucks that have also been purchased through the Contingency Fund, and they will be handed over to the ANP in the next while.

"There is a serious problem of mobility within the ANP. The problem is that the ANP police vehicles don't get regular maintenance. One of the problems is getting funds through the Afghan government for repairs, so when the vehicles break down they tend to sit in a police station yard and no one goes out on patrol. If it's a repair that's manageable cost-wise, we will repair the trucks here in the PRT and put them back on the road. Thus, the police get their mobility back. It's more economical than buying them new ones, and the Afghans learn the idea of responsibility and of maintaining vehicles. Best of all, we have hired some Afghan mechanics and apprentices to maintain the trucks, so we are feeding back into the local economy.

"The Canadian government is committed to the PRT until 2009, so we'll be following up by keeping in contact with all the stations we deal with and all the training programs in order to see what's been successful and what can be improved. Finally, I'm beginning to see that this is an evolutionary process where change comes gradually. Just as with most government departments in Afghanistan, the police have suffered institutional decay over the past 30 years of war, of insurrection, of strife. The infrastructure is very weak right now, and they are not alone. You can take any government department where you can say yes, it needs help in equipment and training, but look at what it's been through. I would suggest that we take our successes where we can find them. The PRT has only been a Canadian endeavour for a few months, and we are making progress. Some people might say at a glacial rate, but in this society it's still progress."

"Without Flash, Glitz, or Bravado"

In January 1841, when the frostbitten British columns retreated through the passes making for the safety of India, Afghan tribesmen picked the Redcoats off with their long-muzzled flintlock *jezails*.[1] Not only were they better marksmen than the British, but their *jezails* far outranged the British muskets, which had remained unchanged since the American War of Independence. As a young officer on the Malakand Field Force in 1896, Winston Churchill marvelled at the ingenuity of the Afghan tribesmen in obtaining weapons. Observing a rudimentary disarmament program, he wrote that of 100 Martini-Henry rifles surrendered by the Afghans, a third bore the British army stamp. Churchill knew they had formerly been "cut up into three pieces under European supervision." What amazed (and frightened) the British army in Churchill's day was that the latest Lee-Metford rifles recently supplied to British troops with their "expansive Dum Dum" (Churchill's own words) bullets had fallen into the hands of the enemy and were being used against the Guides, the British/Indian troops who protected the frontier. "It was a strange instance of the tireless efforts of Supply to meet Demand," the future British prime minister wrote. More than a century later his observations continue to hold true.

Guns, whether flintlocks, rifles, or AK-47s, have always been part of Afghan culture — to be fired in the air instead of firecrackers at weddings and celebrations. Even today it is a rare household in the Afghanistan/Pakistan region that doesn't possess at least one firearm. An integral part of Pashtun culture, especially in the tribal areas, the ownership of guns was a tradition fostered by the British and their successors, the Pakistani government, for their own purposes. Before the tsunami of arms flooded into the country in 1980, the traditional Afghan weapon was the locally made .303 bolt-action rifle. Designed by Lee-Enfield in the 1890s, it was used by Canadian infantrymen in both world wars. British colonial administrators recognized that the Pashtuns loved guns as much as certain American males worshipped cars, so they encouraged gunsmiths along the North-West Frontier Province to manufacture them. It kept tribes on both sides of the border from importing more sophisticated weapons like machine guns. Thus, when the first Soviet tanks rolled across the Oxus River in 1979, tribal leaders had little else to fight them with. "There were seven or eight of us in the beginning," one recalled. "We had a shotgun, a musket, some swords, and knives."

But early into the Soviet invasion, Western media noted that resistance groups were quick to upgrade to the latest imports: AK-47s and RPG-7s from Egypt, recoilless rifles like the Chinese-made 82 mm B-10, and sometimes the odd FN 7.62 or Heckler & Koch G-3 from the Gulf States.[2] As their fathers and grandfathers had before them, village gunsmiths working away in mini-factories on the Pakistani border turned out knock-offs of firearms at bargain prices. When the Soviets withdrew, the CIA-supplied arms caches were never reclaimed by the Americans, and the rifles and semi-automatics served as templates for another generation of Pashtun gunsmiths. In 2006, with an imitation repeating rifle selling for less than US$50 and a G-3 semi-automatic for US$100 in Darra Adam Kheil, a village on the Pakistani/Afghan border, there was little need for the Taliban to go elsewhere. More than a century after Churchill's observation, the ISAF forces were learning what the Afghan government in Kabul has always known: an endless supply of militant Islamists came with an equally inexhaustible supply of weapons.

As for more sophisticated hardware, memorable to television viewers in the 1980s were the staged photo shoots of mujahideen driving captured Soviet tanks and BTR-60 armoured personnel carriers. While these were of little use to the freedom fighters (or their original owners) against the Soviet fighter-bombers and helicopter gunships, the guerrillas did rely on seized, donated, or bought 12.7 mm heavy Soviet machine guns and 14.5 mm ZPU-2s. The breakthrough in the unequal struggle against the armoured Hind gunships took place in January 1982, with the first use of captured Soviet SAM-7s (shoulder-launched surface-to-air missiles). After that the Russians ensured the missiles didn't fall into Afghan hands — government or guerrilla — and in any case, the average tribesman found them too difficult to use. Not so the American equivalent to the Russian SAM-7.

Just as the longbows of Welsh archers transformed warfare by bringing down French armoured knights at the Battle of Agincourt in 1415, so, too, did the introduction of the FIM-92 Stinger in 1983 change combat in Afghanistan. The mujahideen's lack of anti-aircraft weapons caused the United States to supply them with an estimated 2,000 to 2,500 Stingers, allowing them to shoot down an estimated 300 Russian aircraft, many of which were armoured helicopter gunships. Pakistan's Inter-Services Intelligence was put in charge of handing them out, which explains why Ahmed Shah Massoud later claimed they were only available to him at the end of the conflict and all he had were eight, which he sold back to the CIA. Most of the Stingers (by then non-functional) were later repurchased from the warlords by the Bill Clinton administration for between US$80,000 and $150,000 each.[3] Although *Jane's Defence Weekly* reported that the missiles were too old to be effective, as late as January 2005, Afghan intelligence officials were still trying to buy them back — both Stingers and Soviet-era SAM-7s.

Other legacies of the Soviet war in Afghanistan were a plentiful supply of Russian-designed Strela-2M rockets, RPG-7 anti-tank grenade launchers, and TM-57 anti-tank mines. Relatively simple to use and maintain, all were available from stocks of the former Soviet Union and were paid for by the drug trade, which made any arms embargo by the United Nations useless. But, for the most part, the war against the Taliban in the 21st century has been dominated by improvised explosive devices (IEDS).[4] Sometimes radio-controlled, as RCIEDS, they can be buried in highways and detonated with a radio transmitter — anything from a cell phone to a commercially available garage door opener — sending an activation signal to a radio receiver. Cheaper than committing troops to ambush an enemy convoy, IEDS are the weapons of choice for the new generation of Taliban, maximizing damage, instilling fear, and terrorizing victims. Worst of all are suicide improvised explosive devices (SIEDS), which in Afghanistan are divided into human-borne suicide IEDS (SIEDS) and vehicle-borne suicide IEDS (VBIEDS). A recent addition to the current war, these devices are thought to have been imported by Arabs and Pakistanis. Since the suicide terrorist is unconcerned about capture, interrogation (including torture), or trial and imprisonment, there is little in the way of deterrent for either. The only protection against either IEDS or SIEDS for a vehicle convoy, as the Canadian Forces have discovered, is armour.

Ultimately, the enemy's greatest weapon isn't IEDS, rockets, or RPGS, but its faith in martyrdom. As brave as the fighters of the French Resistance were during World War II, none were suicide bombers, and in that conflict only Japanese kamikaze pilots acted as SIEDS. "The Afghans weren't people to us, and vice versa," wrote a Soviet veteran of his war. The British, on the other hand, had a healthy respect for the tribesmen. "To the ferocity of the Zulu are added the craft of the Redskin and the marksmanship of the Boer," wrote Winston Churchill, reflecting a school of thought that continued through to the 1980s when Western media romanticized Afghan warriors as they slaughtered Soviet soldiers. With a coherent ideology fusing modern, resurgent Islam and the centuries-old customs of the Pashtun tribes, the Taliban is said to be motivated by a nostalgia for the simple village life it imagines existed before the Soviets forced Afghans into refugee camps, exile, and war. Mullah Omar, Mullah Dadullah, Akhtar Usmani, Mullah Berader, and others of the latest shura continue to believe, with some justification, that they rescued Afghanistan from the violent anarchy of the post-Soviet years when a corrupt civil service and venal warlords plundered the country.

In 1838, when the British army entered Afghanistan, its officers brought with them all the necessities of campaigning: crates of cigars, bottles of port, and packs of foxhounds for hunting. Special Forces (like

Canada's Joint Task Force 2) apart, the infrastructure required today by foreign governments to maintain their soldiers in the harsh Afghan environment, whether it be PXS or catered meals, has always encumbered their efforts. In contrast, the Taliban is said to live a simple life, surviving on flat *naan* bread, sleeping on rough mats, using turbans for pillows, fighting barefoot, and walking kilometres in the rugged mountains. Thought to be killed off by the American bombing in 2001, the Taliban resurfaced two years later as a catch-all term for any opponent of President Karzai or the Coalition or, if one is to believe the media, for any local casualty.

Today even KHAD, the Afghan intelligence organization, has difficulty defining what the contemporary Taliban is. Identifying three competitors for that title operating out of Pakistan, Lieutenant-General Andrew Leslie pronounced the present-day Taliban "a spectrum … the extreme elements are the ones who actually do us harm. This is the home of the Taliban, the Taliban are a threat to nations around the world, including our own."

The truth is that the Taliban is not a single entity, but a motley assortment of former Taliban leaders such as Mullah Obaidullah, frustrated ex-Northern Alliance fighters, elderly mujahideen like Gulbuddin Hekmatyar, lesser Afghan tribes jockeying for their place against the ruling Popalzai, drug lords, Arab Islamists such as Osama bin Laden, opium farmers, disaffected cannon fodder from Pakistani madrassas, local thugs, and finally those who simply want to protest the corrupt misrule in Kabul. Not to be confused with any of the above are the poor, unemployed men who are simply paid by the Taliban to fight foreigners. The Canadian military classifies these people as Tier One (hardcore) and Tier Two (everyone else). It is the latter that ISAF appeals to, urging them to abandon the cause for promised reconstruction jobs that it will provide.

Today it is as much dollars as any concept of jihad that cements the unholy alliance of religious radicals, drug-running militias, smuggling cartels, and apolitical, unemployed, and unemployable young Afghans. By exploiting the deficiencies of the Karzai regime (corruption, eradication of the poppy crop, and the return of the old warlords) and portraying itself as a kinder, gentler Taliban regime than the one that ruled Afghanistan up to 2001, the new Taliban preys on the impatience of Afghans. And with their armoured vehicles and helicopters, it is easy for the rural population to mistake all ISAF troops as an extension of America's war on terror (or worse the Soviets) rather than a broad international effort to bring stability and prosperity. But what if the foreigners do follow through with real development such as irrigation projects, roads, food, jobs, and security ...?

Winning the hearts and minds of local Afghans may be something for Western foreigners to attempt, but for the Taliban, intimidation such as posting "night letter" leaflets on doors, beheading schoolteachers, and torching schools is a well-tried combination of fear and persuasion. The Taliban's recruiting techniques consist of executing anyone who cooperates with the government and then offering salvation to surviving family members and neighbours. "They ... concentrate their efforts on soft targets, which have such a big bang-for-the-buck impact: buses full of local contract workers, children clustering around soldiers handing out classroom supplies, women's rights activists, humanitarian agencies and journalists," wrote *Toronto Star* columnist Rosie DiManno when embedded with the soldiers in Kandahar. "This is not an insurgency; it's an incursion, an invasion, with dreams of reoccupation," she added.[5]

But Chris Alexander, the former Canadian ambassador to Afghanistan, warned: "We also have to be very careful though about tarring everyone with the same brush. Taliban are religious students. There will always be Taliban in Afghanistan and we should welcome that. The ones who are the problem for NATO and indeed for Afghanistan are the militant ones, the extremist ones, the ones who are fighting and don't show any signs of stepping away from that agenda. But there are thousands, probably tens of thousands, who are willing to join this government to help rebuild their country if they are invited, welcomed, in the right way. And we all need to think about how that hand of cooperation can be extended and how the process of reconciliation in Afghanistan can be deepened."[6]

One thing is certain, however. Whether one calls the current insurgents in Afghanistan "Neo-Taliban" or "Taliban-Lite," as the media have, or dubs them Anti-Coalition Militia (ACM), as NATO does, the enemy this time is not so much an army as an attitude.[7] These guerrillas don't seem particularly awed or worried about the technological might of the

Americans or ISAF ranged against them, and nor were their predecessors in 1839, 1878, or 1979. "The invaders will always be richer and better armed so let them occupy the country. Don't try to hold the cities; fade back into the mountains. Ambush, harass, bleed the foreigners for as long as it takes," wrote Gwynne Dyer about how the Afghans have dealt with foreign conquerors. "Eventually they will cut their losses and go home."[8]

In 1880 a well-armed British/Indian army set out from Kandahar to prevent Ayub Khan from getting rid of London's protégé on the Afghan throne. Mindful of earlier massacre, the British put together a force that was made up of Indian infantry, Afghan levies, and two experienced British regiments of the line — the Gordon Highlanders and the 66th Regiment, both of whom were armed with the latest Martini-Henry repeating rifles. But the soldiers' commanding officer, Brigadier-General George Burrows, was elderly and hadn't seen active service since 1857. He sent out no reconnaissance, and his men had no local knowledge of the terrain. Ominously, the Afghan levies switched sides just as the advance guard reached Maiwand, 75 kilometres from Kandahar. The British discovered that not only did the Afghans outnumber them (25,000 to 2,566), but they also had superior artillery. On July 27 the battle began. Aiming to break the line where the squares of the Gordon Highlanders and the 66th Regiment stood, the Afghans' first attack failed and was blunted. The second time the Afghans identified their enemy's weakness and made straight for the Indian regiments, which were armed with single-shot Snyder rifles. Overwhelmed by the charge, the Indians broke ranks and ran straight into the Highlanders and 66th, destroying their rallying squares. What was left of the British made a final stand in the mud-walled village of Maiwand.[9] Two Victoria Crosses were awarded to the few British gunners who survived, but most of their countrymen were "cut up like sheep," wrote Rudyard Kipling in his poem "That Day":

> I 'eard the knives be'ind me, but I dursn't face my man,
> Nor I don't know where I went to, 'cause I didn't 'alt
>   to see,
> Till I 'eard a beggar squealin' out for quarter as 'e ran,
> An' I thought I knew the voice an' — it was me!

Then, as now, the Afghans' military advantage over all foreigners is an intimate knowledge of a difficult terrain — not knowing the watercourses, Burrows's men suffered from terrible thirst and tore at one another — partnered with a network of relatives and tribesmen who relay to them (today by cell phone) where the enemy is at all times. When, on October 14, 2006, Sergeant Darcy Tedford of CFB Petawawa and Private Blake Williamson from Ottawa were killed west of Kandahar, it was a classic textbook ambush. No matter how many operations are launched to seek him out, in 1880 *and* 2006 it is the Afghan who chooses where and when to fight.

Neither are the insurgents' current weapons limited to RPGs or mines. When the Taliban ruled Afghanistan, its cloistered view was limited to provincial and village affairs with no interest beyond the borders. There were only two official Internet connections — one in Mullah Omar's office and the other at the Foreign Ministry in Kabul. Websites, cell phones, and videotapes have since turned what was an Afghan war into a global one. Today, through television, DVDs, and the Internet, Islamic militants disseminate the struggle of the *umma* (worldwide community of Islam), depicting Palestinian families being evicted by Israeli soldiers, U.S. troops burning Iraqi villages, and Danish cartoons desecrating the Prophet Muhammad, to say nothing of the staged tableaux at Guantánamo. All of these give them better value than any AK-47 could.

But whatever worth RPGs or the Internet have for the Taliban, nothing matches the movement's greatest military advantage — a compliant neighbour. On October 9, 2006, NATO's commander in Afghanistan, Lieutenant-General David Richards, arrived in Islamabad for what were termed "urgent talks" with the Pakistanis. The key items on Richards's agenda were the presence of the Taliban leader Mullah Omar in residence in Quetta and the recently concluded peace accord between the Pakistani military and the Taliban in the tribal areas. Even if ISAF does defeat the insurgents in Afghanistan, it will never destroy them, because they are based in Pakistan. Pakistan's policy of appeasement towards the Taliban and its sympathizers taking shelter along the northwestern border with Afghanistan has played a major role in the dramatic upsurge of violence against Afghan government and NATO forces and civilians. ISAF commanders in the field and the embattled Afghan government have long known this truth. The Taliban uses the safe tribal zone inside Pakistan to lick its wounds, regroup, and rearm for fresh assaults across the border into southeastern Afghanistan.

Pervez Musharraf government's failure to take effective action against its guests will always destabilize Afghanistan. In 2004 the Pakistani president reached a peace accord with Pashtun elders in the lawless border districts of South Waziristan, and in September 2006 a second agreement gave the resident Taliban and its supporters in North Waziristan carte blanche to destabilize Musharraf's neighbour. The local clans, which provide the Taliban with fresh recruits, financial assistance, and supplies, as well as a safe haven, have secured promises from Islamabad that give them the autonomy they have enjoyed since the creation of Pakistan in 1947. The deals were brokered by a pro-Taliban group that has the largest influence in a six-party religious alliance that has thrown its political support to Musharraf. Government troops that entered the rugged region three months after 9/11 were withdrawn from the towns and stopped harassing the tribesmen. The amnesty also extends to "foreign fighters," most of whom have ties to Al Qaeda, the very terrorists the American, British, and Canadian governments are in Afghanistan to root out.

The global think tank Crisis Group warned in a report that since the Pakistani army has virtually retreated to its barracks, this accommodation facilitates the growth of militancy and attacks in Afghanistan by giving pro-Taliban elements a free hand to recruit, train, and arm. To strip the militants of their appeal, Crisis Group urges the Musharraf government to enact political and economic reforms in the deeply impoverished tribal areas, where a colonial-style administration controls the purse strings and the political process, where employment opportunities are scarce, and where desperate people have turned to weapons and drug smuggling. The report also calls on Islamabad to enforce the rule of law in the Waziristans, which means closing the training camps and dismantling the Taliban-type parallel policing and judicial structures set up by the militants. There can never be a military solution to the conflict in Afghanistan, for the mujahideen know they have the immutables on their side: time, a porous border, and a never-ending supply of grievances, recruits, and arms.

Not all of the Taliban's supporters are outside the country, either. By June 2006, with heavy fighting in the south, weaponry destined for battles against the Coalition came from an unlikely source — the Taliban's former foes, the Northern Alliance. The east-west arms transfer from Pakistan was now being crisscrossed by a north-south one. In February, in the northern province of Baghlan, Afghan highway police stopped Toyota pickup trucks loaded with Kalashnikov rifles. The roots of this new development can be traced back to 2004 when, under foreign supervision, the Afghan government's Disarmament, Demobilization, and Reintegration (DDR) program targeted the factional militia commanders in the north for their weapons. Two years later Hamid Karzai's government had decommissioned more than 60,000 former combatants and collected over 35,000 weapons. A second program, Disbandment of Illegally Armed Groups (DIAG), launched in June 2005, collected still more weaponry held by private militias. By the following summer, those of the warlord armies who still possessed weapons preferred to sell them, even to former enemies, rather than hand them over to the Afghan government.

Political analysts have warned that the north-south flow will continue until Kabul finds the will to take on the former Northern Alliance commanders, something the Karzai administration has been reluctant to do so far. The warlords, who from the beginning have opposed the idea of a strong central authority in Kabul, have no incentive to cooperate with either DDR or DIAG, preferring to see the Afghan National Army and ISAF occupied with curbing violence in the south. Such a policy not only increases the price of the warlords' A-47s but also damages two of their potential enemies.

The disarmament and demobilization process, the DDR initiative known as the Afghan New Beginnings Program (ANBP) managed by the United Nations Development Programme (UNDP), is crucial in the creation of conditions for the Karzai government to extend its authority throughout the country. By 2006 the program's fate was uncertain. Even though the Karzai government, with the nagging support of ISAF, had decommissioned the bulk of the heavy weaponry, it had made no inroads in disarming the powerful Tajik-dominated units in Kabul and the Panjshir Valley. Besides, many of the old militia structures had found a new lease on life as police forces or private security guards for provincial governors or district administrators.

The central Afghan government and its international supporters have also been complicit in the maintenance of power by militia commanders. The u.s.-led Coalition has relied on militia commanders in its military operations against Al Qaeda and the Taliban, empowering its local allies militarily and economically and helping them to resist central government control. A major haven for these commanders has been the highway police, with responsibility for securing the ring road linking the country's four major cities as well as the main roads connecting Afghanistan with its neighbours. This arrangement is fraught with risks, not least because it facilitates narcotics trafficking by commanders. A private American security company, United States Protection and Investigations (uspi), pays high wages to highway police commanders to guard the usaid-supported Kabul-Kandahar road project without imposing any apparent accountability on them. The result of these relationships has been to strengthen the commanders politically, militarily, and economically, thus undermining ddr. Besides, military analysts in Afghanistan recognize that there has been a fundamental change in the commanders' priorities during the past three years. Most no longer see the need to maintain large stocks of heavy weaponry, since the Coalition presence precludes the waging of open warfare. Instead, they have opted to maintain leaner, lightly armed forces adequate to protect their political, military, and economic interests, especially narcotics trafficking.

On May 9, 2005, supervised by the Office of National Security Council (onsc), the Afghan government began Program Tahkim-e-Solh (pts), or the Strengthening Peace Program (spp). Set up to repatriate non-criminal former combatants from the Taliban back into Afghan society, the program is aimed at mid-level leaders, since the human-rights records of those at the senior level eliminate them from applying. The Afghan government has emphasized that the program isn't an amnesty but a form of parole to pledge support for it. Those who have taken advantage of this program require supervision, so pts field offices were opened in Hirat, Kandahar, Gardez, Jalalabad, and Konduz. By May 2006 the onsc claimed moderate success — 1,569 former Taliban combatants had been paroled.

As for Afghanistan's military, ISAF's Combined Forces Command Afghanistan (CFC-A) is charged with reconstructing the 35,000-strong Afghan National Army. Much as in Scotland before the English subjugated the clans, Afghan warriors historically owe their loyalty to the tribal chief, not to some far-off president in Kabul, and even less to a nation that encompasses other tribes. As the Soviets did, the United States and now NATO are training an officer corps, mentoring Ministry of Defence officials, and supplying weapons, uniforms, and equipment to establish a working military infrastructure. In March 2006, to help with this training, the Canadian Forces assigned Brigadier-General Gary O'Brien and 13 other Canadian officers, as well as 15 instructors at the Canadian Afghan National Training Centre Detachment (CANTC Det) in Kabul.

Barely four years old, the ANA was beset by poor equipment (patrolling in thin-skinned pickup trucks instead of light armoured vehicles or LAVs), insufficient training, and divided loyalties. Consequently, it was plagued by low retention rates. "One soldier has strong weapons, strong and modern machinery, tanks, jets, bulletproof jackets, and helmets, and the other is fighting with a single weapon that he doesn't even trust," noted an Afghan journalist. The desertion rate among ANA soldiers was 15 percent in November 2006, something U.S. Brigadier-General Douglas Pritt, in charge of training, took some comfort in, since the desertion rate in 2005 had been more than 25 percent.

The causes weren't difficult to imagine. One problem was salary. Although Afghan soldiers had just been given a raise from US$80 to $115 a month, this was a time when day labourers in Kabul's building boom received US$80 monthly. In contrast, the Taliban paid its fighters an equivalent of US$400 a month, and even more, they got to stay near their homes instead of being posted away. Loyalty was another factor: a number of graduates from the Kabul Military Training Centre refused to fight in Kandahar and Helmand provinces. Religion, too, figured into the equation: when Ramadan came, the ANA troops working on a road-building program with Canadian troops suddenly withdrew to go home to their families, leaving the Canadians to fight alone. And then there was lack of trust: although the United States was set to give the ANA 2,500 Humvees, tens of thousands of M-16 assault rifles, and 20,000 flak jackets, any request by the Afghans for armoured vehicles, helicopters, and fighter jets was stonewalled by the Coalition.

It is said that armies are always prepared to fight the previous war, and the Canadian Forces in Afghanistan is no exception. In March 2006, during Stephen Harper's trip to Afghanistan, a Canadian Forces CC-130 Hercules met the prime minister's Airbus at Islamabad Airport to take him and the accompanying media onwards to Kandahar. After struggling into their bulletproof vests, some journalists made the mistake of asking the pilot of the Hercules about the aircraft that was to transport them into a war zone. They were told that the CC-130, while well maintained, was 43 years old and had 43,000 hours of flying time. Developed in the 1950s, the "Herk," designed for the Korean War (1950–53), was the mainstay of the CF air bridge between Kabul/Kandahar and Camp Mirage in the Persian Gulf. Lacking heavy-lift capability, Canada begged lifts from U.S. Air Force C-17 Wings or hired giant Antonov freighters to fly its heavy equipment to Afghanistan. Personnel were ferried to and from CFB Trenton on 437 Squadron's CC-150 Polaris and on commercial aircraft. But without the labours of the Hercules, some of which, ironically, had been bought second-hand from a Middle Eastern air force, there would have been no operations in Afghanistan.

The Canadian Forces' involvement with the Lockheed Martin Hercules began six years after its maiden flight. In the fall of 1960, four C-130B aircraft were purchased by the Royal Canadian Air Force and were designated the CC-130. Later, 24 E-model Hercules were purchased by the Canadian military between 1964 and 1968, and while five of these have been lost in crashes, the other 19 remain in service. Between 1975 and 1996, 16 H-model Hercules were purchased for the Canadian Forces. These represented a number of different sub-models, including five aircraft with an additional configuration for air-to-air refuelling (KC-130, in American terminology) that were acquired in 1991. When the Afghan war began, the Canadian air force had 32 CC-130s operated by five operational squadrons (435 Squadron Winnipeg, Manitoba; 424, 429, and 436 Squadrons Trenton, Ontario; 413 Squadron Greenwood, Nova Scotia) and one training squadron (426 Squadron Trenton).

The last time Canada's air force had taken part in combat resupply operations was during the Korean War. In July 2006 tactical air transport crews from 8 Wing/CFB Trenton were engaged in aerial combat resupply drops over the southern provinces of Afghanistan, using the venerable CC-130 Hercules to support Coalition troops in Operation Mountain Thrust. Usually based at Camp Mirage operating the mail and munitions shuttle to Kandahar, the Hercules crews and maintenance personnel rotated for 18 days through Afghanistan doing the tactical flying operations they had trained for. Up to 16 semi-rigid collapsible containers filled with water, food, blankets, tents, or ammunition were fitted inside the Hercules for aerial delivery, each container weighing up to 1,000 kilograms. The pilots flew the aged aircraft at a constant altitude with a nose-high pitch, relying on the forces of gravity to extract the load out of the fuselage with parachutes deployed automatically via a static line. Known as the container delivery system (CDS), this type of operation required the focus and concentration of all of the crew members as they hugged the Afghan terrain and weaved between hillsides that hid Taliban with shoulder-fired surface-to-air missiles.

Equally dangerous for crew and aircraft that summer was transporting Dutch soldiers from Kandahar to the gravel airstrip at the forward operating base at Tarin Kowt. With "bandit country" only five kilometres away, descents and takeoffs were steeply executed, testing both the aircraft and the crew. "The topography of Tarin Kowt, especially the airstrip, is very much like some of our Arctic outposts in Canada," said Aircraft Commander Major Andy Cook. "Our Canadian tactical training prepared me completely for the challenges of this sortie, and I'm very happy that my crew was able to perform this historic mission and assist our Dutch colleagues."

On November 20, 2006, in what came as no surprise to anyone in the Canadian aviation industry, the Conservative government awarded Lockheed Martin the contract to replace its aged Hercules — with more Hercules. Seventeen of these C-130JS were to be bought for CDN$3.2 billion with a 20-year service contract costing CDN$1.7 billion. It was also no secret that the "J" was favoured by Chief of Defence Staff Rick Hillier over the European A400M air freighter, which hadn't flown yet. Not only would the four Rolls-Royce engines and six-bladed propellers of the J reduce "climb time" out of FOBs by 50 percent, but its cargo floor had been stretched from 12 to nearly 17 metres, allowing for more pallets and troops. However, the factor that ultimately influenced the choice was that the first J could be delivered before 2010, the year in which the Canadian Forces estimated they would have to ground up as many as 14 older Hercules.

The Canadian army had entered World War II with the Universal or Bren gun carrier. Built by Ford in Windsor, Ontario, to provide employment during the Depression, the little armoured vehicle transported four to six soldiers into battle, and because of its tracks, it was able to go anywhere. But the carrier had been designed in 1926, and 15 years later its weaknesses were lethal. It was too lightly armoured (especially its mild steel floor) and its passengers had no overhead protection. Fortunately, by 1944, when the Canadian army landed on the European continent, the Universal had been by and large withdrawn from frontline service. On October 2, 2003, when two Canadian soldiers were killed and three injured because an IED blew a large hole in their Iltis jeep, Opposition Members of Parliament demanded: "Why were our soldiers sent into … self-described 'bad-guy country' in unarmoured, rusted-out dune buggies rather than lightly armoured vehicles?"[10] Chief of Defence Staff General Ray Henault told an Ottawa press conference that though the Iltises offered little combat protection, it was appropriate to use them. "In this case," Henault said, "the decision to go out with the jeep was one that was sound in my view. It was — if you can ever call a threat low in Afghanistan — a low-threat area."

The Universal carrier of Canada's war in Afghanistan, the Iltis (meaning "ferret " in German) had won the multinational competition to create a true Europa Jeep for the resurgent German army in the late 1960s. Volkswagen, known for its World War II Kübelwagen, had just taken over the car manufacturer Auto Union and had entered a variation of the latter's tiny Munga truck, long out of production, into the competition. Because it used commercially available parts and was cheaper than the Mercedes-Benz entry, Volkswagen's bid was successful and production began in 1978 for the Bundeswehr. The Canadian military, too, was looking to replace its M151A2 jeeps, so Bombardier in Quebec bought the manufacturing and marketing rights of the Iltis in October 1981 to build 6,000 vehicles, hoping to export most. With the exception of Cameroon, that didn't happen. But the Department of

National Defence purchased 2,500 of the open, lightly armoured jeeps in 1984 for a total of US$68 million, using them in Operation Desert Storm in Kuwait and in the former Yugoslavia in 1994.

Brought to Afghanistan, the aged vehicles (now 20 years old) were employed as "battlefield taxis" to ferry personnel around and conduct light reconnaissance missions. Since the bulk of Canadian Forces was based in Kabul, the carriers were also used for patrols in areas too narrow for LAV IIIs. The Iltis may have been underpowered for high elevations and showing its age, but it was well suited to Kabul's narrow streets, and its open-top accessibility was ideal for the current "hearts and minds" campaign with the locals. If there were soldiers who liked the easy manoeuvrability of the Iltis, others complained that it had no blast protection and that the fine, powdery Afghan dust clogged the carrier's air filters, making it unreliable.[11] By a stretch of the imagination, the Iltis was described by DND as "lightly armoured," since blast blankets lined its mild steel floorboards. Defence Minister John McCallum even thought that use of the open-top Iltis set Canadian patrols apart from the Americans, who rode around in enclosed, armoured Humvees. In the battle to win over the Afghans, the Iltis did allow its passengers, he told reporters, to interact with locals. But when Major-General Andrew Leslie was asked how much protection the carrier provided travelling through a mined area, he replied, "Quite frankly, the answer is almost none." After October 2003, patrols by Iltis were halted on soft-packed routes where there was a high risk of mines.[12]

The Canadian army had long known that the little jeep was ending its serviceable life, and since 1999 the military had been working towards a replacement under the light utility vehicle wheeled (LUVW) program. With the Iltis's poor reputation featured daily in the media, the request for proposals were pushed through Ottawa's bureaucracy for up to 802 standard military pattern (SMP) LUVWs. The competition winner was the Steyr-Daimler-Puch–built Mercedes-Benz Gelaendenwagen (G-Wagon). Best of all, the Canadian company, Magna International, had acquired Steyr in 1998.[13] With its 5.5-litre Kompressor (supercharger) engine, all-wheel-drive system, front-disc and rear-drum brakes, dual 12- and 24-volt electrical systems, 24-volt starter, solar trickle charger, two-piece wheels with "run flat" tires, strong ladder frame, rigid axles, three electronically locking differentials, low-range off-road gear ratio, and electronic traction control, the G-Wagon was custom-built for the battlefield. In October 2003, Ottawa awarded a US$126-million contract to Mercedes-Benz Canada for 802 long-wheelbase G-Wagons and 118 armour protection systems (APS) kits. The latter was designed to protect the vehicle's crew compartment against small arms, hand grenades, and anti-personnel mines. The APS added a tonne to the 3.9-tonne vehicle but could be installed in the field by three soldiers within eight hours. Nevertheless, since it was fully enclosed and the armoured windows didn't roll down (thus ending the local "friendly" patrols), the G-Wagon was air-conditioned.

Canadians took delivery of the first 60 G-Wagons in Kabul between March 5 and 13, 2004, and immediately put the vehicles on patrols. "You only need to take one look at the new 4x4 to appreciate the sharp and rugged style of the G-Wagon," raved a DND press release. "With its 2.7-litre, 5-cylinder turbocharged diesel engine, near a tonne of plated armour, bulletproof glass, and almost a half-metre of ground clearance," the press release continued, "it has nothing on your normal SUV. Those who had the chance to test-drive it on the 20-kilometre trip from the Kabul airport to Camp Julien were unanimous: the G-Wagon is robust, drives smoothly, and leaves you with a confident feeling of security."[14] Open turrets were then installed on the roofs for machine gun mounts, even though the gunners were unprotected and the additional weight made the G-Wagons unstable. But that was to be the least of the vehicle's problems. The Iltis's replacement wasn't blast-resistant, either, and the purchase process for the vehicle had taken too long to complete. Then the Canadians moved out of Kabul to Kandahar. The following terse list of ensuing casualties speaks for itself:

> 05 Oct. 2005 G-wagon suicide bombing 3 wounded in Kandahar City 04 Dec. 2005 G-wagon suicide bombing 1 wounded outside Kandahar 13 Dec. 2005 G-wagon roadside bomb 3 wounded outside Kandahar 15 Jan. 2006 G-wagon suicide bombing 1 dead/3 wounded near Kandahar 15 Feb. 2006 G-wagon road accident 3 injured just outside Kandahar 25 Feb. 2006 G-wagon RPG attack

1 wounded inside Kandahar City 22 Apr. 2006 G-wagon
roadside bomb 4 dead/0 wounded near Gumbad 11
Aug. 2006 G-wagon suicide VBIED 1 dead/0 wounded
Spin Boldak

In 1898 the young subaltern Winston Churchill wrote that the
Afghan tribesmen picked off the British army's transport animals at
night, killing the camels and mules that were essential to move supplies
through the mountains. "When a certain number are killed, a brigade is
as helpless as a locomotive without coal. It cannot move. Unless it be
assisted it must starve," he noted, warning that the animals should be
better protected. In the 21st century, Afghan insurgents correctly
identified the lightly armoured G-Wagon as the weak link in CF convoys
and targeted them accordingly.

"The G-Wagon is simply an SUV with armour panels attached to a
mild steel body," admitted a military observer. A former second lieutenant in the Armour Branch, now an Opposition MP, was even more
direct. In October 2005, Gordon O'Connor criticized the choice of G-
Wagons in convoy use. He insisted that such vehicles weren't suited to
the Afghan mission: "The government has basically committed our
troops to fight guerrillas in Afghanistan without making sure they had
the equipment." Appointed to cabinet on February 6, 2006, as defence
minister, O'Connor assured Canadians in May that with the lightly
armoured vehicles highly vulnerable to roadside attacks, the military
was restricting its G-Wagons to the compound in Kandahar. However,
Dean Beeby, a reporter for Canadian Press, revealed:

But newly released records indicate the minister's
announcement came as a surprise to military commanders, who had imposed no such restrictions and
continue to use G-Wagons in dangerous convoys.

"It has come to our attention that a statement by
the MND [minister of national defence] ... regarding
G-Wagons was not correct," says an internal e-mail to
the minister's office, the day after the May 30
announcement.

The minister "indicated that in the future we are going to limit nearly all the G-Wagons to the camp, with some exceptions. However, this is not the case.... Please advise the MND not to repeat that statement as G-Wagons will continue to operate outside the camp," public affairs official Aarin Bronson warned.

"The risk here is that we could suffer additional casualties in the G-Wagon while they are operating outside the camp."[15]

During World War II, the Canadian army used the handsome Staghound Armoured Car to protect road convoys. Built by General Motors of Canada, it had a 37 mm gun and an armour thickness of 3.75 centimetres. But its five crew members must have prayed they would never come up against their German equivalent — the Panzerspahwagen Puma. That 8x8 armoured vehicle, with its 50 mm gun and 30 mm armour, easily the best of its day, was the father of all modern LAVs. Yet for its first post-war armoured car, the German Federal Border Guard turned to an unlikely source. Protected by their mountains, the Swiss hadn't fought a war in four centuries, but that didn't prevent MOWAG (Motor-Wagen Fabrik) of Kreuzlingen, Switzerland, from designing the Piranha light armoured vehicle as a private venture. Because the drive train was modular, the LAV could be built in several wheel versions (6x6, 8x8, or 10x10) with different degrees of armour protection and many kinds of turrets. By 2000, Piranha derivatives were troop transports and command vehicles with the militaries of Chile, Sweden, Denmark, Ireland, and Spain and were manufactured under licence in Canada by General Dynamics, in the United Kingdom by BAE Systems Land Systems, in Japan by Komatsu, and in Chile by FAMAE. In February 1977, Canada placed an initial order for 350 Piranhas in the 6x6 configuration, later increasing the purchase to 491 vehicles. Depending on their roles, the Piranha offspring in the CF are known as Huskies, Coyotes, and Bisons, all animals indigenous to Canada.

The Canadian Forces entered the 21st century with approximately 1,200 M113s (in several variants) acquired in the 1960s, 114 Leopard main battle tanks (MBTs), 269 Grizzly armoured personnel carriers (APCs), 195

Cougar direct-fire support/armoured training vehicles, 27 Husky maintenance and recovery vehicles (purchased in the late 1970s/early 1980s), and 199 Bison infantry section carriers, which entered service in 1990–92. In February 2001, as part of its Armoured Personnel Carrier Life Extension program, DND upgraded its APCs to keep them operational until 2015. All 199 Bisons (8x8) and 247 of 269 Grizzlies (6x6) were upgraded at a cost of about CDN$200 million to serve alongside 651 new-production LAV IIIs being delivered. These were the latest of the Piranha family now built by General Dynamics Land Systems — Canada (GDLS), which exported 105 of them to New Zealand between October 2003 and November 2004.

The first deployment of the LAV III with Canadian Forces was during U.N. operations in Eritrea in early 2001, and five years later Canada had 547 of the vehicles in service and an unknown number in Afghanistan.[16] But military analysts warned that the LAV III was built and bought for peacekeeping duties, not warfare. While good on roads, it has little cross-country ability, and worse, its light armour makes it vulnerable to rocket-propelled grenades. To combat the RPG threat in Iraq, the U.S. Army fields its Canadian-built LAV IIIs in slat armour, which looks like a bird cage or a hockey goalie's mask. Installed around the vehicles, the wire mesh causes RPGs to detonate away from it. DND was also said to be actively considering purchasing the Israeli-built Trophy active armour system.[17] In combat the 25 mm gun on the LAV III packs a welcome punch, but the weight of its turret and the Piranha's high centre of gravity may have been the cause of the vehicle's reputation for off-road instability, making it, as the CF discovered on November 24, 2005, unreliable in rough country.

If there is a Jaguar sports car in the Piranha family, it is surely the Coyote. Built by General Motors of Canada specifically for the Canadian Forces, it served in Kosovo and Bosnia in July 1999 as a reconnaissance squadron within the Canadian Battle Group. The Coyotes first arrived in Afghanistan with Lord Strathcona's Horse in 2002 as part of the U.S.-led Operation Enduring Freedom. With a combat weight of 13.4 tonnes and mounting a 25 mm M242 Bushmaster chain gun and two 7.62 mm C6 general-purpose machine guns, it can reach a speed of 120 kilometres per hour. Like its namesake, it is highly manoeuvrable and is able to cross a two-metre trench, climb up to a 60 percent grade, and assist, with a built-in winch, in recovery in rough terrain. The Coyote's hydraulically driven air-conditioning system, which cools equipment and personnel, is especially welcome in Afghanistan, and even if the fuel tank is destroyed, it has sufficient fuel in its lines to power itself for another 30 to 40 kilometres.

The vehicle's surveillance suite was supplied by Computing Devices Canada (now part of General Dynamics Canada) and has three operating modes: surveillance, acquisition, and fall of shot over a one-kilometre area. The radar can detect and locate medium-size targets such as tanks at a distance of up to 12 kilometres, and large vehicles — trains or trucks — out to 24 kilometres. It provides readouts of target grid references, range and bearing, together with clutter maps and a Doppler audio signal. The radar can cue targets to the vehicle's sensors, which have detection ranges in excess of 20 kilometres under good atmospheric conditions. Its magnetic compass system is interfaced with a global positioning system (GPS) receiver.

"These vehicles have given the Canadian soldier a real presence on overseas missions," says Sergeant C.J.E. Stringer, the fire control instructor, Field Artillery School, CFB Gagetown, "proving to those who don't want us around that we are there to make a difference. Over and over again they have taken hits in mine strikes and small-arms fire without great loss on more than one occasion. The sighting systems include optical day sights for both gunner and commander, superior thermal sighting systems for night viewing, night sight for observation, range-finding equipment, and a navigational system. The sighting systems allow for pinpoint accuracy at medium ranges from 100 metres to approximately three kilometres. The challenges to the technicians with this technology can be a hindrance with electronic glitches but overall pays dividends to the fighting soldier."

With their top-heaviness and IED vulnerability, the G-Wagons were to be superseded by larger, fully armoured vehicles similar to the Australian-built Bushmaster (which the Dutch bought for their forces in Afghanistan) or the equally pugnacious-looking RG-31. In contrast to the Swiss, the South African military had been at war until the late 1970s, its armoured vehicles encountering land mines in the Caprivi Strip of

South West Africa/Namibia and in Rhodesia (now Zimbabwe). Designing a vehicle to survive land mines caused South African Land Systems OMG (Olifant Manufacturing Company) to develop a series of light armoured vehicles with v-shaped hulls to deflect blasts and reduce injuries and/or deaths of passengers. Combined with a monocoque hull (cheaper and easier to repair after a land-mine detonation), these LAVs evolved into a mine-resistant series — the Okapi, Kobra, and Mamba, culminating with the RG-31 Nyala.[18]

Thanks to its v-shaped monocoque, welded steel hull, and high suspension designed to resist a blast equivalent to two anti-tank mines, the Nyala soon became the vehicle of choice for U.N. peacekeeping and security forces worldwide. The Canadian Forces were familiar with the South African armoured car, having already bought three RG-31s as route-proving vehicles in Afghanistan. But with the Iltis's death and now the G-Wagon's incapacity, the trio were soon so overused in theatre that their reliability was suspect, and by October 2005 the Canadian Forces were moving quickly to buy more 4x4 armoured patrol vehicles for use in convoys to its PRT and FOBs. Lieutenant-Colonel Paul Ohrt, director of the army's Armoured Vehicle Project Management, said the CF wanted vehicles that were currently in production in order to meet the timeline and that prospective candidates had to have ballistic under-wheel, under-belly protection and a remote weapons station that could carry 7.62 mm and .50 calibre machine guns or a 40 mm automatic grenade launcher. Because of the urgency, delivery would have to be by February-March 2006, just in time for the summer season, which promised to be busy.

The three finalists were General Dynamics Land Systems — Canada with the RG-31 Nyala, Krauss-Maffei Wegmann with the Dingo, and Thales Canada with the Bushmaster Infantry Mobility Vehicle. In November 2005, in what must surely be the quickest bidding process in Ottawa's bureaucratic history, GDLS received a CDN$60.3 million contract to provide 50 RG-31 Nyalas, with an unfunded option to buy 25 more for delivery to Kandahar by June 2006. While the Nyalas would be built by BAE Land Systems OMC's factory in Benoni, South Africa, under the terms, GDLS was to provide program management and engineering and logistics support, basing two experts in Kandahar itself. Learning from the unprotected turret on the G-Wagon, DND ensured that each Nyala had incorporated on its roof the Norwegian-built Kongsberg Protector M151 Remote Weapon Station and had enhanced sidewall armour plate to address any IED threat. As for mine protection, GDLS claimed the Nyala could withstand two TM-57s detonating under any of the wheels and one TM-57 below. A day-and-night sighting system allowed the operator to fire the weapon while remaining protected within the vehicle. Gun ports in the laminated armour glass windows were another option that was provided — equally good for throwing out bottles of water to the Afghans and for firing from. With "sectionalization," the Nyala was also portable in CC-130s and fitted easily into C-17s.

But even the much-vaunted Nyala proved vulnerable to IEDs. The route to Gumbad Platoon House, 90 kilometres northwest of Kandahar, had earned its name "IED Alley" — there had been four IED incidents since January 2006 when the Canadians arrived at the platoon house. While on an early-morning run in the Panjwai district of southern Afghanistan on October 7, 2006, a Canadian patrol using a Nyala hit a roadside bomb. The force of the explosion was such that it penetrated the vehicle's armour and killed the gunner, Trooper Mark Andrew Wilson of the Royal Canadian Dragoons. It wasn't clear why the Nyala blew apart, said CF military spokesperson Lieutenant Sue Stefko — the blast ripped away a wheel. Colonel Fred Lewis, deputy commander of Canada's troops in Afghanistan, couldn't explain how the bomb was able to penetrate the vehicle, commenting that "in this particular case, the enemy got a bit lucky."

The first Canadian military tracked vehicle used in Afghanistan was the most unlikely. Looking like a giant snowmobile that had taken a wrong turn, the BV-206 AMV transported Canadian troops in Operation Anaconda near the Shah-i-Kot Valley, evacuating people and bringing in supplies. Ferried in by U.S. Army CH-47D Chinooks, the six-tonne, four-tracked vehicles built by Sweden's Hagglunds weren't designed for force-on-force combat. In any case, tracked vehicles had a poor record in Afghanistan. During the Soviet invasion, as evidenced by the steel carcasses of T-62s that littered the countryside, the mountainous terrain trapped the heavy, slow-moving Soviet tanks. But the desert region of

Kandahar was better suited for tank warfare; the irrigation canals and mud walls were easily overcome by the tracked monsters.

Somewhere in the genetic makeup of the German-made 105 mm–armed Leopard c1s, main battle tanks that had replaced the British-built Centurions in the Canadian Forces in 1978, was the Tiger, the best tank in World War II. In 1996, with the threat of the Cold War receding, Canada bought 123 ex-German army Leopard 1A5s, had the turrets removed and refurbished by Krauss-Maffei Wegmann, and then shipped them to Canada where they were installed on the existing c1 chassis by DEW Engineering. DND spent US$145 million equipping the tanks with new computers and heat-sensitive equipment. But by 2004 military tactics had changed. The Canadian army was switching to an armoured wheeled vehicle fleet that would be air portable and the Leopards were to be replaced with a wheeled mobile gun system. The remaining Leopards were to be sold off to private collectors, put in museums, or used for target practice, and the military stopped training tank crews at Gagetown.

Defence Minister McCallum and Lieutenant-General Rick Hillier both announced that the metal monsters were to be scrapped. The new, transformed Canadian army, said Hillier, didn't need an MBT. It was "a millstone" that couldn't manoeuvre in urban areas like Kabul, took too long to be shipped to a war zone, and was too heavy for Canadian transport planes to airlift. "Tanks are a perfect example of extremely expensive systems that sit in Canada because they are inappropriate to the operations we conduct daily around the world," Hillier said. Besides, he might have added, the armoured Leopard was hardly conducive to winning over the hearts and minds of Afghans. "On most peace-support operations," Hillier concluded, "it would actually be destabilizing to deploy or employ it."

By the bloody summer of June 2006, though, the remaining Leopards earned a reprieve. After the unexpectedly heavy resistance encountered in Operation Medusa, field commanders wanted more firepower and protection. Besides, their LAVs were being overused and were overdue for a return to Canada for refitting. In August 2006, when there were rumours of military maintenance crews working overtime to prepare the tanks for deployment to Afghanistan, the CF said they were being made ready for an exercise in Wainwright, Alberta. But by the next month, DND Public Affairs could deny no longer. The Leopards would be sent to Afghanistan to provide protection for the PRT convoys. On November 1, 2006, Hillier announced that four Leopards would be flown post-haste into Kandahar by U.S. Air Force C-17 and that 11 more would follow.

Asked about the change of heart, the chief of defence staff replied, "With a tank, to go back to that old Bell Telephone commercial, you can reach out and touch somebody at a long way's away." Fire support from the Leopard's 105 mm could pierce mud-brick walls, and a plough mounted on its front could clear mines. And, for a tank, the Leopard C2 was very fast. It could reach speeds of up to 65 kilometres per hour on good roads or about 45 kilometres per hour cross-country, which made it useful as a convoy escort.

On December 2, 2006, a squadron of Leopards rolled through Panjwai, the scene of recent fighting, in a display of force, firing their cannons for the first time in decades. If the Soviet tanks had been nick-named the "beasts" almost 30 years before, for the Taliban the Leopards were the "super beasts." But even the mighty Leopard wasn't invulnerable, and in late November 2006, one hit a mine in a training exercise in Kandahar that blew its tracks off. Their Cold War armoury now almost depleted, the Canadian Forces also announced they would use their tracked M113s in Afghanistan. Several were already in Kandahar, and 40 more were to be shipped from Canada in 2007. Unlike the LAVs, they could roll over the irrigation ditches that had stopped the wheeled vehicles.

In the Third Afghan War in 1919, rather than mount an army expedition to subdue the rebellious tribes, the British used a Royal Air Force Handley Page v/1500 bomber, sending it on a six-hour flight from Kohat, India, to bomb Kabul.[19] London realized the potential for "policing" difficult corners of the empire with aircraft, and through the 1920s, bombing runs over errant Afghan villages were cheaper and quicker than mounting an overland expedition. Like the Doolittle Raid staged by the Americans against the Japanese mainland in 1942, little damage would be done in the bombing, but the lesson taught to the enemy was of inestimable value. Beginning in 1927, RAF fighters delivered swift retribution against the Fakir of Ipi after British armoured cars and 40,000 troops had been unable to capture him. Again, in 1938, when the Fakir (his real name was Mirza Ali Khan) was receiving military aid from the Axis, the RAF undertook the first scorched-earth raid in Afghanistan's history against the Pashtun guerrillas. Jerry cans of petrol were dropped onto crops and set ablaze, and British air power alone prevented a Pashtun uprising.[20]

Without their own air-support element in Afghanistan, the Canadians called up aircraft from other NATO forces, notably, U.S. Army A-10 Thunderbolts from Bagram and Royal Air Force GR.7 Harriers at Kandahar. Nicknamed "Warthog," the Thunderbolt could fire 3,900 rounds per minute from its main 30 mm cannon and was especially useful against Taliban strongholds. In the bloody summer of 2006, NATO close-air-support aircraft were flying "roughly 800 missions in August alone, using their weapons in about 450 of them," said a spokesperson. The small Royal Air Force detachment was increased to seven Harrier GR.7s in September 2006 because of a "surge in demand from international troops for air support at Kandahar." A British Harrier pilot called the Canadians "their best customers," and British Defence Secretary Des Browne announced that the "temporary deployment" would be extended when in 2008 the RAF intended to deploy its ground-attack Eurofighter Typhoons equipped with precision-guided bombs.

Inevitably, chaotic situations on the battlefield led to what the British, who had suffered the A-10's attention in Iraq, called " blue on blue" incidents. On July 8, 2006, an American B-2 bomber dropped a laser-guided 225-kilogram bomb on a Canadian position. While evoking painful memories of the "friendly fire" Tarnak Farm incident in 2002, this time the soft ground prevented any deaths, but not injuries. Not so fortunate was the Canadian platoon early on September 4 when two A-10s mistakenly strafed it, killing one soldier and injuring dozens of others. Thus the rumour that six CF-18s, like the Leopards, were Afghanistan-bound was welcome news. But the fighters had only been earmarked for NATO's Rapid Reaction Force, and Defence Minister Gordon O'Connor told the House of Commons on October 31, 2006, that there was no plan "in the works" to send the jets overseas. "They will not be deployed," he said, "unless there is an operational requirement, and at this time there is no operational requirement." But if no

CF-18s were to be deployed to Kandahar, the hope was that Canadian helicopters soon would be.

In Operation Athena, when the Royal Canadian Horse Artillery's LG-1 MK II 105 mm howitzer was to be lifted by helicopter, it was hooked up to a German army C-53 at Kabul Airport. Without their own helicopters in Afghanistan, the Canadians were forced to " thumb rides" in British and Dutch Chinooks. It hadn't always been like that. Many of the troops could remember when the CF operated the "Heavy Hooker," the CH-147 Chinook that could lift 11 tonnes of cargo or carry 44 troops. When Brian Mulroney's Conservative government put the CH-147s up for sale in 1991, the Netherlands was pleased to take them off its hands.[21]

For Chief of Defence Staff Rick Hillier, the acquisition of heavy- to medium-lift helicopters was a priority. In June 28, 2006, the government announced that it would purchase a fleet of 16 aircraft with a 20-year service contract, sufficient to sustain three deployed helicopters based at two main operating bases — Edmonton and Petawawa. To be signed with Boeing in July 2007, the US$4.7 billion order was for medium- to heavy-lift Chinook helicopters that could accommodate an infantry platoon of 30 soldiers with full combat equipment, be able to externally lift multiple loads, including a lightweight field howitzer, and be delivered no later than 36 months after contract award with final aircraft delivery no later than 60 months after.

Hillier always had the Chinook in mind for Afghanistan where, with the thin mountain air and summer temperatures of 50 degrees Celsius, lift is hard to achieve and tail rotors lose their stabilizing effect. The counter-rotating Chinook didn't have a tail rotor, and the spinning blades of its rear rotor were also high above the troops getting in or out. Unfortunately, as with the Nyala purchase, the Canadian Forces were competing with other countries for the latest model, the CH-47F. Even with a price tag of US$40 million each, the most recent Chinook was much in demand.[22] But so desperate was the need for medium-lift helicopters that the media reported that soldiers about to deploy to Afghanistan were training on the navy's ancient Sea Kings, which had been stripped of their anti-submarine gear and equipped with troop seats. Questioned whether the Sea Kings, with their poor safety record, were to be sent to Afghanistan caused DND to issue denials, but it was noted that the government had amended the contract with the manufacturer of the navy's new Cyclone helicopters to ensure they could take on troop-carrying roles.

CC-130s apart, there had been Canadian aircraft in Afghanistan since October 2003 — of a sort. Military aviation had its origins in the observation balloons first used in campaigns by the Duke of Wellington "to see over the hill," which is exactly what modern unmanned aerial vehicles (UAVs) are designed to do. Canada had lost several opportunities to develop its own UAVs (or drones, as they were then called) when, in the 1950s, the Royal Canadian Air Force conducted cold-weather tests for the U.S. Air Force's KDA-4 Firebee and was invited to join in the development. The Firebee was subsequently used around the world, but the RCAF had no interest in it.

In 1959, when the cancellation of the Avro Arrow meant that Canadair had lost out on the sales of its Sparrow missiles, the company took the technology to design the CL-89. Here was a UAV in its simplest form. Launched from a truck, it flew a pre-programmed course, took photos, and then returned to land on a homing beacon. The CL-89 was bought by Germany, France, Italy, and Britain (which used them in the 1991 Gulf War), but not by the Canadian Forces. Buoyed by the exports, Canadair updated the CL-89 to the CL-289 surveillance drone, and in 1987 sold the system to the French and German governments for $411 million, both European militaries using it extensively in Bosnia and Kosovo. But once more, lack of its own government's interest forced Canadair to shelve its promising lead in unmanned platform technology.

The CL-289 was the forerunner of the tactical "Sperwer" UAV system, which was developed by the French SAGEM (Société d'Applications Générales de l'Electricité et de la Mécanique) and sold to the Dutch army, hence the name Sperwer, which is Dutch for "sparrow hawk." In August 2003, fulfilling a promise made to NATO for UAV operations, Canada placed a US$33.8 million order for the Sperwer UAV to support ISAF in Afghanistan, and Canadian Oerlikon-Contraves, the prime contractor for the project, was made responsible for the integrated logistics support package. The contract was for one system of six air vehicles, two control stations, and training and support. Twenty-five Canadian Forces soldiers were sent to SAGEM's training facility in France to prepare them to take over the UAV when it was delivered to Afghanistan in October 2003. They may have been buoyed to know that, besides its origins, there was some Canadian content in the Sperwer: it was propelled in the air by a Rotax 982 engine, the two-cylinder, lightly modified snowmobile engine built by Bombardier's European division giving it a characteristic Ski-Doo sound.

The ground station contained, among other classified assets, 3D terrain modelling and flight path presentation on a geographical data system, as well as image processing, interpretation and connection to networks, and compatibility with communications networks. Equipped with digital band datalink (15GHZ), transponder/IFF, and VHF relay for integration in controlled airspace, the Sperwer provided high-resolution day-and-night imagery and target location with an accuracy of 20 metres. Carrying an electro-optical/infrared sensor, it had a mission radius of 200 kilometres and loiter time of six hours.

Captain Richard Little of Intelligence, Surveillance, Targeting, and Acquisition (ISTAR) arrived in Kabul with the UAV organization in the last week of October 2003. "Our operations were progressing so well," he said, "that the Dutch sent over four soldiers from their Sperwer unit to learn from us, the Danes sent over the leadership from their Sperwer platoons to glean what they could, and the German commander of their artillery forces, Oberstleutnant Tilmann Roehricht, was so thrilled at seeing a Sperwer fly that he was present for every launch made within a two-week span. By about the first week of December, we were just about to be fully operational. About this time we also had our first crash. The UAV was coming in for a landing, and the parachute didn't extract from the air vehicle [AV], making the AV glide right into the ground. The AV and sensor were completely destroyed. An investigation team was dispatched from Ottawa. A spring had broken, which held back the extractor mechanism for the parachute. But while awaiting this investigation, other problems came to light. Spare parts.

"The Sperwer weighs 750 pounds at takeoff and it lands just a bit lighter. In order to prevent damage to highly sensitive and exposed components, such as the payload, a parachute and airbags deploy. However, there are other parts that will absorb the shock of landing, damaging themselves. When this happens, spares are needed, and the Sperwer in Kabul was using more spares than were estimated. With the decreased air density at the 6,000-foot altitude, the parachute wasn't slowing the descent enough, and more parts were breaking than our supply system could handle at the time. Coupled with that was that the launch mechanism had to launch at top pressure every time to ensure that flight velocity was achieved. This put too much pressure on some parts of the launcher, causing small cracks.

"In January we had our second crash. Because the AV was no longer coming down in its landing zone, we conducted an examination of the landing procedure. The Sperwer had been designed to fly and be recovered in Europe, especially the areas within France, but the mountains around Kabul gave it wind patterns that were too unfamiliar for its computer to decode. So, when it popped its parachute to land, because of unforeseen wind, it didn't come down in a predicted spot. We switched to manual recovery. In this mode, the recovery is initiated by the operator, rather than the machine. The operator determines a parachute-release point, flies over it, releases, and the AV comes to the ground. In our trials, it all went extremely well, except for the last time. Because the AV needs to be a fixed height above ground for recovery, the operator must drop its altitude. Unfortunately, on this flight, the operator dropped the altitude too early and the AV hit a hill. A pair of Coyote LAVs were dispatched to provide overwatch, but it took over two days to get to the AV and recover it."

After the crash of a sixth and last Sperwer, the Canadians had no more UAV capability.[23] Major Dyrald Cross, ISTAR commander, explained to the media: "Kabul is more or less in a bowl surrounded by mountains," which produce wind shears and turbulence. The "challenge was trying to come in on an approach that brings you as far away from those [mountains] as you can get and still manage to fly the path necessary" to land on ground that is as hard as concrete.

In December 2005, with the move to Kandahar, the Department of National Defence renewed its faith in UAVs, and five additional Sperwers at a cost of US$15 million were bought from Oerlikon-Contraves Canada and delivered in early 2006. With the deactivation of the Danish army Sperwer unit in Kabul, Canada acquired the Danish systems, as well.

Ultimately, the unchanging truth of warfare is that only soldiers, Taliban or Coalition, can conquer the enemy. Leopards can offer improved firepower, protection, and mobility, and the A-10 Warthogs and Harriers can be called up to neutralize any insurgent stronghold, but only people (the infantry), as author Tom Clancy says, "can take up residency there."

A Final Word

It took Prime Minister Stephen Harper's appeal at the NATO Summit in Riga, Latvia, echoed by that of John McNee (Canada's ambassador to the United Nations) at the U.N. Security Council on December 7, 2006, for Canadians to understand. To much of the world, the Afghan mission is discretionary, a sideshow. Nowhere is this attitude more evident than in the body count, with three countries — the United States, Canada, and Britain accounting for 90 percent of NATO's combat casualties. Americans killed in action account for half of the total, followed by Canada with 25 percent and Britain with 15 percent.

Sending troops to, for example, Lebanon or Kosovo, is viewed as more critical to global outcomes. And even in Washington and London, Afghanistan is less of a priority compared with the fiasco of Iraq. The 37 countries that contribute 32,800 troops to ISAF (as of November 10, 2006) consist of all 26 NATO members, nine partner nations, and two non-members. Four years after the U.S. Marines swooped into Kandahar to get Osama bin Laden "dead or alive," the United States remains the largest contributor (11,800) followed by the United Kingdom (6,000), Germany (2,700), Canada (2,500), and the Dutch (2,000). The French, having just withdrawn their 200 Special Forces from the volatile Kandahar region, now have 975 soldiers. Austria and Switzerland have five nationals each, fewer than the number of Austrian and Swiss flags flying at ISAF headquarters. Many of those contributions are of token support only — a few soldiers to 200 — and would be too small to be effective in combat even if they were deployed in the south.

When asked why his country had more sizable forces in southern Lebanon, Kosovo, and Africa, Daniel Jouanneau, the French ambassador to Canada, explained: "Kosovo is at our doors, its a neighbour country. It is very close to France. So the future of Kosovo, the future of the Balkans' stability, is a first priority for us."[1] His country, he said, was committed to staying in the Afghan capital, "which was indispensable to the security of the country." On hearing this statement, Colonel Fred Lewis, the deputy contingent commander, asked, "How many battalions does it take to protect Kabul Airport?"

There is also the political unwillingness of most NATO nations to allow their soldiers to be sent into combat in Kandahar Province. As in Iraq, troop presence in Afghanistan appears more to be about demonstrating an alliance with the United States in response to 9/11, rather than meeting the country's needs. And those nations, like Germany, with the third-largest military contingent in Afghanistan, Italy (1,800), and Spain (650), countries that have combat-ready contingents in the country, have hobbled them with restrictions that prevent them from fighting. Spain, for example, even after the Madrid bombings, has kept its soldiers in Badghis in northern Afghanistan. Germany, which also has large numbers of its troops in Lebanon and Kosovo, can't deploy into the south without approval of its parliament. Only Poland responded to the appeal by NATO Secretary-General Jaap de Hoop Scheffer at the Riga NATO Summit to send 1,100 soldiers who will fight wherever ISAF needs them. The Polish ambassador to Canada, Piotr Ogrodzinski, said, "We want to see the ISAF operation be successful. The more flexibility in the possible use of troops, the better." The intervention in Afghanistan was done on the cheap. Compared even to the recent post-conflict situations (Bosnia, Kosovo), it was given proportionately many fewer peacekeepers and less resources, and Afghanistan has never been a post-conflict situation. Even the numbers don't tell the full story, since force protection, rather than the creation of durable security, seems to be the first priority for most NATO members.

Then there is Pakistan. At a ceremony held at CFB Petawawa on September 8, 2006, to honour five fallen Canadian soldiers, Lieutenant-General Andrew Leslie eulogized: "They were willing to fight and die to let young girls go to school. These outstanding Canadians represent the very best that we as a nation have to offer." Speaking of the same Canadian dead, Pakistani President Pervez Musharraf said: "So you suffered two dead, and there's a crying and shout all around the place that there are coffins. Well, we've had 500 coffins." His government's continual appeasement of Taliban sympathizers has resulted in a base for the insurgents in Pakistan's Pashtun-majority Federally Administered Tribal Areas (FATA) from where the militants rest and rearm. President Musharraf has been reluctant to take more consequential action there because his government depends on support from radical religious groups and must appease them if he wants to extend his power as his term ends in 2007. Consequently, he has bought them off, giving them control over the North-West Frontier Province and Baluchistan.

To Pakistan, Afghanistan has been since 1947 its rightful client state. Its real and historic enemy is India, whose growing influence in Afghanistan it fears. President Karzai was, after all, educated in India and has allowed the Indian government to open consulates in Kandahar and Jalalabad, Pashtun strongholds that Pakistan considers its own neighbourhood. Besides seducing Afghan youth with Bollywood movies and music, India has a large food-aid program and is also building the new Afghan parliament buildings. What is worse, many Pakistanis believe that New Delhi is financing the Baluch insurgency in Pakistan's far south, which would sabotage the new Chinese-built port of Gwadar. Since the terrible massacres at Indian independence in 1947 when over 12 million Hindus and Muslims were said to have been killed, Pakistan (and especially its military) sees itself as the protector and refuge of all Muslims in Southeast Asia. Musharraf himself, a former general, knows that his military won't kill fellow Muslims, especially in the tribal Waziristan where the Taliban has become the Afghan government in exile. According to NATO sources, it was only after Musharraf's accord with the militants in the summer of 2006 that attacks against ISAF rose by 300 percent. Finally, keeping Afghanistan unstable means a continued ISAF presence in the region, an effective counterbalance to India on Pakistan's other border.

The West would like to see Pakistan institute broad political and economic measures to curb extremism, beginning by integrating FATA into the North-West Frontier Province. It wants Pakistan to disarm the Taliban and open FATA to the media and human-rights monitors. Washington, London, and Ottawa fear that without democratic change very soon, extremism may take over the entire region. Because the lives of NATO and Afghan soldiers and the future of the democratically elected government in Kabul depend on it, Western governments are increasing the pressure on Musharraf to choke off the insurgency. Canada's leverage on Pakistan is no longer nuclear-related but in the large Pakistani community in Canada. That community would like Pakistan International Airlines to be granted more frequent flights between Islamabad and Toronto and a faster turnaround time in visa issuance for Pakistani students who wish to study in Canada.

The poor security, especially in the south of Afghanistan, has meant that many of the reconstruction programs are faltering or have been entirely suspended. This problem is especially critical for the education and immunization programs, allowing polio to return and 35 percent of the schools to remain closed. The military alone can't overcome insecurity. The Afghan people see that corrupt or absent local officials have contributed to the incapacity of the Karzai government to deliver on the promises it has made, so they turn to the Taliban for answers. The employment creation programs that would have alleviated poverty have almost stopped, since the insecurity has also scared away the necessary public investments that would enable private-sector growth. The few commercial successes in the fruit-processing and horticulture industries, hotel and tourism management, and telecommunications are confined to heavily protected Kabul and the north and west of the country.

At the Second Regional Economic Cooperation Conference held in New Delhi on November 18–19, 2006, the focus was on developing investment opportunities in Afghanistan. The hope has always been that the Afghan Diaspora would invest in kick-starting the economic climate, but barriers to private-sector investment (besides the all-encompassing plague of corruption) include limited access to financing, an unreliable electrical supply, land-titling legalities that are incomplete, and a distorted labour market.

All is not doom and gloom for the country, since in 2006 the government was on track to meet the target for domestic revenues of us$520 million, a significant increase over the us$467 million in 2005. With this sum it was able to meet 63 percent of the operating-budget expenditure forecast, a giant step towards fiscal stability. Almost 50 percent of these revenues come from customs collection, aided by donor-funded computerized systems and training for the customs officials at 13 priority border crossings.

What has brought Afghanistan to its present state, says Crisis Group, the Brussels-headquartered NGO that seeks resolutions to deadly conflicts, is the West's desire for a quick, cheap war followed by a quick, cheap peace. Rather than confronting the Taliban or the Pakistanis, the United States and the Karzai government opted for short-term measures such as relying on ill-trained and poorly disciplined militias and warlords from past eras. In late 2006, after the bloody summer, political strategy moved towards making a deal with the Taliban. That is a terrible idea. The key to restoring peace and stability in Afghanistan is not making concessions to the violent extremists but meeting the legitimate grievances of the population, which for the most part has eagerly supported democratization. Crisis Group warns that fighting the Taliban, drug lords, and corrupt officials while nation-building is mutually reinforcing and that some short-term pain is inevitable. The Afghan government and the donors must continue to hold their nerve to pursue deep-rooted, substantive reform. The current violence is an urgent wake-up call for remedial action, not an excuse to give up at the hopelessness of it all. There is nothing inevitable about failure in Afghanistan. However, without rethinking policies, there is equally nothing inevitable about success. Crisis Group recommends:

- that the Government of Afghanistan launch an anti-corruption drive, headed by the president, that includes in its targets those involved in the narcotics trade;

- that it require all provincial governors, heads of provincial councils, and members of the National Assembly to declare their assets annually and take legal action when impropriety is found, without regard to the position or status of the suspected offender;

• that it assemble a top-level team at the Ministry of Foreign Affairs to guide the relationship with Pakistan;

• that it hold regular meetings of the signatories of the Kabul Declaration on Good Neighbourly Relations (Afghanistan, China, Iran, Pakistan, Tajikistan, Turkmenistan, and Uzbekistan) to work towards a regional conflict resolution plan.

Crisis Group further recommends that donor governments:

• insist that due process is followed on senior appointments and in police reform;

• emphasize rule of law in commitments by embedding substantial numbers of police trainers in every province, and by providing significantly more funds for the judicial sector;

• aid capacity-building of the new representative institutions, including the Provincial Councils and the National Assembly committees, and ensure that their voices are heard in decision-making.

Crisis Group also recommends that NATO/ISAF governments:

• ensure sustained diplomatic pressure on Pakistan to try in court or hand over Taliban leaders, to end political and military sanctuary for insurgents, reform the madrassa sector, and strengthen progressive and democratic forces through free and fair elections in 2007;

• publicly release monthly figures on militant incursions from Pakistan, meet the force requirements of the ISAF Operational Plan by sending additional troops and equipment urgently to

Afghanistan as requested by the NATO secretary-general, and conduct a fresh audit of required troop numbers and resources, with the United States taking the lead in increasing commitments;

• remove national caveats that impede interoperability so that all international troops in Afghanistan can be used where and as needed in the country.[2]

For Canadians, who since 2002 have lost 44 of their soldiers and one diplomat, it is disingenuous to separate "the mission" from "the soldiers." Whoever Canada sends there *is* the mission. That what we are doing in Afghanistan is not a peacekeeping mission, and was never designed to be one, is only now coming home to most Canadians. When involvement with that far-off country began in 2002, 75 percent of the Canadians polled by Environics Research Group approved what the Canadian Forces were doing there. In November 2006, only 50 percent did. The same poll showed that 59 percent of those polled wanted all Canadian troops out of Afghanistan in 2009. Reconstruction has faltered drastically in Kandahar, and for every ramp ceremony, domestic support drops further still. As yet war-battered Afghans are immensely brave and resilient. If more Canadians shared their stamina, their spine, we would be a greater people. If not for Afghanistan, then for us. Or have Canadians so quickly forgotten what happened in Afghanistan the last time the world turned a blind eye, when the Taliban ruled, when Al Qaeda was embraced, and the seeds of 9/11 were sown? Should Canadians break faith with Afghans and forfeit the passion that rages against injustice, the Taliban will be proven de facto right: the treacherous West can never be trusted.

Notes

Chapter 1: "The Petri Dish of Afghanistan"

1. The titles of all the chapters in this book are taken directly from an article "Thinking Outside the Box: Communicating for Success" by Chief of Defence Staff General Rick Hillier in the March/April 2006 issue of *FRONTLINE* magazine.

2. When British Prime Minister Tony Blair paid a surprise visit to British troops in southern Afghanistan in 2006, he declared, "Here in this extraordinary piece of desert is where the fate of world security in the early 21st century is going to be decided." Afghanistan, as a previous British statesman had said, remains the cockpit of the world.

3. According to a recent U.N. Food and Agriculture Organization report, Afghanistan's annual available surface water is 84,000 million m^3. Even after bordering countries take their share, Afghanistan is left with 57,000 million m^3 or 2,500 m^3 per person annually, which is comparable to its neighbours.

4. Pomegranates, like apples in the biblical sense, are more than just a fruit in Afghanistan. They are a national treasure, and President Karzai, who grew up in the southern part of the country, has even taken them to the White House. The leathery fruit is juicy and ruby-red inside and is found everywhere in Afghanistan, but the ones grown in the bomb-shattered gardens of Kandahar are the best. With their sweet taste and size — some as much as a kilogram —

Kabul hopes that farmers will substitute growing the fruit instead of poppies. Unfortunately, a kilogram of dry opium can bring a Kandahar farmer US$140, according to a February report by the U.N. drugs office and the Afghan government. The same amount of pomegranates fetches about US$2 in Kabul and less than 50 cents in rural centres. The other advantage of opium is that it can be stored for long periods, unlike pomegranates. Until 2006, Kandahar had no facilities to store the fruit to export them off-season for a better price. A new cold-storage system has just been built by the Indian government that can house up to 50,000 tonnes of fruit. Afghans cut the fruit into quarters and bite into the seedy flesh, the red juice staining their hands and mouths. The seeds are used for diarrhea, the skin for anemia, and its fruit for thousands of disorders. In Afghanistan's rich heritage of poetry, the sexual nature of pomegranates figures in verse surprisingly immodest in this religious country. "God may take my life for pomegranates. They remind me of my lover's breasts," says an old Pashto poem. And a women's folk song is even better: "Put your hand through the slit of my collar, oh sweet, if you want to touch the pomegranates of Kandahar."

5. Canadian troops in Afghanistan have stumbled across forests of three-metre-high marijuana plants that Taliban fighters use as cover. Since marijuana plants absorb heat very readily, they are difficult to penetrate with thermal devices, making it impossible to locate the Taliban. The Canadian military has tried burning them with white phosphorous and with diesel fuel, but because the plants are so full of water, neither has worked. Even when they do incinerate, there are problems. As Chief of Defence Staff Rick Hiller noted: "A couple of brown plants on the edges of some of those [forests] did catch on fire. But a section of soldiers that was downwind from that had some ill effects and decided that was probably not the right course of action."

6. Wrote Jason Burke, the veteran correspondent for the *Manchester Guardian,* on November 21, 2001: "We are told that the Americans have knocked out the Taliban 'command and control centres.' I have

seen many of these. They largely consist of a man sitting on a rug with a radio, an ancient, unconnected telephone and the mother of all teapots."

7. To the relief of all those who have suffered in the ramshackle old Soviet-built terminal, on November 20, 2006, with US$35 million funding from Japan, construction of the new terminal at Kabul International Airport was begun. President Hamid Karzai and the Japanese ambassador, Junichi Kosuge, laid the foundation stone of the project. Minister for Transportation Niamatullah Ehsan Javed said the project would be completed by 2008.

8. Philip Mason, *A Matter of Honour: An Account of the Indian Army, Its Officers and Men* (London: Trinity Press, 1974), 335.

9. Honour killings are the murder of women or girls by their own family members because they have refused to participate in arranged marriages or give up what the family thinks are inappropriate relationships.

10. John Fullerton, *The Soviet Occupation of Afghanistan* (Hong Kong: South China Morning Post Book, 1984).

11. Allan Woods, "War Stories Soldiers Share Grisly Details of Afghan Mission Via Internet," *Winnipeg Free Press*, October 14, 2006.

12. Instead of a crown, to show their loyalty to him at the Loya Jirga, the tribal leaders wrapped a turban around Ahmad Shah Abdali's head and placed blades of grass in it.

13. In a joint venture between Deutscher Entwicklungsdienst and the German military Supply Company 2, Afghanistan was recently reminded of its short-lived railway. Soldiers from the International Security Assistance Force recovery unit used a crane and a heavy multi-purpose truck to move a locomotive (one of three remaining in the country) that lay neglected in the backyard of Kabul's

National Museum. Today, almost 80 years after it was last used, this locomotive resides in front of the museum directly opposite Darulaman Palace.

14. The Canada Aviation Museum's Hawker Hind aircraft was built in 1937 as a light bomber for Britain's Royal Air Force. In 1938 it was one of 19 Hinds delivered to the Royal Afghan Air Force. It served with the RAAF into the 1940s and was an instructional airframe in the 1950s. By 1975 it was derelict and noticed in the first Canadian-Afghan bilateral relations, then was donated by the Afghan government to the Canada Aviation Museum.

15. The first American president to visit Afghanistan was Dwight Eisenhower, who arrived on December 9, 1959, to meet King Mohammed Zahir Shah, who promptly asked him for American aid to counter that of the Soviet Union. The visit lasted less than 24 hours, and the king remembered that nothing came out of it. President Bill Clinton made it as far as Islamabad, bringing two "doubles" of himself to avert assassination attempts. The next American president to arrive in Kabul was George W. Bush. His flight, for reasons of security, was unannounced until he touched down on March 1, 2006.

16. In a quotation that came back to haunt his countrymen on September 11, 2001, Zbigniew Brzezinski is supposed to have said: "What is more important in the worldview of history? A few stirred-up Muslims or the liberation of Central Europe and the end of the Cold War?" In 1995, in a twist of fate, Jimmy Carter's former national security adviser turned up as a lobbyist for the American oil consortium to develop pipelines from the Caspian Sea region and Afghanistan.

17. The CIA, the Pentagon, and the State Department resisted the move from the White House in 1986 to supply Stinger missiles to the mujahideen, noting that if they could shoot down Russian helicopters they could also do the same to airliners.

18. Sarah Chayes, *The Punishment of Virtue: Inside Afghanistan After the Taliban* (London: Penguin, 2006), 188.

19. The term *jihad* has come to be associated in the West with a Muslim war against all non-believers. While it is a holy war to spread the faith, on a personal level, jihad is an exercise in self-examination for a Muslim to better himself and his community. It is a moral struggle to live under religious laws as a better human being.

20. On the question of recognition of the new government, the Canadian position has always been to recognize states rather than governments and to establish diplomatic relations with governments once certain criteria are met, for example, effective control of territory by the regime and the humanitarian nature of that regime. As a result, Canada didn't have diplomatic relations with any regime in Afghanistan since 1979.

21. Annie, if that really was her name, was a blond former high-school teacher who arrived in Peshawar with her boyfriend and a collection of remote-controlled model aircraft. She claimed they could fly over the Bagram airbase and bomb the ranks of MIGs — the technology predating today's armed Predators. The boyfriend vanished and the Pakistani Inter-Services Intelligence put a cramp on her sales. When Annie couldn't pay her hotel bill, the model aircraft were used as security until her husband arrived to take her home.

22. The war in Afghanistan had a strong impact on domestic politics in the Soviet Union and was one of the key factors in the dissolution of Communist Party rule. It stirred up religious, nationalist, and ethnic striving among the predominately Islamic populace of the Central Asian Soviet republics. The Red Army was demoralized as a result of repeatedly being castigated as invaders. Academician Andrei Sakharov publicly denounced the activities of the Soviet army in Afghanistan. The war scarred the national psyche much as the Vietnam War did in the United States. It was only in 2006 that the first Russian movie made about the Afghan war was released:

Company 9, a story about the sole survivor of a Russian airborne unit in Afghanistan.

23. When General Dostum and his Uzbek militia fled Kabul in March 1992, Mohammad Najibullah's time ran out. In April, Kabul fell to the mujahideen, and the former president sought shelter in a U.N. compound. He remained there under U.N. protection until 1996, writing his memoirs and refusing to leave even when the Taliban captured the city and the remainder of the government had fled. The Taliban had no respect for U.N. immunity, and a special delegation broke into the compound, kidnapped Najibullah, drove him to the Presidential Palace where he was beaten, castrated him, and then dragged him behind a pickup truck before killing him. His body was hung outside the palace.

24. Ahmed Shah Massoud stars in Ken Follett's *Lie Down with Lions*, a novel about the Soviet invasion of Afghanistan (in French the book was released as *Les Lions du Panjshir*). The guerrilla leader was a good customer of the shadowy Russian air freight owner Viktor Bout, as was the Taliban. The ex-Russian air force officer (not yet 40) turned entrepreneur when the Soviet Union collapsed, bought three old Antonovs (some say he was given them by his former employer) and, basing himself in the United Arab Emirates in 1992, began flying in arms to Massoud. When a Taliban fighter aircraft forced one of his planes to land at Kandahar, Bout negotiated its release by working for the mullahs, as well. Because the United Arab Emirates was one of three countries to recognize the Taliban, and because Bout's aircraft were registered in Equatorial Guinea, he went on to supply the Taliban with everything from arms to satellite phones until the collapse of the regime in 2001. Then his much-expanded fleet got a contract to fly in supplies for Coalition forces and secured a FedEx contract in Iraq. When Hamid Karzai's government went through Taliban records, it discovered that Bout had been paid more than US$50 million by the Taliban over the years and that his aircraft had been used by them to fly out terrorists, opium, and hard cash.

25. Ismail Khan's title, "Minister of Darkness," doesn't stem from his poor human-rights record of torture but from his days as the minister responsible for electricity in Kabul under President Karzai. Suffering under daily power cuts that led to a popular business in generators, the citizens of Kabul, with a sense of wry humour, bestowed the title on Khan.

26. A shura is a council meeting attended by those who have a leadership role for a geographic area or functional area.

27. Rather improbably, Jalalabad is twinned with San Diego, California.

28. *Kandahar* (also titled *The Sun Behind the Moon*) is the only movie made about living under the Taliban, and it has a slight Canadian connection. Iranian director Mohsen Makhmalbaf set the film in Afghanistan during the Taliban era. It is about a refugee (played by Nelofer Pazira) from Canada who returns to Afghanistan after receiving a letter from her sister, who was left behind when the family escaped and plans to commit suicide on the last solar eclipse of the millennium. *Kandahar* was filmed in Iran, but some parts were secretly done in Afghanistan itself and few actors were used. Nelofer Pazira, in fact, plays herself. The film premiered at the 2001 Cannes Film Festival but didn't get much attention initially. After the events of 9/11, everyone wanted to know about the Taliban, including President George W. Bush, who saw the movie.

29. There is an anecdote that may or may not be apocryphal. In 1998, after persecuting the u.n. aid agencies, the Taliban suddenly asked for their help with a certain high-profile project. In a magnanimous gesture, to give their subjects some relief, the Taliban asked that Kabul's old football stadium, which had been bombed into ruin, be repaired for use. With visions of cheering crowds and Afghanistan entering a team in the World Cup (the Afghan Sports Federation had just been formed), the aid agencies seized on the project. Grounds were checked for unexploded ordnance, and the turf and stands were rebuilt. Three weeks later all was ready and an inaugural soccer

match was advertised. Strangely enough, none of the expatriate aid agencies was invited (or women). There was no game. What took place were public executions, floggings, and torture. It later transpired that everyone in Kabul, except the aid agencies, had always known what refurbishing the stadium was for.

30. In the First Gulf War, the Saudis did ask the mujahideen to send their experienced warriors to help fight Iraq. It would not only be a demonstration of Muslim solidarity and a return on the millions of dollars in Saudi funds invested but would also show the Arab world that it didn't depend totally on the West. Every Afghan faction refused.

31. In 2003 the United Nations designated the Bamiyan ruins as a World Heritage Site because of their fragile condition, vulnerability to looting, and pressure from the construction boom due to the tourism industry.

32. In June 2006, in a move that bodes well for the future, President Karzai had Gul Agha Shirzai, the corrupt Kandahari warlord, moved to Jalalabad and replaced him with Asadullah Khalid, the warlord from Ghazni. The swap put Shirzai, the Chicago-style boss of Kandahar, in a city where he had no influence. "Why did we switch?" Khalid said in an interview. "Because a governor who is not from the area he is serving will be better, more honest, cleaner. In Ghazni I have my own tribe, my own friends. And when I serve in office, I am looking to the tribe, to the district of the tribe, and not to all the people. But in Kandahar, I have no such obligations. I can look to law and justice for all the people."

33. The print media in Afghanistan has suffered not only because of censorship but financially. Newspapers are financially dependent on one of the three main factions: the former mujahideen supporters of King Mohammed Zahir Shah or those of President Karzai.

Chapter 2: "We Face an Enemy That Lacks a Postal Code"

1. Captain Nicole Meszaros, "8 Wing/CFB Trenton Pays Late-Night Tribute to a Fallen Soldier," *Contact*, May 26, 2006, 1.

2. Two days after Captain Goddard's death, Minister of Defence Gordon O'Connor announced that the Memorial Cross would be awarded to Mr. Beam. "The Memorial Cross is Canada's way of showing our profound gratitude to the loved ones of those who die in the defence of this country," the minister said in a released statement. Traditionally, the Memorial Cross, a token of loss and sacrifice given by a grateful Canadian government, is presented only to the mothers and widows of those killed in action.

3. In November 1979, when Ambassador Ken Taylor and his staff at the Canadian embassy in Tehran smuggled six Americans out of Iran on Canadian passports, the audacity of the "Canadian Caper," as it became known, seemed wholly out of character for Canadians, especially their External Affairs diplomats.

4. Igor Gouzenko was a cipher clerk in the Soviet embassy in Ottawa after World War II who defected to the West with information about a large number of Soviet spies in North America.

5. Canada's record in selling Pakistan nuclear technology came home to roost in September 2006 when Defence Minister Gordon O'Connor flew into Islamabad on a three-day visit to pressure Pakistan to curb the Taliban. Although the Chinese had replaced Canada in the field building reactors at Chashma and Khushab, nuclear technology was the only bargaining chip available to Ottawa's urgent diplomatic efforts to win Islamabad's support for the war against the Taliban. Besides, the Canadian CANDU reactor at Karachi had barely worked since 2002 and needed upgrading. Since President Musharraf was out of the country, O'Connor's schedule listed appointments with Ashfaq Kiani, director-general of Inter-Services Intelligence, and General Ehsanul Haq, chairman of the Joint Chiefs of Staff.

6. Greater only than the aid and development industry in war-torn countries are the armoured SUV dealerships. During the Soviet occupation, Russian jeeps were plentiful, and one was even taken apart and transported over the mountains by mule for the use of Ahmed Shah Massoud. Because it was the only vehicle in the Panjshir Valley, it quickly became a target for Soviet helicopters and soon resembled a pepper pot on wheels. When the Soviets left, the British-built Land Rover, due to colonial connections, originally had the monopoly in Pakistan and later Afghanistan. Pakistani and Afghan shops could armour it adequately, and it wasn't too high-tech. Not so the Mercedes G-Wagon, which featured too many computerized parts that failed in the Afghan dust and had a single-frame body that cracked on local roads. U.S.-built Chevy Suburbans not only identified passengers as North American but spare parts from General Motors were obtainable only from the Persian Gulf states. All of these pale in comparison to the current onslaught of armoured Toyota Land Cruisers into Afghanistan, which every U.N., NGO, and embassy official now has.

7. Richard Foot, "War on Terror," *Ottawa Citizen*, September 4, 2006, A6.

8. The very first act in the war against terrorism that the Canadian Forces did was to provide relief to 23,921 passengers aboard 142 civilian flights diverted from the United States to six Canadian airports immediately following the attacks.

9. The U.S. campaign was initially named Operation Infinite Justice, but when U.S. and Afghan clerics pointed out that only God, and not the president, could dispense infinite justice, it was renamed Enduring Freedom.

10. This article states that any attack on a NATO nation launched from outside that nation shall be interpreted as an attack on all NATO nations.

11. Canadian peacekeeping efforts during the U.N. Somalia mission were tainted by charges of torture and murder. On March 4, 1993, Canadian sentries at Belet Huen shot two Somali infiltrators, one fatally, while stationed at a U.N. famine-relief mission. Almost two weeks later troops captured, tortured, and killed 16-year-old Shidane Arone, who was caught sneaking into the compound by Canadians. Private Elvin Kyle Brown was convicted in 1993 for the beating-death. Allegations of a military cover-up also prompted a formal public inquiry in 1995. Later that year, in a precedent-setting move, Defence Minister David Collenette disbanded the Canadian Airborne Regiment, saying the troops had irretrievably lost the public's trust.

12. In December 2001, between 250 to 5,000 Taliban prisoners being transferred by U.S. and Afghan National Army soldiers from Kunduz to Sherberghan Prison in northern Afghanistan were shot or dumped in metal truck containers in the desert where they suffocated.

13. Four years later, Jakob Kellenberger, head of the International Committee of the Red Cross, said that he was satisfied that Canadian troops in Afghanistan had been following the rules of the Geneva Conventions when they took prisoners. Canadian soldiers worried that Afghan authorities mistreated prisoners handed over to them, and Kellenberger praised the Canadians for pressuring the Afghan government to treat them properly.

14. Eddie Goldenberg, "The Afghan War: Bush and Chrétien Meet in the White House," *Embassy*, September 27, 2006, 9.

15. U.S. Air Force Major Harry Schmidt, one of the pilots involved in the "friendly fire" incident that killed four Canadians in Afghanistan, maintains he wasn't briefed on the Canadian exercise before the flight. He says he was told in the briefing that the Taliban was active in the area. Schmidt was found guilty of dereliction of duty on July 6, 2004, in what the U.S. military calls a "non-judicial hearing" before a senior

officer. The maximum penalty he had faced was 30 days of house arrest. He was reprimanded and forfeited more than US$5,000 in pay. Schmidt later appealed the verdict, but the appeal was rejected. He also filed a lawsuit against the U.S. Air Force, saying it released his letter of reprimand to the media in violation of his privacy. Schmidt had made a deal in June 2004 so he could avoid a full court martial.

16. Those who think that the traditional peacekeeping operations Canadian troops have been involved in are bloodless have short memories. In 1974, during the Turkish invasion of Cyprus, Canadian soldiers fought Turks at Nicosia's airport, and in 1993 there was the "forgotten" battle at the Medak Pocket in Croatia. That Canadians are the world's foremost peacekeepers is a myth. In 2006, of the 68,000 troops deployed around the world on U.N. peacekeeping missions, fewer than 60 were Canadian.

17. Even as the conference was taking place, a bus carrying local people to a picnic in central Afghanistan hit a mine and 13 passengers died. Authorities said the driver disregarded passengers' warnings and risked a two-hour route rather than take a six-hour detour.

18. Hansard Commons Debate 4243, March 17, 2003.

19. Camp Warehouse served as both the Multinational Brigade Headquarters and as the German base camp. It was called Warehouse because many of the buildings had been part of a warehouse complex. The brigade staff building was the office for the Warehouse complex. Camp Julien was the primary camp for the Canadian Battle Group and national command element. There were some elements in Julien that belonged to the brigade, the Intelligence, Surveillance, Targeting, and Acquisition company, for example, but for the most part, if you lived in Julien, you were either with the battle group or with national command or support.

20. Major-General Lewis MacKenzie (Retired), "Why Colonel Murphy Died in Afghanistan," *National Post*, February 2, 2004.

21. Sharon Hobson, "Interview: General Rick Hillier, Canadian Forces Chief of Defence Staff," *Jane's Defence Weekly*, August 9, 2006.

22. David Pugliese, "The Teflon General," *Ottawa Citizen*, May 20, 2006, Saturday Observer, Section B.

23. Andrew Clark, "Mission Impossible," *Saturday Night*, November 2005, 33.

24. Eric S. Margolis, a war correspondent who covered Afghanistan and the war for years, warned as much in his book *War at the Top of the World: The Struggle for Afghanistan and Asia* (Toronto: Key Porter Books, 2002).

25. Like all Welshmen, Glyn Berry loved singing and rugby. A colleague remembers him in Afghanistan singing "Alouette" with the French troops. On November 17, 2006, when Wales met Canada in rugby at Millennium Stadium, Cardiff, Wales, a trophy was named in his honour. In that match, Wales beat Canada 61 to 26.

26. A chalk is basically how the military refers to a flight and its contents.

27. Graeme Smith, "A Country Where Blood Is Everything," *Globe and Mail*, December 11, 2006, A9.

28. Martello Towers are fortifications that were built by the British army from Ireland to Canada for coastal defence against invasion by Napoleon. The name Martello and the idea came from a circular stone tower built in Corsica at Mortella Point. In 1794 two Royal Navy ships sailed close to the Mortella Tower, garrisoned by the French, to destroy it. Not only did their shot bounce off the tower walls, but they were themselves fired on and suffered 60 casualties. The tower was eventually captured, but its strength impressed the British, who built similar structures all over their empire.

29. All quotations are taken from Richard Foot's superbly researched article "War on Terror: The Canadian Toll," *Ottawa Citizen*, September 4, 2006.

30. The Star of Military Valour and the Medal of Military Valour were created by Her Majesty Queen Elizabeth II on January 1, 1993. Her Excellency the Right Honourable Michaëlle Jean, governor general and commander-in-chief of Canada, announced on October 27, 2006, the awarding of the first four Military Valour Decorations to members of the Canadian Forces who have displayed gallantry and devotion to duty in combat. Military Valour Decorations are national honours awarded to recognize acts of valour, self-sacrifice, or devotion to duty in the presence of the enemy. They consist of the Victoria Cross, the Star of Military Valour, and the Medal of Military Valour. This occasion marked the first time that these decorations have been awarded.

31. At about 5:30 a.m. on September 4, 2006, U.S. warplanes supporting Operation Medusa mistakenly strafed Canadian Forces camped on a hillside near the south bank of the Arghandab River. The soldiers were just waking up when at least one of the two A-10 Thunderbolts attacked. The strike killed Private Mark Anthony Graham and injured more than 30, including five seriously.

32. MASCAL is a mass casualty situation. It is any time that the number of casualties overwhelms the capacity of the facility. On each of the three incidents mentioned here, a MASCAL occurred and some casualties had to be sent to other facilities. There are actually three "priorities" to describe patients who are coming into the facility. Priority 1 means surgery is required immediately to save life, limb, or eyesight; Priority 2 means surgery is required but is not urgent; and Priority 3 is the walking wounded.

33. "One of the aspects about working here is there are a few funny, albeit tragic for the individual, methods of injury," Major Bradley wrote. "We had the Brit who put a hole through his chin and knocked out a

few teeth, playing with a flare. An American shot himself in the buttocks while climbing out of his vehicle. I can just imagine his kids asking him, 'Daddy, where did you get shot?' The reply, 'In Afghanistan, son.' Just yesterday we had another guy inadvertently shoot himself. While climbing out of a vehicle he shot himself in the scrotum. (You can imagine the cringing around our command post when we heard about this one.) This guy was lucky in his bad luck. Other than two holes in his scrotum, and unlimited embarrassment, he will be fine. The all-time winner, though, has to be one that we did not receive but watched with interest on the operations chat board four days ago. There was a lady who had a broken arm caused by a camel bite. The camel dragged her along, then sat on her."

34. Many of Major James Bradley's observations while serving at the Multinational Medical Unit at Kandahar Airfield can be found on the website for the magazine *Armchair General* (*www.armchair-general.com*), particularly his dispatches for October 2, 2006 ("Another Busy Day"), and November 20, 2006 ("And Then All Hell Broke Loose").

Chapter 3: "Where Security Means Not Dying"

1. "It's like showing up on Christmas Day and expecting people to come into work for you," said Canadian aid worker Norine MacDonald of the Verner drop-in visit.

Chapter 4: "Without Flash, Glitz, or Bravado"

1. As a flintlock, the *jezail* was better suited to Afghanistan. It could be carried at any angle and fired in rain or snow. There is a *jezail* on display at the Museum of the Royal Electrical and Mechanical Engineers at Aborfield, near Reading, Berkshire, England.

2. While the ubiquitous RPG-7 remains the man-portable anti-armour weapon of choice worldwide, Russian defence contractors continue to dominate the RPG market, accounting in 2006

for over 69 percent of man-portable anti-armour weapon production. Today the Russian RPG-26 and RPG-27 account for 55.04 percent of all new production, worth 31.59 percent of the total market value.

3. To fire the Stinger missile, a battery must be inserted into the hand guard. This powers the acquisition indicators, IFF antenna, and missile. The batteries are sensitive and without proper maintenance become unserviceable. What Stingers there might be in use today in Afghanistan are Iranian, since that country learned to copy them in 1990.

4. IEDS as mines have been described as the perfect terrorists. They wait in silence, possibly forever, for their victims, they never give up until used, and they require no maintenance. IEDS are easy to sow, and without maps, impossible to find because they shift with the rains. The mines in Afghanistan include clumsy World War II Soviet models adapted from older British designs, U.S. Claymores, and bright yellow plastic TC/6s, which are favourites. Designed by Tecnovar Italian SpA, and also produced in Egypt and Portugal, the TC-6 is now no longer in production, but stocks remain in Afghanistan, Chad, Ecuador, and Tajikistan.

5. Rosie DiManno, "Why We Should Care About Afghanistan," *Toronto Star*, October 9, 2006.

6. Interview with Chris Alexander, NATO Headquarters, Brussels, November 2, 2006.

7. As with any organization, the Taliban has directives for disciplining its recruits. Some of the 30 new rules agreed to by the 33-member shura during the 2006 Eid religious holiday wouldn't be out of place in IBM, the Catholic Church, or Foreign Affairs Canada, such as taking office equipment home for personal use. "Taliban may not use jihad equipment or property for personal ends," declares rule 9, referring to recreational use of AK-47s or RPG-7 rocket launchers at

weddings. Another rule urges mujahideen to quit smoking and live longer, and a third declares that "mujahideen are not allowed to take young boys with no facial hair into their private quarters." Some rules are coldly legal. While theft, unauthorized house searches, and murder are forbidden, traitors and government employees must be treated without mercy and killed. If there are to be trials before killing, witnesses must have a "good psychological condition and possess an untarnished religious reputation." Schools that ignore warnings to close must be burned, "but all religious books must be secured beforehand," while the teachers working there must first be warned of the folly of working for the "puppet regime" of President Karzai, "because this strengthens the system of the infidels." If they refuse, they must be beaten. And if the teacher "continues to instruct contrary to the principles of Islam," the handbook declares, "the district commander or a group leader must kill him." Rule 30 declares that "the above 29 rules are obligatory."

8. Gwynne Dyer "Same War, Different Players," *Toronto Star*, July 12, 2006.

9. Neither regiment received official recognition for valour at Maiwand, and since the battle was a defeat, no battle honour was ever given. Of the two Victoria Crosses awarded, one was taken back because the soldier was found guilty of bigamy, and it took His Majesty Edward VII (who knew a thing or two about bigamy) to restore the medal. Dr. John H. Watson, fictional companion of Sherlock Holmes, was wounded in the Battle of Maiwand (as described in the opening chapter of Sir Arthur Conan Doyle's *A Study in Scarlet*) and was invalided out of the British army.

10. The anti-tank mine that killed the two soldiers in the Iltis on October 2, 2003, were planted by Hezb-e-Islami Gulbuddin (HIG), the resistance group of Gulbuddin Hekmatyar, the former Afghan prime minister. In October 2006, HIG was designated a terrorist group under the Criminal Code of Canada. Its Canadian assets can now be seized, and Canadians who aid it can now be imprisoned.

11. The Iltis was also the only vehicle in the Canadian fleet that used gasoline, not diesel fuel, which most of the vehicles of Canada's allies used.

12. Camp Julien had an "Iltis graveyard" that fascinated journalists. They counted over 100 Iltis jeeps dumped there when G-Wagons began to replace them. The German army gave their Iltises to the newly independent formerly Soviet Baltic states where they are still to be seen. But when Canada offered their Iltises to the Afghan National Army as a gift, they were refused — unless each Iltis came with a year's supply of gasoline!

13. The G-Class was conceived in 1975 to be a luxury SUV as part of a huge order by the Shah of Iran, and a factory was built in Graz, Austria, for that purpose. When the Shah's government fell, most of the G-Class vehicles were bought by other nations for military use, and its manufacturer realized that it had a potential money-maker.

14. To replace the Iltis in Canada, 1,061 militarized commercial off-the-shelf (MILCOTS) Silverado (4x4) vehicles in three variants — basic, cable layers, and military police — were acquired from General Motors to be distributed to both regular and reserve force units across the country.

15. Dean Beeby, "Minister's Statement Surprised Military," *Ottawa Citizen*, August 14, 2006, A9. The contradiction between the minister's statement and the military commanders in Kandahar who hadn't imposed restrictions on the use of the G-Wagon became even more confusing when Public Affairs put out a press release that said the G-Wagons would continue to be used when and where deemed appropriate within and without Kandahar Airfield "based on threat assessments made in theatre."

16. In the U.S. Army, the LAV III is known as the Stryker, named in honour of Specialist 4 Robert F. Stryker, who received the Medal of Honor for his actions during the Vietnam War, and Private First

Class Stuart S. Stryker, who received the award for his actions during World War II. Both men were killed in action.

17. With their long experience in countering IEDS and RPGS, the Israelis lead the world in armour defence. Unveiled by Rafael and Elta on March 8, 2005, Trophy has four radars mounted on a LAV to detect an incoming RPG round. It tracks, classifies, and estimates the "optimal insertion point" in the LAV. Having done so, within a second, Trophy then puts up a wall of metal pellets that shred the grenade without igniting it. Marketed in North America by General Dynamics, Trophy was developed for use on the LAV III (Stryker). Its drawback is that, once fired, it has no reloading capability, leaving the vehicle defenceless. Worse, because of the spray of metal shards, it can't be used in an urban area, which is possibly why Trophy wasn't used in Lebanon in the summer of 2006.

18. *Nyala* is Swahili for a shy antelope that spends much of its time hiding in the grass to escape predators. Why the South Africans chose to name the RG-31 (actually the Mamba MK 2) is unknown. No wonder when the Americans bought the vehicles they rechristened them "Charger" and "Armadillo."

19. The story of that particular aircraft (painted pink) appears in my book *Gateways: Airports of Canada* (East Lawrencetown, NS: Pottersfield Press, 1996).

20. An integral part of the survival gear for Royal Air Force pilots bombing the Afghans in the 1920s were "Ransom Chits." These were written in 12 local dialects, promising that if the pilot was returned unharmed to the nearest British post, the bearer would be rewarded with 10,000 rupees, an enormous sum then. Because the DH9s used by the RAF were very vulnerable to a single shot from the ground, and the Afghans were known to have mastered the art of deflection shooting, the fear was being shot down and falling into the hands of the tribesmen. The pilots had heard that the Afghans

had a nasty ritual that entailed cutting off an enemy's testicles and stuffing them in his mouth. No wonder the RAF called the Ransom Chits the "Gooley Chits."

21. Of the remaining 11 Royal Netherlands Air Force Chinooks, two had crashed in Afghanistan. But it wasn't only the Dutch Chinooks that had Canadian connections. On July 17, 2006, RAF Flying Officer Christopher Hasler guided his Chinook under heavy fire in tight quarters to resupply British paratroopers at the Taliban stronghold of Sangin, later receiving the Distinguished Flying Cross from Queen Elizabeth II at Buckingham Palace. The 26-year-old Hasler was born in Jasper, Alberta, and grew up in Halifax. When he applied to join the Canadian Forces out of high school, he was rejected. Hasler was on his third two-month tour of duty in Afghanistan.

22. To ensure Canada remains a strong ally in Afghanistan, the U.S. military has offered to come to the rescue with its Cargo Helicopter Alternate Program (CHAP), making ex-U.S. Army CH-47DS available instead until the F model is available.

23. SAGEM was worried by allegations in the Canadian media about the reliability of their UAV. A company spokesperson said that "cracks" in the wings of the two UAVs sent back for repair were really scratches that required a coat of paint to put right. Sperwer's deployment in Afghanistan was its first appearance in a conflict zone, and SAGEM suggested that losses in rough terrain or dangerous conditions were only to be expected. No official suggestion was made that the Canadian operators of the UAVs lacked expertise, and that since the Sperwer was the first UAV to enter Canadian service, human error might be at fault.

A Final Word

1. Lee Berthiaume, "Little Hope for More Troops," *Embassy*, November 29, 2006, 11.

2. The reader can find Crisis Group's full set of recommendations concerning Afghanistan by accessing "Countering Afghanistan's Insurgency: No Quick Fixes," Asia Report No. 123 (November 2, 2006) at Crisis Group's website: *www.crisisgroup.org*.

Bibliography

Chayes, Sarah. *The Punishment of Virtue: Inside Afghanistan After the Taliban*. New York: Penguin, 2006.

Dyer, Gwynne. *Ignorant Armies: Sliding into War in Iraq*. Toronto: McClelland & Stewart, 2003.

Elliot, Jason. *An Unexpected Light: Travels in Afghanistan*. New York: Picador, 1999.

Ewans, Martin. *Afghanistan: A Short History of Its People and Politics*. New York: HarperCollins Perennial, 2002.

Friedman, George. *America's Secret War: Inside the Hidden Worldwide Struggle Between America and Its Enemies*. New York: Doubleday, 2004.

Fullerton, John. *The Soviet Occupation of Afghanistan*. Hong Kong: South China Morning Post Book, 1984.

Prosser, David. *Out of Afghanistan*. Montreal: Eden Press, 1987.

Rashid, Ahmed. *Taliban: Militant Islam, Oil and Fundamentalism in Central Asia*. New Haven, CT: Yale University Press, 2000.

Glossary of Acronyms

AAG	Arrival Assistance Group
ACM	Anti-Coalition Militia
ACP	Ammunition Consolidation Point
AMV	Armoured Modular Vehicle
ANA	Afghan National Army
ANBP	Afghan New Beginnings Program
ANDS	Afghanistan National Development Strategy
ANP	Afghan National Police
AOR	Area of Responsibility
APC	Armoured Personnel Carrier
APS	Armour Protection System
ARTHUR	Artillery Hunting Radar
AV	Air Vehicle
AWACS	Airborne Warning and Control System
CADPAT	Canadian Disruptive PATtern
CANTC Det	Canadian Afghan National Training Centre Detachment
CCF	Commander's Contingency Fund
CDS	Container Delivery System
CEFCOM	Canadian Expeditionary Force Command
CERP	Commander's Emergency Response Program
CF	Canadian Forces
CFC—A	Combined Forces Command Afghanistan
CFPSA	Canadian Forces Personnel Support Agency
CIA	Central Intelligence Agency
CIDA	Canadian International Development Agency
CIMIC	Canadian Forces Civil Military Cooperation
CNS	Camp Nathan Smith
CUB	Commander's Update Briefing

DDR	Disarmament, Demobilization, and Reintegration
DFAIT	Department of Foreign Affairs and International Trade
DFID UK	Department for International Development United Kingdom
DIAG	Disbandment of Illegally Armed Groups
DND	Department of National Defence
DRA	Democratic Republic of Afghanistan
EBO	Effects-Based Operations
FAO	Food and Agriculture Organization
FATA	Federally Administered Tribal Area
FOB	Forward Operating Base
GDLS	General Dynamics Land Systems
GOA	Government of Afghanistan
GPS	Global Positioning System
HIG	Hezb-e-Islami Gulbuddin
ICRC	International Committee of the Red Cross
ICU	Intensive Care Unit
IDLO	International Development Law Organization
IED	Improvised Explosive Device
IMF	International Monetary Fund
IO	Information Officer, International Organization
IRF	Immediate Reaction Force
ISAF	International Security Assistance Force
ISI	Inter-Services Intelligence
ISTAR	Intelligence, Surveillance, Targeting, and Acquisition
JICA	Japan International Cooperation Agency
JICS	Japan International Construction System
JTF2	Joint Task Force 2
JUI	Jamiat Ulema-e-Islam
KAF	Kandahar Airfield
KAIA	Kabul International Airport
KHAD	Khidamate Aetilaati Daulati

KIA	Killed in Action
KMNB	Kabul Multinational Brigade
KPRT	Kandahar Provincial Reconstruction Team
LAV	Light Armoured Vehicle
LUTW	Light Up the World
LUVW	Light Utility Vehicle Wheeled
MA	Matériel Assistance
MAA	Matériel Assistance to Afghanistan
MASCAL	Mass Casualty Evacuation
MBT	Main Battle Tank
MND	Minister of National Defence
MP	Member of Parliament, Military Police
MRO	Maintenance Response Operation
MRRD	Ministry of Rural Rehabilitation and Development
NATO	North Atlantic Treaty Organisation
NGO	Non-Governmental Organization
NPF	Non-Public Fund
OC	Operations Centre, Operations Command
OGD	Other Government Department
ONSC	Office of National Security Council
PDPA	People's Democratic Party of Afghanistan
PD	Police District
PM	Prime Minister
PPCLI	Princess Patricia's Canadian Light Infantry
PRT	Provincial Reconstruction Team
PTS	Program Tahkim-e-Solh
PUB	PRT Update Briefing
PUC	Person Under Custody
QIP	Quick Impact Project
QRF	Quick Reaction Force
RAF	Royal Air Force

RCAF	Royal Canadian Air Force
RCIED	Radio-Controlled Improvised Explosive Device
RCMP	Royal Canadian Mounted Police
RPG	Rocket-Propelled Grenade
RSM	Regimental Sergeant Major
SAM	Surface-to-Air Missile
SAT	Strategic Advisory Team
SIED	Suicide Improvised Explosive Device
SMP	Standard Military Pattern
SPP	Strengthening Peace Program
SRT	Strategic Reconnaissance Team
SUV	Sport Utility Vehicle
TCN	Troop Contributing Nation
TFA	Task Force Afghanistan
UAE	United Arab Emirates
UAV	Unmanned Aerial Vehicle
UIFSA	United Islamic Front for the Salvation of Afghanistan
UNAMA	United Nations Assistance Mission in Afghanistan
UNCOHA	United Nations Coordinator of Humanitarian Assistance
UNESCO	United Nations Educational, Scientific and Cultural Organization
UNODC	United Nations Office on Drugs and Crime
UNWFP	United Nations World Food Programme
USAF	United States Air Force
USAID	United States Agency for International Development
USPI	United States Protection and Investigations
VBIED	Vehicle-Borne Improvised Explosive Device
VMO	Village Medical Outreach

Index